WALEED ALY is a lecturer in politics at Monash University, working primarily within the Global Terrorism Research Centre. A former commercial lawyer, he also has experience in human rights and family law.

Waleed was a board member of the Islamic Council of Victoria for over four years, and is frequently sought for comment by media outlets across Australia on a broad range of issues relating to Islam and Western Muslims. He has contributed regularly to *The Australian*, *The Australian Financial Review*, *The Sydney Morning Herald* and *The Age*, and he has been commended at both the Walkley Awards and the Quill Awards for his commentary. Waleed is also a co-host of *The Conversation Hour* with Jon Faine on ABC radio in Melbourne.

In 2005, Waleed was made a White Ribbon Day Ambassador for the United Nations' International Day for the Elimination of Violence Against Women. The following year he was one of 90 young Australians chosen to attend the Australian Future Directions Forum to generate ideas for the next twenty years of Australia's future. In 2007, he was named one of *The Bulletin* magazine's 'Smart 100'.

He is married with two children.

PEOPLE LIKE US

How arrogance is dividing Islam and the West

Waleed Aly

Pan Macmillan Australia

First published 2007 in Picador by Pan Macmillan Australia Pty Limited
1 Market Street, Sydney

Reprinted 2007

Copyright © Waleed Aly 2007
The moral right of the author has been asserted

All rights reserved. No part of this book may be reproduced or transmitted by any person or entity (including Google, Amazon or similar organisations), in any form or by any means, electronic or mechanical, including photocopying, recording, scanning or by any information storage and retrieval system, without prior permission in writing from the publisher.

National Library of Australia
Cataloguing-in-Publication data:

Aly, Waleed.
People like us : how arrogance is dividing Islam and the West.

ISBN 978 0 3304 2380 9 (pbk.).

1. Islam and secularism. 2. Islam and state. 3. Civilization, Western. 4. Civilization, Islamic. 5. Islam and world politics. I. Title.

297.27

Typeset in 11.5/15.5 pt Sabon by Midland Typesetters, Australia
Printed by McPherson's Printing Group

Papers used by Pan Macmillan Australia Pty Ltd are natural, recyclable products made from wood grown in sustainable forests. The manufacturing processes conform to the environmental regulations of the country of origin.

For Aisha and Zayd

May your world realise its potential,
not complete its trajectory

Contents

Notes on Arabic transliteration ... ix

Introduction ... xi

1 A Danish snapshot ... 1

2 How did we get here? ... 17

3 Don't call me a moderate! ... 54

4 Save our secular souls ... 71

5 Women as a battlefield ... 104

6 The war on jihad ... 147

7 What is so medieval about al-Qa'ida? ... 178

8 Reformists, Reformation and Renaissance ... 208

9 Seeking the human ... 236

Notes on sources ... 265

Acknowledgements ... 275

Notes on Arabic transliteration

Owing to the subject matter of this book, it has been necessary on occasion to transliterate Arabic terms and names in the text. In doing so, I have adopted the standard method of transliteration, using macrons for long vowels, and dots under consonants that do not exist in English and have no uniquely corresponding letter.

With terms and names that have been incorporated into English language, or which refer to authors of books published in English, I have dispensed with this standard transliteration and the italics, and instead adopted a popular spelling. Examples include: hijab, jihad, Qur'an, al-Qa'ida, Sayyid Qutb, Osama bin Laden and Al-Jazeera.

I have followed this pattern, even where the name is identical: thus, I write 'Muhammad' when referring to the Prophet, an oft-mentioned figure in the English language, but 'Muḥammad' when referring to Muḥammad ibn Idrīs al-Shāfi'ī. Conversely, I have employed standard transliteration for well-known words where they form part of a larger phrase, such as *jihād al-nafs* or *dār al-Islām*.

Introduction

Hanging on a wall in the chambers of Justice Joseph Kay in the Family Court of Australia is a framed cover of *The New Yorker* from 13 November 2000. I spent my first year out of university working as Justice Kay's legal associate. Much of that time was spent in his chambers. More time than I care to admit was spent gazing into that picture.

It is a cartoon entirely in black and white. The scene, I imagine, is a swank, high-rise New York apartment. In the foreground is an arguing couple. The man is on the left side of the picture, the woman, on the right. Each is yelling at the other.

From the man's mouth comes a black speech bubble containing only a white square. From the woman's, the exact opposite: a white speech bubble containing a black square.

The contrasting shades express brilliantly this couple's deep failure to communicate. It captures more than a marital disagreement. These are two people with completely and fundamentally different ways of seeing the world, or at least this argument. Their communication problem is deeply ingrained and apparently insoluble. Samuel Beckett could have written about them in *Waiting for Godot*. They talk, but they do not communicate. They use the same words, but they are not speaking the same language. It is obviously a perfect fit in the Family Court. But it captures the essence of any dysfunctional relationship.

So it has been lately between the Muslim and Western worlds. No two civilisations have spoken so many words to and about each other in recent years as those of Islam and the West. And no two seem to have communicated less.

Perhaps it is my experience as a Muslim born and raised in the West that makes me keenly alive to this fact. I do not pretend to be a disinterested observer, which I consider to be an important disclosure in an age where commentators often claim objectivity when they are in fact dogmatically, ideologically, biased. But if I must have a subjective view, my vantage point comes with at least one distinct advantage. Through no conscious determination of my own, I stand at the intersection of these two conceptual entities we very loosely call 'Islam' and the 'West'. We tend to conceive of a gulf existing between them, and to a significant degree in today's world that is true. But there is also an overlap, and I presently find myself dwelling in it. Those who occupy this space are decidedly more familiar with the Islamic tradition than are most Westerners, and with Western societies, culture and politics than are most Muslims. That is not a qualification. People in this position can be ignorant, too. But it does provide unique opportunities.

From this vantage point, I see a world of exasperating nonsense. The public conversations that surround Islam and the West often reveal little more than the deep inability of each to comprehend the other; a world of much mutual stereotyping and consequent ignorance. Ignorance can, with will and effort, be cured. More intractably problematic is the fact that so many of the voices in this sermonising – for it is rarely a dialogue – merely talk across each other. Often they proceed from a different set of assumptions that are not explicitly stated or acknowledged.

INTRODUCTION

Within their own frames of reference, they may make perfect sense. The problem is that we are often unable to see the limitations of our own frame of reference. When we take this habit into a conversation across civilisations, the result is only mutual confusion. This has become a world of radical misunderstandings. At this moment, I see in it the intelligible expression of that cover from *The New Yorker*. The caricature is intensely frustrating. I confess that this book is a product of that frustration.

This book started life as a discussion of what I considered a verbal ocean of nonsense. And in such pursuits, snappy catch-phrases such as 'the clash of civilisations' provide a good place to start. It was Princeton University Professor Bernard Lewis who first used this expression in a 1990 article for *The Atlantic Monthly*, and indeed his diagnosis has become absorbed in much Western commentary, as if by ideological osmosis. For Lewis, the problem of Islam is simple: it never modernised, and it never cleaved Church from State. For political scientist Samuel Huntington, who borrowed Lewis' phrase in writing 'The Clash of Civilizations?', published in the prominent American journal *Foreign Affairs* in 1993, the modern world is built on cultural and religious fault lines, which define civilisations that are destined for conflict. Huntington's theory applied to a range of civilisations: Islamic, Confucianist, Hindu, Japanese, Slavic-Orthodox, Latin American, African and, of course, Western. But his obvious focus was on the Muslim world: a world characterised in his view by 'bloody borders', which provocatively hints at an inherent Muslim murderousness.

For Huntington, the clash inhered in attitudes towards 'individualism, liberalism, constitutionalism, human rights, equality, liberty, the rule of law, democracy, free markets, [and] the separation of church and state'. Perhaps gender and sexuality was already implied in this, but in any event, it was explicitly added by Ronald Inglehart and Pippa Norris, who argued in *Foreign Policy* in 2003 that it was in Muslim attitudes on such matters that the true clash of civilisations could be found.

So, the conceptual battle lines are clearly drawn: secularism, women, violence and modernity. And who can deny that these are the very concepts that have come to dominate Western thinking on Islam and the Muslim world? So pervasive, so thoroughly dominant are these ideas in the discourse that it is almost impossible to speak of Islam or Muslims in alternative terms, such as spirituality. Even those unfamiliar with the Huntington thesis habitually consider the Muslim world through these very concepts.

But as I found myself unpacking the layers of nonsense I saw surrounding public discourse on these subjects, it became clear to me that they sprang from two distinct but related problems: egocentricity and dehumanisation. By egocentricity I mean the inability to understand the world from the perspective of another. It is egocentricity that leads us to assume our own historical and social experiences are universal; to assume that the solutions to our problems are the solutions to everyone else's, even when the circumstances surrounding them are entirely different; to assume that the world would be so much better if only everyone was like us. There is an arrogance here, but it is rarely conscious. It can be very difficult to spot one's own egocentricity. We often fail to appreciate that our views of the world are shaped – even created – by the experiences we have had and the environment in which we live. It is precisely this failure that causes us to assume our worldview is natural and objective. It is very rare indeed that we recognise the limits of our own horizons. And when we don't, we tend to show no great concern for the inherited wisdoms and histories of others.

This is readily observable in the most popular Western prescriptions, deriving much momentum from Huntington and Lewis, for the treatment of the Muslim world's ills. It must secularise, which in turn precipitates the emancipation of women and the rejection of jihad, and ushers in an Islamic Reformation and the transition to modernity. What is immediately striking about this narrative is that it is so inherently a Western one. It neatly summarises the progression of Western history: the cleavage of Church and State, the rejection of 'holy war', Reformation, Enlightenment, modernity. What the Western world is suggesting when it proposes these solutions is that the Muslim world becomes its duplicate. That is profoundly egocentric. And it therefore inevitably makes a series of impossibly crude, and often misleading, approximations along the way. While the separation of Church and State is so axiomatic in contemporary Western political thought, the Islamic tradition, particularly in its majority Sunni expression, does not have the concept of a 'Church' from which to separate the State. The binary terms of secularity versus theocracy, often used as though they exhaust all possible modes of government, are in many ways meaningless in an Islamic context. Several Western commentators fixate stubbornly upon the veils worn by some Muslim women, presuming them to be inherently oppressive irrespective of what Muslim women might say. These commentators would not choose to dress this way themselves, and simply cannot fathom how anyone else could. Jihad is presumed unthinkingly, and falsely, to be synonymous with the medieval Christian doctrine of holy war. Accordingly, terrorism and Muslim radicalism are determined to be medieval, perhaps because they resemble in some way the excesses of the medieval Church, when in fact they are not remotely medieval in Islamic terms, but radically modern, both operationally and philosophically. Still, Western calls for an Islamic Reformation grow predictably and irrepressibly stronger, while those familiar with the Islamic tradition easily observe that radical and terrorist groups, such as al-Qa'ida and the Taliban, cannot be cured by Reformation for the very simple fact that they *are* the Reformation.

Confusions abound, and the assumptions fall at every hurdle. Yet, we remain oblivious to this, and even perpetuate it. Even Muslims themselves become direct, unknowing contributors. Secularism is either embraced or rejected, often without anyone apparently understanding what it means. Western calls for women's equality, usually perceived as a form of cultural hegemony, are resisted for precisely that reason, perpetuating oppressive norms and further validating Western criticism. Muslim apologists embrace the fiction that jihad is a purely spiritual term with no military dimension; while less apologetic voices, with little to no knowledge of the holy war doctrine in medieval Christianity, assert that it truly is synonymous with the Islamic concept of 'jihad', despite the clear and crucial differences. Meanwhile, radical ideologues do indeed employ medieval language, making it very difficult for many Western observers to see beyond this superficiality and into the true modernity of their nature.

And so it seems that the more we attempt to describe and analyse the other, the more we end up describing little but ourselves. Yet, in spite of this, and more likely because of it, this discourse is often thoroughly dehumanising. At the very simplest, most obvious level, we do this the minute we frame the discussion in simple terms of 'Islam' or 'the Muslim world' and 'the West' as though each is a coherent singular entity. This immediately collapses vast, diverse regions and populations into one-dimensional political fictions. It recognises no difference between Indonesia and Saudi Arabia, Albania and Somalia, Afghanistan and the Maldives. It crudely equates Utah with the red-light district of Amsterdam, France with the United States, Denmark with Spain. Even the moderately discerning must be moved to ask: what, precisely, is the Muslim world? Does it include the large Muslim minorities in India and China? Does it include the millions of Muslims who live in smaller minorities in Europe and the United States? And what, precisely, is the West? Does it include Greece? Poland? Russia? Is it defined by democracy? Does it include India? Or is it defined by capitalism? Does it include Japan? Does it include Western Muslims? Is it possible for Islam to *be* the West, and to what extent? What do we make of the unavoidable historical fact, and inevitable occurrence in the future, of intercivilisational exchange? Can the West really be considered an entity independent from the Muslim world when they trade together, share labour, and interact through the arts

INTRODUCTION

and immigration as they have for centuries? How we answer such questions could profoundly change almost any analysis.

Yet, for Bernard Lewis, the clash of civilisations results from the fact that Muslims are enraged at Western modernity. Lewis only fleetingly acknowledges that this probably does not describe most Muslims before proceeding to speak in the most generalised terms of the 'resentment and anger of the Muslim masses', and the 'perhaps irrational but surely historic reaction of an ancient rival against our Judeo–Christian heritage [and] our secular present'. Lewis appears to consider this Muslim rage at modernity as an expression of Islam's internal logic; what he calls its 'religious culture'. The flabbergasting, dehumanising superficiality of this argument must surely be enormously clear. Here is the reductive description of one-fifth of humanity – a mass of 1.3 billion people across five continents who speak innumerable languages, and connect to innumerable cultures that have grown out of innumerable histories – all funnelled into one singular rage. Forget diversity. Forget the internal tensions that exist in every human society. Forget that perhaps, just perhaps, vast numbers of Muslims have more pressing concerns than life in the Western world. Theirs is a narrow but uniform rage at Western modernity, as though such a singular condition meaningfully exists.

Here, Lewis manages to essentialise both the Muslim world and the West. And he is far from alone in this. It is no exaggeration to state that prevailing rhetoric, both from Westerners and Muslims, depends to a very large degree on essentialising the societies of the other, and often themselves. The result is a view of the world that is static and simple. In short, it is a view that is profoundly inhuman. Human societies are dynamic and complex. They are not vessels for a singular culture or religion; they are arenas in which myriad cultures, countercultures, orthodoxies and heresies compete perpetually for the public imagination.

This is frequently invisible to those who view the world through Huntingtonian spectacles. That includes some Muslims gazing at the West. Among both Western and Muslim voices are those that fall into the trap of pretending social complexity does not exist. Moreover, they find willing audiences among those keen to bolster their prejudices. What is in fact appalling generalisation and simplicity is easily and often celebrated as straight-talking pragmatism. From there, the descent into nonsense is inexorable.

This posture is hardwired for conflict. The nature of the clash of civilisations is that it is a self-fulfilling prophecy. Opposing, dehumanising discourses share a symbiotic relationship with one another, inspiring mutual rhetoric of superiority and separateness. As some Western discourses take a position of condescension and arrogance towards a stereotyped Muslim world, some Muslims, often harbouring feelings of humiliation, latch on to a defensive cultural antagonism against a stereotyped West. Those speaking from a position of power may seek to preserve and rationalise their self-proclaimed superiority, while those in a position of weakness dehumanise the other as a way of restoring independence and honour, of repudiating inferiority.

Hence, *People Like Us*. The phrase embodies both problem and solution. Our stubborn egocentricities lead us to believe that the world must be run according to our own templates; that all would be well with the world if only it were populated with *people like us*. But our dehumanised apprehension of the unfamiliar points directly to the resolution. Only when we come to understand, or even just acknowledge, each other's complexities can comprehension begin. Only when we apprehend each other as human, with all the contradictions, beauty and frailty that implies, and consider each other's conduct in that light; only once we internalise that those we do not immediately understand are nevertheless *people like us* – will the world begin to make sense.

And it all begins with words. Our conversations are laden with words and imagery that inevitably colour our apprehension of the world. Sometimes an attitude is subtly, almost subliminally conveyed: we talk, for instance, of Western 'public opinion', but of the 'Arab street'. Other times we are trapped in the emptiness of our own vocabulary. The example discussed in this book is the incurable tendency in much Western discourse to divide Muslims into fundamentalists and moderates. Both terms are devoid of meaning, yet they often come to define the entire Muslim landscape. It is impossible to grasp the humanity of Muslims in these terms.

The inherent impossibility of speaking of 'the Muslim world' and 'the West' with the kind of singularity that is commonly found bears heavily on my mind here. I have sought throughout this book to avoid doing so without qualification, but so essentialised is our thought and discourse that we lack the nomenclature to convey nuance. Thus, the use of 'the Muslim world' and 'the West' is sadly unavoidable. This places a deeply unsatisfactory limitation on what follows, and I have no choice but to accept it. I take comfort in the fact that this is not intended to be a scholarly work. It is a work of passion, and it necessarily contains analysis. But I confess to painting in broad brushstrokes here. I ask only that what follows is read with that in mind.

If the process of writing this book has led me to one moral lesson, it is that humility is among the world's most undervalued virtues. Never can we conquer our egocentricity without it. Never will we be able to suspend our own ideological interests and allow others their humanity without first discovering it. In some ways, our collective confusion is a disease of the heart before it is one of the intellect. We all have prejudices. It takes more than clarity to overcome them. It takes courage.

This, like any book, is merely a snapshot of a single intellect at a single point in time. Books may endure, but they do not so easily live or evolve. Yet the intellect that produced this book, whatever its quality, is living and dynamic. It does constantly evolve. The limitation on books is that they cannot reflect this. I must accept that my views may change. In a world of rapid developments, perhaps this is inevitable. I confess that this daunts me. How often during the writing of this book have I dwelt upon the famous saying of the prophet Muhammad: 'He who is silent is saved.' To write is to break silence. Despite the deluge of words that flood our contemporary lives, it is a weighty thing to do. In that case, might I borrow from the classical scholars of my tradition: If there is any good to be found in this book, it comes from God. Whatever ill in it comes from me.

1

A Danish snapshot

Another mob. Another riot. Another embassy in ruins. A series of small fires burn where windows once were, and black smoke spirals skyward as if into the ether. Flags and banners are shaken vigorously, and the yelling by now is thunderous as the mob grows ever more passionate, raucous and senseless.

This time the embassy is Danish. Or possibly Norwegian. Madness is satisfied with such approximations. Certainly it is Scandinavian. Or at least European. Danish flags are being defiled and burned simultaneously in nations spanning several continents. In Gaza, gunmen storm the European Union's office and are warning all Danes, Norwegians and Swedes to flee. Bomb threats are made to offices of various European newspapers.

But the mob mentality also infects government. A diplomatic crisis is brewing. Saudi Arabia, Iran, Libya and Syria all recall their ambassadors from Copenhagen. The Arab League, a collection of nations with endless overwhelming problems to confront, can find nothing more pressing than this incident to discuss when they meet in January 2006. Together with the Organisation of the

Islamic Conference (OIC), they consider the situation so dire they call for a United Nations resolution, backed by possible sanctions, to protect religions. Incredibly, Danish prime minister Anders Fogh Rasmussen describes the situation as Denmark's worst international crisis since World War II.

Boycotts of Danish products spread throughout the Arab world. Shelves in supermarkets from Saudi Arabia and the Gulf to Egypt are suddenly bare of Danish butter. A hemisphere away, my inbox is inundated daily with messages imploring me to boycott Danish brands. Attached always is a colourful display of the trademarks of every Danish product I am likely to encounter: Lego, Lurpak, Klovborg, Kinder (which isn't even Danish). Apparently, so grave is the initial offence that it warrants collective punishment. The employees of Emborg Foods must face the prospect of losing their jobs in retribution.

What could be behind this vehement outrage? A political assassination? A declaration of war? A human rights abuse scandal?

A cartoon.

Or twelve, to be precise. The story goes that Kåre Bluitgen, a Danish author, had written a children's book about the prophet Muhammad but found tremendous difficulty finding artists willing to illustrate it. It appears this was because the artists believed it was offensive to Muslims to depict the image of the Prophet, and feared violent reprisal. It is possible, though, that they simply did not want to touch a book on Islam by Bluitgen. A staggeringly ignored fact is that Bluitgen is infamous among Danish Muslims for his 2002 book, *For the Benefit of the Blacks: Veiled Eyes in the Danish Immigration Debate*, in which he appallingly, genuinely advocated that the Qur'an be publicly desecrated with menstrual blood.

In any event, the story incensed Flemming Rose, the cultural editor of the conservative Danish newspaper *Jyllands-Posten*, who, in order to see 'how deep this self-censorship lies in the Danish public', contacted 40 cartoonists and asked them to draw the Prophet. Twelve responded, and in late September 2005, they were published.

As it happens, not all of the cartoons were intended to be offensive. Indeed, one was a pointed attack on the newspaper's stunt. It featured a boy named Muhammad, pointing to a statement written in Farsi on a schoolroom blackboard, which says: 'The editorial team of *Jyllands-Posten* is a bunch of reactionary provocateurs.' Of course, none of this mattered to the protestors, most of whom probably never even saw the cartoons. As we shall see, the cartoons really had nothing to do with it.

Some of them, it must be said, were unquestionably designed to offend. The most infamous cartoon depicted the Prophet wearing a turban in the form of a bomb, while another had him turning suicide bombers back from the gates of paradise, saying: 'Stop. Stop. We have run out of virgins.' That was about as witty as it got. Another cartoon simply showed Muhammad standing in front of two darkly shrouded women, brandishing a sword, his face bearing a sinister, murderous expression.

Now was a time for Huntingtonians to rejoice and claim analytical victory. This looked suspiciously like the clash of two defining principles; where Muslim reverence for, and desire to preserve, an inviolable, sacred domain had conflicted with the West's support for an absolute, inalienable right to freedom of expression. The apocalyptic global battle had begun. The clash of civilisations, in all its terrible glory, was graphically, demonstrably upon us.

There is a superficial truth to this. Muslim societies tend to have a strong sense of the sacred. The Qur'an forbids Muslims from insulting the deities of others, lest that inspires others to disparage God. The imperative is to avoid a social dynamic characterised by mutual violations of that which people hold dearest. It is a vision that recognises how the sacred realm is often what defines one's very being. To insult the sacred is not merely offensive; it carries with it a denial of the other's humanity. It conveys a desire that the other ceases to exist. To be so insulted is to be utterly dehumanised.

This, of course, is all very alien to a Western civilisation that, to simplify glibly, seems by now to hold little sacred, except perhaps the ideal of free expression itself. From within this paradigm, deep offence at a cartoon, let alone this strength of response, is nothing short of absurd. Instructively, perhaps the Western country with among the greatest retention of the sacred sphere, the United States, most unequivocally criticised the publication of the offending cartoons at the time.

So, a philosophical dissonance was apparent. Certainly, that was the combined narrative of the main protagonists in this thoroughly contemptible episode. Each side's rhetorical hook was one of principle. Each portrayed itself as the defender of what defines them. But there is good reason to be suspicious of this portrait. Any analysis that stops here is irredeemably shallow.

The publication of such gratuitously offensive material was defended staunchly on the basis of free speech; that bedrock of the Enlightenment on which Western civilisation purports to be built. Yet, their publication only made a mockery of Western civilisation's most important value by reducing it to a gimmick. In the rhetorical fracas that followed, no one seemed inspired to defend the cartoons' wit or satirical quality. By consensus, they were dull, amateurish, and on another day, probably unworthy of precious mass media space. Reflecting on the violent madness they had ostensibly inspired, Bill Leak, a considerably wittier cartoonist from *The Australian*, quipped: 'Imagine the consequences had the cartoons been any good.' This was publishing for publishing's sake. It is sadly impoverishing when media publishes material not for its quality or substantive importance, but for its mere existence. Free speech is such a crucial ideal because it allows us to say what matters. Anyone who valued the public conversation had reason to feel cheated.

But the free speech defence looked suspicious anyway. Is it conceivable that a newspaper would seek to make a point about child sex abuse in the Catholic priesthood by publishing a cartoon depicting the Pope or, say, Jesus raping a child? A graphic image, indeed. Too graphic for the sensibilities of many. And one, I suspect, too offensive for mass media consumption. How ironic that, in the 1980s, *Jyllands-Posten* had vehemently denounced a mural depicting a naked Christ with an erection, demanding its removal and flippantly dismissing objections about free speech. How ironic, too, that in 2003 the Sunday editor of *Jyllands-Posten* had refused to publish a comparatively inoffensive cartoon dealing with the resurrection of Jesus, explaining to the cartoonist by email: 'I don't think *Jyllands-Posten*'s readers will enjoy the drawings. As a matter of fact, I think that they will provoke an outcry. Therefore, I will not use them.' When news of this surfaced, the newspaper argued that the editor's statement was a diplomatic untruth. They were not so much concerned with offending their readership, as with offending the freelance cartoonist. The real reason for rejecting the cartoon, we were told, was that it was simply no good. Which incidentally, as noted above, seems to have been most people's assessment of the cartoons of Muhammad.

But perhaps more to the point, Denmark and other European nations (some of which republished the cartoons) already have quite significant legal restrictions on speech. Danish Muslims explored taking legal action against *Jyllands-Posten* after the cartoons' publication, precisely because the Danish criminal code contains laws that allow for up to four months' imprisonment for demeaning a 'recognised religious community'. Norway, where the cartoons were reproduced by a Christian publication called *Magazinet*, had cheerfully banned Monty Python's classic film *The Life of Brian* because of its blasphemous overtones. In France, Germany, Austria, Italy, Switzerland, Hungary and the Czech Republic, laws forbid the denial of genocide. So, for example, newspapers in these countries publish material denying the Jewish Holocaust at their peril. Within weeks of the Danish circus, an Austrian court sentenced the British pseudo-historian David Irving to three years' imprisonment for denying the Holocaust during a stopover in that country in 1989.

Frankly, I have little sympathy for those who deny the Holocaust, such is the repugnance of their rhetoric. Moreover, I understand entirely why a country such as Austria, which still bears the scars of its involvement in the sickening horror of the Holocaust while under Nazi control, would see a need to limit speech in this way. As Hans Rauscher, a columnist with Vienna's *Standard* newspaper, explained, the intention of the law, which was introduced after World War II, was not so much to ban Holocaust denial as to prevent the return of National Socialism. 'People who deny the crimes of National Socialism are always trying to get Nazi ideas back into the mainstream,' he said. 'My position is that people like David Irving don't have an opinion. They are liars, and they know what they are saying is untrue. Free speech doesn't come into it. The Holocaust is proven, and anyone who says it was different is not giving an opinion, they are guilty of a hate crime.'

It is therefore not my intention here to quibble with the existence of these laws in much of Europe. The policy behind them is entirely reasonable, even if contestable. But their mere presence precludes any notion of absolute free speech. Such laws do not merely forbid extreme modes of expression; they forbid certain ideas entering into the public space. They do not merely set ground rules for fair play; they interfere in the marketplace of ideas, because they forcibly limit the scope of what is available there. They run directly counter to the most powerful argument advanced in favour of the principle of free speech: that the ascertainment of truth is best achieved by allowing free competition between all ideas, even the most stupid and offensive. Bad ideas are defeated by exposure and refutation, not censorship. Good ideas will ultimately prevail. By extension, this holds the powerful to public account and militates against dictatorship.

The fact that Holocaust denial is uncivilised nonsense is therefore not the reason for its illegality in these European countries. Speech can scarcely be said to be free where stupid arguments are forbidden. Rather, law-makers make an assessment that the denial of genocide is of such grave offence and danger that its public utterance is unjustifiable. That is, the imperative of free speech is outweighed by some other consideration. It is not absolute.

Indeed, this has always been true. Whether owing to defamation laws or more authoritarian measures, it is difficult to think of even one example of a society in human history that has not limited speech in some way. Even the modern-day United States, with its constitution being a celebrated monument to free speech, has its limitations. American defamation lawyers continue to thrive. The simple fact is that freedom of speech is always qualified by a country's historical experiences, traditions and political currents.

And in the context of media, the reality is that self-censorship is a daily, inevitable fact of life. Every hour of every day, newspaper editors make decisions about what is, and is not, fit for print. Swearing is rarely reproduced in full. Photographs are regularly deemed too graphic, too violent, or too sexually explicit, whether for the front page or elsewhere. Flemming Rose himself admitted as much when, in explaining why he published the cartoons, he wrote: '*Jyllands-Posten* would not publish pornographic images or graphic details of dead bodies; swear words rarely make it into our pages.' None of this daily media business is perceived as a threat to free speech, and rightly so. As *The Age* editorialised when explaining that its decision not to publish the *Jyllands-Posten* cartoons was a matter of editorial judgment: 'The Danish cartoons were neither insightful nor effective, just stereotypical smears. At the level of content, there was little justification to run them. Even given their curiosity value, such material carries a responsibility to consider whether the point of publication outweighs any likely offence. Having the freedom to publish does not mean we must publish to prove it.' This statement typifies this kind of self-censorship. It is usually made on the basis of value judgments about which publications would be justified, and which would not. And in the case of highly offensive material, editors are forced to ask themselves whether the reasons for publishing are sufficient to warrant the offence.

People who make these decisions cannot hide behind the laudable concept of free speech to escape scrutiny for the value judgments they make in this process. In the Danish cartoon episode, what so few advocates of the free speech defence acknowledged were the implicit judgments that validated a gratuitous insult to Muslims. It is these judgments, and not the cartoons themselves, that constituted the true offence of *Jyllands-Posten*'s actions. Put another way, there was more at work here than a principled stance on free speech. There always is. Otherwise, editors would have little function.

So, what lurked beneath the surface here? This is readily revealed by the social context in which the original offending cartoons were published. It is only superficially true to say the saga began with Bluitgen's difficulty in finding an illustrator for his children's book. The preceding few years had seen increased public contempt in Denmark for, and prejudice towards, Islam. Two members of the Danish Parliament from the Danish People's Party in parliamentary speeches had labelled Muslims 'a cancer on Danish society' and faced no public outcry. Such xenophobia coming directly from Parliament was no longer considered extreme in Denmark. Indeed, the People's Party, from whom such sentiments are common, can no longer simply be dismissed as a radical fringe element. It is part of a parliamentary coalition that supports the government. Prime Minister Rasmussen has never distanced himself from such anti-Muslim tirades coming from the People's Party.

Meanwhile, Kay Wilhelmsen, a Danish radio announcer, had advocated violence against, and the expulsion of, Muslims in Western Europe. Around the time the cartoons were published, Brian Mikkelsen, the Danish minister for cultural affairs, argued that the next phase of the culture wars in Denmark was the battle against the acceptance of Muslim norms and ways of thought through cultural restoration. By the time the cartoons came around, no one would flinch when public debate in Denmark threw up proposals that Danish converts to Islam should be deported, or arguments that conversion to Islam is a sign of mental illness. It was just symptomatic of a political shift to greater xenophobia. Immigration had become a flashpoint for this discourse, as exemplified by People's Party representative and Church of Denmark vicar Søren Krarup's hysterical outburst in Parliament against the naturalisation of certain foreign residents: 'Danes are increasingly becoming foreigners in their own country . . . Parliament is permitting the slow extermination of the Danish people.' Continuing, he predicted that 'our descendants' will 'curse' those politicians who are responsible for fostering the 'alienation of Danes in Denmark'.

So, *Jyllands-Posten*'s chagrin was not truly about the difficulties surrounding the illustration of a children's book. It was reflective of a broader narrative centred on immigration and the Muslim menace. Here, Muslims are relentlessly conceived of and portrayed as a threat to the very essence of Western civilisation, or at least Danish society. Brewing tensions between Muslims and non-Muslims in Europe in general, and Denmark in particular, had merely delivered us to this point. A landmark was the murder of Dutch filmmaker Theo van Gogh in November 2004 by a young Muslim whose Muslim sensibilities, he felt, had been insulted by one of Van Gogh's films. In reality, *Jyllands-Posten*'s provocation was probably inspired more by this event than by the production difficulties of any children's book. Along with the London bombings of July 2005, it had unleashed an enormous amount of anti-Muslim sentiment in Europe. In the Netherlands, Muslim schools and mosques were burned.

Thus, in Germany, the state of Baden-Württemberg proposed a citizenship test that would elicit immigrants' attitudes on forced marriage, homosexuality and women's rights. The state of Hesse followed suit, proposing a test to determine an applicant's belief in Israel's right to exist and views on whether a woman should be allowed out in public without the accompaniment of a male relative. These are questions quite clearly aimed at the stereotypical attitudes of the Muslim bogeyman, which is why the proposed tests were quickly dubbed 'Muslim tests'.

The Dutch went even further, introducing a specific entry test for 'non-Western' immigrants that requires them to know that nude bathing is legal in the Netherlands. Applicants must watch videos of topless female bathers and gay men kissing, and pay over €400 for the privilege. This hideously expensive process is plainly calculated to exclude non-Western (read Muslim) immigrants. Germany's interior minister, Wolfgang Schäuble, was mightily impressed, and thought immediately about how Germany might adopt something similar at a federal level.

Suddenly, it is not so surprising that in France, then interior minister (and later, president) Nicolas Sarkozy could repeatedly refer to the young men of Paris' suburbs, the vast majority of them French-born citizens of North African descent and Muslim backgrounds, as 'scum' ('*racaille*') whom he was going to 'pressure hose' ('*nettoyer à Kärcher*') out of urban communities. All over Europe, the mood was grim and the tension high.

Such resentment always has the potential to exclude maligned social groups from social norms that otherwise apply. Belligerent and offensive conduct becomes acceptable towards Muslims where it is not acceptable towards others. Sometimes this double standard is subtle. In the case of the Danish cartoons, it was not. Thus, in a highly unusual fashion for a newspaper, the limits of Muslim tolerance are to be *tested*, while other sectors of the community benefit from prevailing norms of civility. The cartoons were only possible because Muslims had, over time, become a despised Other in Denmark as in other parts of Europe.

There was very good reason, therefore, for Muslims to feel offended. But the Danish prime minister was clearly not concerned. He repudiated the cartoons in only the most general of language, and otherwise refused to condemn them explicitly. Freedom of speech may mean it was not his business to punish the cartoonists, but it also gives him the freedom to state his disgust frankly. A good statesman would have done so, recognising the offence that had been caused, and how his cool response would play to an interconnected global audience. But chances are Rasmussen was thinking domestically, and was more concerned with alienating the xenophobic political elements on which his government relies for support. Matters only worsened when he refused to meet with ambassadors of several Muslim-majority countries who had requested an opportunity to discuss their concerns. This only sent the message to the Muslim world that the Danish government was indifferent, or even antagonistic, to Muslim concerns. It was only once the Muslim boycott of Danish goods began to bite economically that Rasmussen thought better of his decision, and agreed to a meeting with Muslim representatives. Either he had realised his mis-judgment, or he only became interested once there was money on the line.

Not that the rioting mobs were any more principled. The game was up when the inevitable clamour of Muslim talking heads argued that free speech could not justify causing offence to others. Obviously, this demonstrates a thorough ignorance of what freedom of speech implies: free speech means precisely nothing if it does *not* provide the freedom to offend. And a Syrian Foreign Ministry official merely confirmed the extent of this ignorance when he demanded that the Danish government punish those responsible for publishing the cartoons. Perhaps he was expecting Denmark to behave like Jordan, which arrested the editor of the tabloid *Al-Shihan* after it had printed three of the cartoons. Of course, in a free society, one in which free speech actually means something, governments do not control what newspapers publish. In the absence of a breach of the law, which Danish Muslims had already explored, there was nothing for the government to do. Arab governments should understand this. The independence of the press is regularly the first shield behind which they hide when confronted about the publication of cartoons that move beyond criticism of Israel and enter the realm of rampant anti-Semitism. Only in this case, it is a furphy, because most of the Arab press is government controlled.

Critics are amply justified in pointing to the rancid anti-Semitic cartoons in parts of the Arab and Persian press as evidence of hypocrisy. As if to illustrate this point on cue, the government-controlled *Hamshahri* newspaper in Iran responded by running a competition soliciting cartoons denying the Holocaust. Suddenly the Jews, who had nothing to do with this circus, were dragged into it only for the purpose of being insulted. *Hamshahri*'s point was to test the West's commitment to free speech, but what of its own opposition to offensive speech?

Not even the principle that revered symbols should be off limits could be invoked here. To burn and defile the Danish flag is a highly symbolic act calculated to insult that which is emblematic of the nation. By happily doing so, protestors have indulged in what, in a secular context, is the very equivalent of violating another's deity – a point made by influential American Muslim scholar Hamza Yusuf soon after September 11, 2001.

The more you ponder the detail, the more senseless this episode becomes. Ostensibly offended at the suggestion Islam was inherently violent, protesters in London raised banners calling for Denmark to be nuked. Others were more graphic: 'Behead those who insult Islam' and 'Exterminate those who slander Islam'. Meanwhile, at least a dozen people died in mass protests in Afghanistan, Libya and Nigeria. In Pakistan, rioters torched and looted a Kentucky Fried Chicken outlet, and draped it in banners carrying Qur'anic verses. What possible reason is there for this? One of the rioters, Arshad Khan, made the astonishingly stupid claim that 'firing gunshots and putting flags on fire will book us a place in paradise'. It would be more appropriate for such conduct to book him a place in prison.

But the hypocrisy pervaded even non-violent forms of protest. The Muslim world was rightly outraged by the collective punishment of the United Nations' sanctions on Iraq, because the people suffered for the sins of their government. Yet, in addition to the Arab League and the OIC's call for sanctions, collective punishment was firmly on the agenda of those who carried out a boycott of Danish goods in response to the conduct of one privately owned publication. Now, employees of Lego, including many Muslims around the world, must suffer economic punishment for something completely outside of their control.

The hypocrisy becomes transparent when observing the selectivity of this pious outrage. No boycotts in the Muslim world followed the hugely unpopular, and far deadlier, invasion of Iraq. Nor were there boycotts of, for example, Turkish or French products when those countries banned headscarves in public educational institutions, or in Turkey's case, governmental institutions as well. Similar inconsistencies are most explicit in the case of suddenly outraged Arab governments who, over decades, have built a reputation for repressing Islamic preaching and political participation. Suddenly they have a burning desire to demonstrate their Islamic credentials by taking up the fight against Denmark, and portraying themselves as defenders of the faith that many of their populations feel they continue to conspire to destroy. To massacre tens of thousands of one's own citizens in Hama, Syria, in 1982 in a crackdown on the banned Muslim Brotherhood is apparently of no account, but to draw an offensive cartoon of the Prophet simply cannot be tolerated.

But then, it should surprise no one that the Danish cartoons became a flashpoint for political exploitation. It is telling that the cartoons were published in September 2005, but the anger only ignited in February 2006. In several of the countries where riots took place, rioting is nigh on impossible without government knowledge and acquiescence (at least). This led many commentators to conclude that the violent reactions were orchestrated by governments. Moreover, Danish imam Ahmed Abu Laban burst into the limelight as a spokesman for Danish Muslims, and toured the Middle East to whip up angry support. In the process, he brandished a hideous picture of a pig-like man, captioned 'Muhammad'. The impression spread widely throughout the Middle East that this was one of the offensive depictions of Muhammad published by *Jyllands-Posten*, but Abu Laban insisted he only ever claimed it was an example of hate mail he had received. Suddenly, Abu Laban stood accused of spreading lies to orchestrate a frenzy.

In Malaysia, journalists complained that the Pan-Malaysian Islamic Party was capitalising on the cartoons to roll back the fragile and hard-won freedom of the press still fledgling in the post-Mahathir era. Malaysian Opposition leader Lim Kit Siang argued there were bigger political battles behind the scenes, particularly between supporters of Prime Minister Abdullah Badawi's reform program and the powerful interest groups hankering for a return to the previous order. All of which indicates that the cartoons were not truly the issue, but were being exploited for political points.

And in places such as Pakistan, there is an audience for the most bellicose religious messages, particularly among the poor and the illiterate. The youth organisation of the political party Jamaat-e-Islami placed a bounty of €7000 on the cartoonists' heads. Not to be outdone, Pakistani would-be imam Mohammed Yousuf Qureshi offered a US$1 million bounty for killing the cartoonists. It was undoubtedly a good look for them: such vacuous chest-thumping appeals to the regressive, ignorant margins. It boosts one's credentials in the quest for religious authority, which is vital for political support. Similarly, the then humiliated Taliban in Afghanistan called for a jihad in response to the cartoons, as though desperate to show signs of life.

Of course, we were asked to believe that all of this was for the sake of 'defending' the Prophet and Islam. Yet, this is a manifestly absurd notion on every level. The prophet Muhammad is dead and beyond harm. His status before God is hardly going to be affected by the inane, humourless scribblings of some obscure Danish cartoonists. Nor will the affection in which Muslims hold him be diminished. He doesn't need our protection, and neither does the message he brought – certainly not from such trivial drivel.

Alternatively, it was meant to be a show of strength – at least that's how the endless emails calling for a boycott put it. But if this was the intention of the response, it was a dismal failure.

Responding so hysterically to a cartoon is far more likely to be interpreted as a sign of profound weakness and insecurity. Violence and anger are the language of the disempowered; those who, in their weakness, are incapable of thoughtful or reasonable reply. The response was just as unsuccessful as a statement of religious identity. The disproportionate obsession with these cartoons, at a time when the Muslim world has a raft of genuine problems to confront, only entrenches a perception that the Muslim world is ultimately beholden to the imperatives of Western public discourse, even if only through vitriolic reaction.

Indeed, if we are honest, we will recognise that this deeply internalised weakness was probably the main driving force behind the reaction. This is why the most extreme responses in the Muslim world tended to occur in those nations mired in the greatest political turmoil, where humiliation and Western political hostility is an internalised dynamic. As Olivier Roy, research director at the French National Center for Scientific Research, observed in *Newsweek* as the controversy erupted: 'Except for a small fringe of radicals who presume to speak for Islam, mainstream Muslims, especially in Europe, have reacted with impressive moderation.' The cartoons only became so controversial once they entered the Arab world's consciousness. For five months after initial publication, this was not even a story.

It is not difficult to imagine the true grievances driving the rioting. In Gaza, the dynamics of perpetual political crisis obviously lend themselves to this kind of reactionary behaviour. In Iran, anti-Americanism, which is often crudely conflated with anti-Western and anti-Israeli attitudes, would have played its part. (Hence the response of dragging the Holocaust into this mess.) In Saudi Arabia, Sheikh Badr bin Nader al-Mashar demonstrated this confusion, and a considerable amount of bluff, by calling the cartoon episode 'part of the war waged by the decadent West against the triumphant Islam'. In Pakistan, too, much anger is referable to disenfranchisement with the government, which many view as too compliant with US demands.

Rioters in Pakistan yelled 'Death to America!' and bashed an effigy of President George W. Bush over what some thought were the American cartoons. Similar anti-American sentiment was expressed at violent protests in Afghanistan. Rioters in Indonesia targeted the US embassy. Clearly, there was far more to the grievances behind these protests than met the eye. There is a difference between what *triggers* a riot, and what *causes* it.

Similarly, it comes as no surprise that the protests were most raucous in countries with limited freedom of expression. Marginalised people with no constructive outlet for their frustrations will often find a destructive one. As Robert Wright, author and senior fellow at the New America Foundation, wrote in *The New York Times*, this is precisely what happened in the urban riots of black Americans in the 1960s. It began with the Watts Riots in 1965, in which 34 people were killed. The rioting was triggered by police handling of a traffic stop in Watts, a black suburb of Los Angeles; however, as the Kerner Commission, set up by then president Lyndon Johnson in the aftermath of the riot, found, it really had more to do with poverty, discrimination and unequal education.

The details of the detestable Danish cartoons debacle could continue to be listed, but the pattern is clear. The whole affair was besieged by hypocrisy from every angle. For all the pious ranting on both sides of this controversy, there was nothing virtuous about either protagonist. It had little to do with principle. If you will, it was a clash of hypocrisies. Not a clash of civilisations, but rather a clash of the uncivilised.

The grandstanding about inviolable principles was now exposed as little more than cover for the expression of pre-existing prejudices. Mutual tensions between Muslims and the West had built to the point of dangerous volatility. What the world witnessed here was simply the eruption of this gestating animosity. The depth of that animosity is the real issue. The cartoons merely provided the excuse.

How did we get here?

2

How did we get here?

And the admiral calls upon Apollo
And Tervagant and Mahomet, prays and speaks:
'My lords and gods, I've done you much service;
Your images, in gold I'll fashion each;
Against Carlun give me your warranty!'
– Le Chanson de Roland; stanza CCLIII

Perhaps it is symbolic that *Le Chanson de Roland*, a song written in Old French at the time of the First Crusade, is one of the classic pieces of literature produced in Western civilisation. Today it is obscure. One could hardly assert that it is widely read, recited or in any other way looms large in the collective consciousness of the West. But it was wildly popular in its day, and while its verses are largely forgotten, it does capture the kind of ignorance of Islam that has so endured in the Western world.

Throughout this epic song, we see the Crusaders' Muslim enemy depicted as an idol-worshipper, bowing before a concocted pagan trinity: Apollo, Tervagant and Mahomet. The above verses are a vivid case in point. The Muslim admiral calls upon this trinity, his 'lords and gods', and promises to make golden idols of them in return for divine favour. It is difficult to know where to begin.

Perhaps with the fact that Islam is emphatically not a trinitarian faith. Several Qur'anic verses specifically address the concept of the Trinity and make abundantly clear that it forms no part of Islam. It is true that the Qur'anic verses in question are directed specifically at Trinitarian Christianity, but it is simply unarguable that the Qur'an, or any other Islamic text, sanctions the idea of any trinity, much less three separate pagan gods. There can simply be no denial of the Qur'an's clarity on the point that it accepts the existence of only one, indivisible, unitary God. There is no talk even of one God in multiple manifestations. It is monotheism at its simplest.

This imaginary trinity includes Mahomet, an occidental rendering of 'Muhammad', the name of Islam's last and greatest prophet. Ironically, the suggestion that he might be an object of Muslim worship is an incredible blunder that would have angered Muhammad more than anyone else. Throughout his time on Earth, the Prophet made it emphatically clear that he was no more than a man. He happily admitted his limitations, sometimes even emphasising them to his companions. He sought the advice of others on a range of issues. He gave agricultural advice that ultimately didn't work: he was a prophet, not a farmer; a man like his companions, except that he had been deemed worthy to receive and pass on a divine message.

As his death approached, he made a point of his humanity even more stridently. Having lived in a pagan society when almost anything could become an object of worship, he was at pains to prevent people deifying him when he was gone. He was keenly aware that the deification of spiritual leaders after their death was common all over world. How could a man, who brought to pagan Arabia a revolutionary message that there was nothing worthy of worship except God, tolerate being worshipped himself?

This is not esoteric theology. We are talking about the most basic premise of the Islamic tradition, yet it was clearly alien to the composers of *Le Chanson de Roland*. To argue that the song's composers were merely taking poetic licence, and that this was understood by their audience, simply won't do. This distortion is so extreme, the ideas so fictional, that it cannot be explained away by exuberant creativity. Even if some level of poetic licence is assumed, hyperbole must have some remote connection with fact to be convincing. This is quite simply fabrication for an audience who knew no better. We live in an age of endless misunderstandings and mutual, cross-civilisational ignorance. Clearly, that ignorance has a long lineage.

Given the Danish controversy, it is fitting that at the centre of this long-entrenched ignorance has always been the figure of the prophet Muhammad. Since the earliest Western biographies of the Prophet, such as the ninth-century work written at the Monastery of San Salvador de Leyre in Navarra, Spain, or in the writings of Isadore of Seville in the same century, the advent of Islam has been accommodated into an eschatological vision of the second coming of Jesus. This line of thought drew on the prophecy of the 'Great Apostasy' mentioned in the New Testament book of II Thessalonians, and the descriptions of the Beast 666 from the Book of Revelation. This Beast would come to rule the world from the Temple Mount. Islam, to which many Christians would convert, became the prophesied Great Apostasy. Indeed the Muslims conquered Jerusalem, and to those in the region must have looked like they really did rule the world. It all made for a convenient argument that Islam and its prophet was the Beast. Thus we find the legendary St John of Damascus designating Muhammad as the Antichrist. Remarkably, St John would later be condemned by the Church for being 'Saracen-minded' and too positively disposed towards Islam.

The character of Muhammad was portrayed as a fraud; an impostor who deceived the world, or at least the Arabs, into believing in his prophethood for his own material gain. He was a violent womaniser; a man of blood and lust. It is a myth that remains alive and well in the dimmer parts of the Western imagination. Whether it be modern-day evangelical and Pentecostal Christians, or disbelieving rationalists, many – I would venture to say most – who have an opinion on the matter dismiss the prophet Muhammad's life as a tactic in his quest for power and wealth, without ever feeling the need to think in any depth about it.

It is an absurd theory when you consider the facts. Muhammad refused to take charity, and died poor – largely by his own choice. As a young man in his sexual prime, he married Khadīja, a woman fifteen years his senior, and in a society that practised unlimited polygyny, stayed monogamous until Khadīja's death some 25 years later. Thereafter, Muhammad would have multiple marriages, though most were to widows who had no support, or to women from rival tribes as a means of creating political alliances.

Well before Islam obtained a position of strength, Arabia's most powerful tribe had already offered him all the power, wealth and women he could contemplate. The offer came with only one condition: that he cease preaching his message. Muhammad flatly refused, without the slightest hesitation, retorting: 'I swear by God, if they place the sun in my right hand and the moon in my left hand on the condition that I abandon this matter, I would not leave it unless I perish in defence of this truth or God decides whatever He pleases.' Indeed, such exchanges occurred regularly between the pagan Arabs and the Prophet. Clearly, Muhammad felt his message was more important than any amount of wealth or power. Whatever people might (and do) say about him, Muhammad was a man who clearly believed his own message.

The fictional Muhammad of medieval Christendom came to greater prominence as Europe began to re-emerge as a significant political force. As Christian armies began to launch military attacks on the Muslim world, and to take back whatever land they could, they were fuelled in part by the myth of Muhammad: the constructed Antichrist. By the twelfth century, the mythical

Muhammad was entrenched in European folklore along with a host of even more bizarre accompanying myths. One example has Muhammad training a dove to peck peas from his ears, with the aim of making it appear the Holy Spirit was giving him revelation. This story is entirely fabricated, but draws heavily on New Testament descriptions of the Holy Spirit appearing in the form of a dove. Muhammad's mysticism was simply explained away as epilepsy, the Qur'an being the product of his mutterings during epileptic fits. That, of course, fails dismally to explain the coherence of the Qur'an. Even if you think the Qur'an contains nothing but error, it is not the kind of speech people utter while in the grip of an epileptic fit.

The myth-making pervaded even the Prophet's death. Contrary to all historical reports, and apparently seeking to concoct the most pointedly dishonourable story imaginable, Hildebert of Tours wrote, in his vastly popular Latin poem *Historia de Muhamete*, that the Prophet was ripped apart by a herd of pigs after having returned home in a drunken stupor and fallen into a dunghill.

By the turn of the thirteenth century, and with the Church coming to rule over Muslim (and Jewish) populations, Christendom had instituted a series of highly persecutory laws before Pope Clement V simply declared their existence in Christendom an affront to God. This historical trail leads to the Spanish Inquisition.

In noting such belligerence, I am not dwelling on the extreme margins of the Western Christian thought of the day. Such attitudes, being promoted as they were by popes and kings, were the orthodoxy of Western Christendom. There are, of course, examples of more constructive exchanges. Christian rulers occasionally invited Muslim armies to provide protection for their cities. In eighth-century France, Duke Eudes forged a political alliance by giving his daughter in marriage to the Muslim ruler of nearby Cerdaña. Around this time, France had better diplomatic relations with Baghdad than with the Christians of Byzantium.

But sometimes, even where some positive stance towards Muslims was evident, it would be outweighed by vitriol. Spain saw periods of coexistence under Christian rule, but also the Inquisition. Peter the Venerable, who commissioned Muslim and Christian scholars to work together in translating a range of Islamic texts – including the Qur'an – in order to reach out to Muslims 'not in hatred, but in love', wrote a polemic *Against the Loathsome Heresy of the Sect of the Saracens* and was a passionate supporter of the Second Crusade. Dante considered both Ibn Rushd (known in the West as Averroes) and the great Muslim warrior and general, Saladin, who fought the Crusaders, to be good unbelievers in *The Divine Comedy*, but assigned to the prophet Muhammad himself a most sickeningly repulsive punishment in the darkest depths of hell.

This belligerence is unremarkable. After all, it was common in the medieval world. But what is clear throughout this period leading up to the Reformation is just how little Christendom knew about Islam or Muslims, except how much it hated them. 'Islam' became shorthand for all that was contemptible in religion. To be likened to Muslims was to suffer a grievous insult. Christian reformers would condemn the pope for being similar to Muhammad, and the Church for duplicating the evil shortcomings of Islam. In the sixteenth century, Martin Luther considered whether or not Islam was the Antichrist, and concluded that it was too grotesque even for that title. That title was to be reserved for the Church.

Some Catholics responded in kind. In his book *Islam and the West*, Norman Daniel quotes a seventeenth-century Catholic missionary named M. Lefebvre damning 'Muhammadan Protestants', while Protestant writer Leonhart Rauwolff denounced 'Muhammadan Catholics'. Catholic commentators argued that Muslims, like Protestants, sought salvation through faith alone, while their Protestant counterparts argued that Muslims believed in salvation through deeds, just like Catholics. Almost certainly, neither had any idea what they were talking about.

It was only as Western Europe approached the Enlightenment

that meaningful trends in the opposite direction began to emerge. In the eighteenth century, Voltaire wrote of Muhammad as a great political thinker, and praised Islam as a rational religion, in apparent contradistinction to Christianity. Voltaire also noted that Islamic governments were famously more tolerant than their Christian counterparts. Of course, Enlightenment thinkers did not take Muhammad's claim to prophethood seriously, if indeed they noticed it at all. For Voltaire and many others, Islam was to be admired in comparison with Christianity precisely because, in their view, it was not so much a religion as the product of reason. Of course, lying superficially beneath the surface of this discourse was the old, stubborn image of Muhammad as a manipulative, ambitious, power-hungry politician. For all Voltaire's positive sentiments, in his play *Mahomet*, he still used Muhammad as an example of a fraud who had enslaved masses to religion by masterful deceit. Here he has Muhammad convincing his slave, Seid, to murder his own father before Muhammad has Seid poisoned. Voltaire himself admitted in a letter to Frederick King of Prussia that Muhammad 'did not actually commit that particular crime which is the subject of this tragedy', but was not discouraged by this because, in Voltaire's view, this was entirely consistent with Muhammad's character. In the Western imagination, with little exception, this man and his followers were still driven by blood, power, wealth and lust. Only an irrational, superstitious people – like the Arabs – would believe otherwise, and as several European writers argued, Europe was too intellectually sophisticated for that.

So, the basic currency of Western mythology on Islam remained essentially unchanged. Islam and its Prophet were still deceitful, violent and sexually lewd. The only difference was that at one time this tradition fuelled fear, while subsequently, it came to breed arrogant contempt. The latter attitude came to lie at the heart of colonialism. Everything to do with the colonised was constructed as incurably primitive, which of course justified, or even mandated, that Western Europeans act as benevolent saviours by replacing these backward cultures and norms with their own. Islam naturally resumed its position as a violent, ignorant cult that was incompatible with civilisation, but now, even the Arabic language was held in contempt. Along with Hebrew, it was deemed incapable of linguistic progression. The Semitic nations were incomplete and simple. As French philologist Ernest Renan explained, the Semites were 'to the Indo-European family what a pencil sketch is to a painting'.

Thus, we read colonialists such as Lord Cromer, the British consul-general in Egypt from 1883 to 1907, stating as though it were indisputable, observable fact, that the Arab mind is not concerned with accuracy. European man (and almost certainly not woman) is a man of reason; a man who values precision, accuracy, truth. The Arab mind wanders from hyperbole and imprecision, eventually to dishonesty. It is incapable of rational argument or even rudimentary reasoning. One can only assume this was a modern affliction that somehow suddenly infected the Arab world. After all, it was Arab and Islamic civilisations that for so long led the world in the most precise pursuits, such as astronomy and mathematics, to say nothing of the arts.

Sadly, the spirit of *Le Chanson de Roland* lives on beyond its popular memory. The most rabid evangelical Christian literature and lectures replicate its ignorance in almost precise terms. I will never forget hearing Anis Sharrosh, a Palestinian-American Christian evangelist, argue in a debate that the Qur'an spoke of a trinity no fewer than 114 times. His evidence for this startling claim was that, preceding all but one chapter of the Qur'an, we read: 'In the name of God, the Most Gracious, the Most Merciful.' The mind boggles at such impressive stupidity. Presumably, Sharrosh thinks that Alexander the Great was two people.

Similarly, one finds the most extraordinary attempts to maintain the myth of Islamic paganism. Christian literature asserting that Allah is an ancient Arabian pagan moon god worshipped by Muslims is staggeringly common in some Pentecostal circles. The fact that no Muslim has ever said this, or even that no pagan Arab ever said this, seems to present no deterrent to the persistent peddling of this drivel.

Nor, of course, does the fact that Arab Christians will also say they worship 'Allah'. Open any Arabic translation of the Bible and you will find 'Allah' throughout it. This is hardly surprising. It is the Arabic word for 'God'. The equivalent in Hebrew, Arabic's sister language, is '*Eloh*', which appears in several places in the Hebrew Bible and bears clear semantic similarities. It takes an active imagination, or wilful and hostile ignorance, to maintain the ridiculous moon-god theory.

Yet, such muck does not dwell merely on an irrelevant fringe of the Christian communities. It is stocked by the biggest Christian bookshops attached to some of the biggest, richest, highest-profile churches. And particularly in the United States, anti-Islamic vitriol is coming from some of the most influential Christian preachers, with strong links to the Bush administration. Whether it is televangelist Pat Robertson labelling Islam a 'bloody, brutal type of religion', or the Reverend Franklin Graham, son of Billy Graham, calling it 'a very evil and wicked religion', the spirit of medieval belligerence seems alive and well.

And just as *Le Chanson de Roland* lent fervour to political hostility towards the Muslim world, the spectacular ignorance of the modern-day Crusader also tends to accompany a very hostile political stance. The very same people who devour this vacuous literature are likely also to oppose Muslim immigration, and shriek about an insidious Muslim plot to overrun Western democracies with their pagan barbarism. It comes as no surprise that the most bigoted comments about Muslims from the Danish People's Party come, sadly, from people who are also senior figures in churches with similar outlooks.

This narrative is often very supportive of any military campaign in the Muslim world, and in particular of the recent invasions of Afghanistan and Iraq. The most extreme example is perhaps that of conservative Christian and high-profile syndicated US columnist, author and media personality Ann Coulter, who famously wrote that, as for Muslims: 'We should invade their countries, kill their leaders and convert them to Christianity. We weren't punctilious about locating and punishing only Hitler and his top officers. We carpet-bombed German cities; we killed civilians. That's war. And this is war.' This is a woman for whom 'Christianity fuels everything I write'.

We can take some heart in the fact that for all Coulter's prominence, her nuttiness is widely acknowledged. More troubling, though, is the recent emergence of similarly hostile voices in North America that carry more credible reputations, particularly among conservatives. An example is Robert Spencer, author of six books on Islam, including two bestsellers, in all of which the hostility is plain. 'Islam itself is an incomplete, misleading, and often downright false revelation' that 'constitutes a threat to the world at large,' he wrote in *Inside Islam: A Guide for Catholics*, a theme from which he scarcely departs. These could be the words of any medieval Church figure. Spencer's familiarly medieval thesis is that Islam is a pathologically violent, repressive, malevolent blight that begins with its barbaric prophet, Muhammad. The title of his 2006 book, *The Truth About Muhammad: Founder of the World's Most Intolerant Religion*, neatly captures his position. And it is from this position that Spencer regularly assumes the role of expert commentator for media outlets and organisations such as the FBI.

But he is far from alone. Spencer finds influential allies in similarly regarded commentators like Ibn Warraq, Daniel Pipes and Bat Ye'or. For her part, Ye'or draws on kindred assumptions in advancing her increasingly popular *Eurabia* thesis, which posits that Europe is evolving into a post-Judeo-Christian civilisation increasingly subjugated to the jihadi ideology of Muslim immigrants. Where once the Islamic threat was of a military invasion, now it is a demographic one: as though Muslims are plotting to invade and conquer Europe through migration. This, too, is a reinvention of the medieval Christian fear of Muslim invasion – only that fear was less fantastic.

Ye'or's conspiracy theory has been embraced heartily by Canadian columnist Mark Steyn, who has emerged as a darling of heavyweight business and government conservatives in the US and Australia (whose government funded and hosted his tour of the country in 2006). His first political book, *America Alone: The End of the World as We Know It*, proceeds from an imaginary sketch of 'Eurabia' in 2020, where Muslims have seized political control of many European cities. It is a clear appropriation of Ye'or's Eurabian hallucination that assumes a singular Muslim plot to overrun a sick, self-loathing, relativist Europe with numbers and an absolutist, supremacist will. Steyn's solution is relatively simple: Europe must abandon 'the dull opiate of multiculturalism' in favour of assimilation, return to religion (particularly Christianity), sacrifice human rights, forsake the welfare policies of the social-democratic state and, frankly, breed prolifically.

Accordingly, it is America's 'comparatively robust demographics' which, in Steyn's estimation, will enable it alone to resist the Muslim demographic invasion: American women breed at a higher rate than their European or Canadian counterparts. Should his prescription fail, Steyn foresees 'unthinkable solutions' being necessary. Precisely what they might be is unclear, but Steyn's chilling invocation of the Balkans conflict hints at a very dark forecast:

> In a democratic age, you can't buck demography – except through civil war. The Serbs figured that out – as other Continentals will in the years ahead: if you can't outbreed the enemy, cull 'em. The problem Europe faces is that Bosnia's demographic profile is now the model for the entire continent.

Is this where Steyn's analysis leads?

It is in no way surprising that such pundits adopt a hawkish orientation. This is most famously true of Steyn who, if he criticises America's military activity at all, tends to do so on the basis that it has been too restrained, apologetic and benevolent. Steyn argues that the Iraq war has been fought 'under absurd degrees of self-imposed etiquette' and in a mistakenly 'compassionate' way. He advocates an invasion of Syria, and advises generally that the US should '[s]trike [the Muslim world] militarily when the opportunity presents itself'. Meanwhile, he complains that the US treats detainees at Guantanamo Bay 'with kid gloves'.

Steyn does not baulk at the prospect of widespread warfare. For him, such instability is a constant to be embraced. '[I]n the old days, the white man settled the Indian territory', he writes with a hint of happiness. For Steyn, this is more attractive than the only alternative he can imagine: that 'the followers of the badland's radical imams' will colonise Europe. Europe will, in Steyn's words, become 'reprimitivized' by its 'laughably primitive enemy'.

There is a worryingly neocolonialist resonance in these more bellicose discourses – not that this would bother Steyn, whose criticism of America is that it is not colonialist enough. It was Coulter, again, who asked rhetorically if 'conventions of civilized behavior, personal hygiene and grooming' are 'inapplicable when Muslims are involved'. Perhaps Coulter had been reading the preliminary results of a survey conducted by the Australian Catholic University, which found that nearly 40 per cent of Victorian schoolchildren agreed that Muslims are unclean. It is such perceptions of Muslims as subhuman that permit Republican Senator Saxby Chambliss to tell law officers in his state of Georgia, in the United States, to 'turn [the sheriff] loose and have him arrest every Muslim that crosses the state line'. His Republican colleague, Senator Conrad Burns, managed to compress a mass of stereotypical confusion into one thought when he spoke of America's 'faceless enemy' of terrorists who 'drive taxi cabs in the daytime and kill at night'.

Meanwhile, in *The Australian*, former Treasury secretary and National Party senator John Stone called for the establishment of the Queen Isabella Society; named after the woman who drove the Moors from Spain and established an infamous reign of persecution of non-Christians (and Christians) with her husband Ferdinand of Aragon, culminating in the Inquisition. In the United States, the Reverend Rod Parsley, a man with links to senior state politicians in Ohio, has argued that 'America was founded, in part, with the intention of seeing this false religion [Islam] destroyed'.

But perhaps most deeply colonialist is the collection of essays, edited by Ibn Warraq, in *The Quest for the Historical Muhammad*. Here, collectively, is an argument that early Islamic history as we know it is probably a lie. Muhammad never preached in Mecca, or perhaps never lived at all. Arabic may not have been the language of the Arabian peninsula. Muslim accounts of their own history are fabrications made to create a myth of their own salvation. Muslims, it seems, are quite prepared to fabricate entire histories for their own self-validation. Their historical accounts are therefore less reliable than even the most marginal non-Muslim accounts (on which this argument often relies), presumably because non-Muslims are historically objective, while the Muslim mind is incapable of reaching such levels of dispassion. Meanwhile, Steyn argues dismissively that even the great civilisations of Islamic history 'were in large part living off the energy of others'. For Steyn, Muslims cannot even claim their own successes; they must owe them to the presence of non-Muslims. It is like Lord Cromer in Egypt all over again.

At this point, however, two qualifiers are necessary. The first is that the recent advent of terrorist attacks on Western soil in Islam's name bears significant responsibility for much anti-Islamic sentiment there. In some cases, such sentiment is merely an extension of ancient, inherited prejudices. In others it is not so sinister. As American scholar Hamza Yusuf told a London Muslim audience in September 2005: 'I don't like the term Islamophobia because a phobia is an irrational fear. I think many people have instead a rational fear of Islam and Muslims in that they have valid reasons to be worried.' It is difficult to disagree. The second is that a number of non-Muslim Western thinkers and writers have emerged in recent decades, resisting the tide. They may not have the mass communications machinery of Fox News, but they are prominent in their fields and their work is particularly important. Perhaps the archetype is John Esposito, professor of religion and international affairs, and of Islamic studies, at Georgetown University in the United States, and founding director of the Center for Muslim–Christian Understanding, but several others could be cited here: Oxford University's James Piscatori being but one other.

Of course, in very few dysfunctional relationships (and the prevailing Islam–West relationship is that) does blame rest entirely on one party. When Indonesia's infamous Abu Bakr Bashir says a 'ravine of hate' will forever exist between Muslims and the Western world, it is obvious that there are people on all sides of the equation doing their best to keep the animosity fuelled. There can be no honest denial of the fact that within the contemporary Muslim world, there is a high degree of (often indiscriminate) antipathy towards the West. The examples are too numerous to mention. Just as Muslim societies are caricatured as violent, repressive and backward, Western societies are often caricatured as greedy, godless, immoral, imperial and inhumane.

The significant difference is that, where Western animosity has a long lineage, this sort of attitude is a relatively modern phenomenon in the Muslim world. Indeed, medieval Muslims in the East, who did not come into regular contact with Christians, were largely apathetic towards Western Christendom and paid little attention to it. They were perhaps inclined to dismiss this part of the world as remote and culturally barren, but even so, the West was not significant enough to them to arouse their passions.

Islamic civilisation simply did not, for the most part, exhibit the kind of blind, myth-based vitriol it received from medieval Christendom, and with very good reason. Because Muslims did not regard Islam as a new religion, but rather as the final expression of the faith brought by Abraham, Moses and Jesus, Muslims saw themselves as being from the same theological stock as Christians. The Qur'an mandated that Muslims believe in the scriptures brought by these messengers, which immediately created a connection with those the Qur'an calls 'people of the Book': a term commonly understood to refer to Jews and Christians. It was therefore impossible for Muslims to demonise Christianity's central figure, Jesus, in the same way Christians did Muhammad, because Jesus was himself a highly revered figure in the Islamic tradition. As medieval Christian historian Otto of Freising noted, the Muslims did not attack Jesus or the Apostles.

Naturally, this did not mean that major theological differences did not exist. The Qur'an specifically denies core elements of the Christian narrative such as the crucifixion, the divinity of Jesus and the Trinity. But while Muslims may have regarded the Trinity as a deviation, they were simply not at liberty to disparage Christianity – or Judaism, for that matter – as inherently evil and satanic in the way Christendom often portrayed Islam. Muslims understood implicitly that Christians and Muslims worshipped the same God, even if they had differences in what they believed about that God. This was a proposition resoundingly rejected in medieval Christian thought, and to this day, a significant number of Christians, particularly from more conservative and evangelical denominations, will fervently deny it as though it is a defining feature of their theology.

Moreover, the history of Muslim–Christian relations began with the prophet Muhammad's charter for the monks of St Catherine near Mount Sinai, in which the Prophet undertook to protect Christians under his care, and to defend their churches and the residences of their priests. Their freedom of religion was guaranteed to the extent that they had the right to regulate their own affairs in accordance with their own laws. This meant, for example, that while Muslims were not permitted to consume alcohol, Christians were. The Prophet made plain that any

Muslim who violated these terms was violating God's covenant and transgressing against his or her own faith.

This certainly did not mean Muslims never took adversarial, or even venomous, attitudes towards Christians at various points in history. Indeed, dissertations against Christianity were quite common, and clearly in an environment of military hostility, as prevailed during the Crusades, warfare was backed by hostile polemic. Yet, these polemics would still distinguish between the Crusaders and those Christians who were not hostile to the Muslims. In the case of those living under Islamic rule, the prevailing attitude of the Muslims was one of pride and honour in being charged with their protection. This is why, when the Mongols invaded Muslim lands and took many Christians captive, the medieval Islamic jurist Aḥmad ibn Taymiyya famously demanded that the Christian prisoners be returned to the Muslims as part of any treaty, and refused any offer that failed to guarantee this. To do otherwise would have violated the Muslims' duty to protect their Christian subjects and fight on their behalf for as long as necessary. Eventually, the Mongols relented, and thousands of Christians were released. To draw a general picture, even accounting for more hostile circumstances, the Muslim attitude towards the Christian tradition itself, even if not all Christians, was generally one of qualified respect. The doctrine of the Trinity was regarded with some disdain, but otherwise, Muslims displayed a markedly more respectful (and informed) attitude than flowed in the opposite direction. Christians often occupied high government posts, or worked as physicians, architects, engineers or translators of the Caliph. Ibn Taymiyya even argued that Christians who, unaware of the message of Muhammad, followed what they believed was the truth of Jesus' message were eligible for paradise. It is inconceivable that such a comment could have come from his Christian contemporaries.

Today, the Muslim world hosts much anti-Western sentiment. True, there is a big difference between old Christendom and the contemporary West, but the historical continuity between the two is indisputable, and in any event, I have been surprised at the extent to which people in the Muslim world tend to conflate the West with Christianity. So, what went wrong? Why would the Muslim world become so hostile to the 'Christian' West?

The tempting, and common, conclusion is to reduce the shift in Muslim attitudes towards the Western world to a post-colonial phenomenon. And certainly, no reasonable person can deny the scar that colonialism has left on the psyche of the colonised. As far as many Muslims are concerned, from Asia through to the Middle East and Africa, colonialism was an experience that ravaged societies and dismantled prized social institutions. It is therefore easy to say that any animosity is simply to be expected, or even that terrorism is ultimately a result of the havoc wrought on the East by Western colonial powers. That was precisely the argument made by Ken Livingstone, lord mayor of London, immediately after the terrorist attacks on London in July 2005, when he linked the attacks to '80 years of Western intervention into predominantly Arab lands because of the Western need for oil'.

But it is neither that simple, nor, for Muslims, that convenient. Particularly for Muslims born and raised in the West, there seems to be some deeper psychological malaise that causes many to take a more defensively hostile posture. My very strong suspicion is that Muslim rhetoric of opposition to the West is as much a function of identity politics as anything else. It may draw on the contemptible history of colonialism and the foreign policies of contemporary Western states, but this merely fuels the fire. Those facts alone are only inflamed because they are received within a certain mental framework.

The starting point is to acknowledge the presence of a victim mentality throughout much of the Muslim world. The May 2006 Gallup survey revealed that, overwhelmingly, Muslims feel demonised and disrespected by the West. They feel dismissed as inferior and barbaric. A subsequent survey in January 2007 found that, more than anything, Muslims desire from the West that it 'respect Islam'. In April 2007, a University of Maryland study found 90 per cent of Egyptians expressed a desire 'to stand up to America and affirm the dignity of the Islamic people'. Such feelings are likely only to be intensified among Muslim communities in the West where, often, public hostility is part of life.

And indeed, Muslim populations have every reason to feel oppressed, particularly by their own rulers. Especially in the Arab world and Africa, there is almost no meaningful intellectual freedom, let alone freedom of political expression. Rulers are generally entrenched for life, whether as monarch (see Saudi Arabia), or republican president (see Egypt). Mass illiteracy means change from the people is unlikely. And many in the Muslim world will have noticed that, often, these oppressive rulers act under the approving gaze of their Western allies.

In such circumstances, it becomes easy, natural even, to shift blame furiously to the rich and powerful West. And indeed, many of the grievances raised are perfectly valid. The impact of past colonialism and present Western hegemony on the Muslim world is a relevant and worthy topic of discussion, however much Western political leaders and their cheerleading analysts insist otherwise. The problem is when Muslims use these arguments as the vehicle for eschewing all responsibility for our own dismal condition. That is an argument for inaction, and ultimately, continued humiliation.

This attitude creates a vicious circle. People who have internalised and become consumed with anger and humiliation become incapable of constructive action. What begins with a refusal to take responsibility and become something greater ends with the inability to do so. Such people are so engulfed in their humiliation that they cannot escape it. It becomes a central reference point in their lives. Their existence is defined by it. But because they have failed to claim responsibility for their own condition, preferring instead to find an external source for the humiliation that defines them, they have relinquished control of their own identities. They have no choice but to become fixated on their constructed oppressor. In attempting to assert themselves and their own identity, they find themselves, probably unconsciously, incapable of any independent existence. They adopt what Chicago-based Islamic scholar Umar Abd-Allah precisely calls 'a shallow, parochial understanding of Islam as a counter-cultural identity religion'. Their very existence is defined by their proclaimed enemy. The more they assert resistance and control, the less control they really have. All their attempts are inevitably defined by reference to their oppressors. Hence the response to the Danish cartoons.

This is why the disenfranchised so often emphasise what it is that makes them different from whatever is socially or politically dominant. The sensible solution to alienation would be to look for points of commonality and use them to connect, but this does not appeal to the person whose very identity lies in difference. How hideous this condition is. It is a negative existence, where your identity has little to do with who you *are*, and a lot to do with who you are *not*. For all the huff of resistance and liberation that abounds in this context, there is nothing liberating about it. It is an existence still yoked to the dictates of the Other.

So, a young man sends a query to a website looking for religious guidance on an issue. This seems, tragically, to be the latest forum for gaining an Islamic ruling on some aspect of one's life. Once upon a time, religious advice would be given by people who would get to understand you, and your circumstances, intimately; someone who understands your culture and social environment because they share it. Now it is given by an internet sheikh who has never met you and knows nothing of your life or society. It is possible he does not even speak your language. It is to Islamic thought what McDonald's is to cuisine: drive-through religious advice.

On this occasion, the young man wants to know if it is permissible for him to wear an earring. The answer is unequivocally in the negative. Earrings, he is told, are exclusively for women, as though this were a matter of absolute, immutable truth rather than a question of culture. But of relevance here, earrings are also sinful for men because they are an imitation of the 'disbelievers'. The response opines:

> Finally, we would say that any Muslim man who wears jewelry is making himself look like the disbelievers, because this is known to be their style of adornment; the latest fashion among them is to wear earrings and the like in their ears, noses, lips, cheeks and other parts of the body (so-called 'body-piercing') . . .
>
> Whoever does this should repent to Allah and not engage in the futile defence of falsehood. He should be distinct in both his personality and his dress from the disbelievers, as Islam has commanded us to be.

It is a message reiterated in response to a surprising array of questions. What colour should a Muslim wear to a funeral? White, because non-Muslims wear black. Can we celebrate birthdays? No, because non-Muslims do; or perhaps yes, but not with candles and a cake like non-Muslims. Can we have step haircuts? No, because non-Muslims do. Can we wear suits and ties? The pattern continues.

What matters here are not the conclusions advanced in these rulings, but the reasoning that leads to them. There may well be compelling grounds to hold that Muslim men cannot wear earrings, but the fact that non-Muslim men wear jewellery is not among them. It is true that Islamic thought has always frowned upon 'imitating the disbelievers', but traditionally this concept was not applied so broadly, and certainly never intruded on cultural norms not specific to another religion. Were it otherwise, Muslim communities in places such as India would have retained none of their previous customs, on the basis that the non-Muslims surrounding them also practised them. The concept of imitation concerned a situation where one's subjective intention was to imitate, or where it involved a matter intrinsic to another religion. So, for example, a Muslim would not wear a cross.

The traditional attitude, then, was really one of knowing who you are. The above examples represent a new regression, where imitation becomes a central reference point, and is interpreted so broadly that life becomes frighteningly insular. It achieves the exact opposite of the classical approach. It is about defining yourself through opposition to others.

This is the phenomenon of what I call 'negative Islam', and it is rife in Muslim communities in the West. This is a dynamic inherently set up for conflict. Where your very identity is one of differentiation, any attempt to look for points of connection, to build bridges, very quickly becomes an act of treachery. Accordingly, it is now common in the Muslim conversation for ideas and arguments to be dismissed on the grounds not that they lack merit, but that they are 'Western', and hence automatically a corrupting, 'un-Islamic' influence. While theological opponents in medieval Christendom would disparage each other by labelling one another 'Islamic', and therefore heretical, some Muslims are now using the label of 'Western' in the same rhetorical manner. History repeats – in reverse.

This sort of attitude was notably absent from the proudest eras of Islamic civilisation. As Islam spread rapidly out of the Arabian peninsula, Muslims came into contact with many ancient non-Muslim societies, yet were quite prepared to receive the accumulated wisdoms of these civilisations. Indeed, their mindset seemed to be the precise opposite of its prevailing contemporary counterpart. They were humble enough to recognise that other peoples had much to teach them, and confident enough not to feel threatened by, or insecure because of, this fact. They did not employ binary terms such as 'Islamic' and 'un-Islamic', as though the world is split in two, and everything that does not have its origin in Islam is corrupt and bereft of wisdom.

I call this 'confident humility'. It is one of life's great truths that confident, successful people are usually secure enough within themselves to be open to the thoughts and experiences of others. Thus, Muslim theologians not only received the philosophy of the ancient Greek masters, but they engaged with it. They translated it, preserved it, defended it, critiqued it and expanded upon it. In his tenth-century thesis on the features of the hypothetical 'Virtuous City', master Islamic political theorist Abū Naṣr al-Fārābī explicitly took guidance from Socrates and Plato. Islamic philosophers came to call Aristotle *shaykh al-ra'īs*, the First Master, and had protracted debates about his ideas. While the brilliant Abū Ḥāmid al-Ghazālī attacked Aristotelian thought in *The Incoherence of the Philosophers*, Ibn Rushd retorted forthrightly with *The Incoherence of the Incoherence*. These were men with a passion for knowledge, whatever its source. As the prophet Muhammad had said before them, 'wisdom is the lost property of the believer.' They would rejoice wherever they found it. This allowed the early Muslims to experience rapid intellectual growth.

But, it seems, modern-day Abu Dhabi has little to do with medieval Islamic Spain. As Abdelwahab Meddeb recounts in *Islam and its Discontents*:

> When I was at Abu Dhabi in May 2001, a number of my interlocutors, of various Arab communities (Lebanese, Syrian, Sudanese, etc.), confirmed the warning, spread by the local newspapers, to the public of the countries of the Near East not to buy the very inexpensive belts with the label *Made in Thailand*. These belts, the people told me, were actually Israeli products in disguise and carried a kind of flea that propagated an incurable disease: one more Zionist trick to weaken Arab bodies, if not eliminate them. These interlocutors, otherwise reasonable and likable, gave credit to information as fantastic as that.

Traditionally educated Islamic scholar and Cambridge theologian Abdal Hakim Murad cites this as an example of 'a kind of Islamic McCarthyism' that has become prevalent in the Muslim world. And indeed, sadly, this kind of conspiratorial madness is far from an isolated incident. In September 1997, when Princess Diana died in a car crash in a Paris tunnel, rumour spread wildly throughout the Muslim world, and among Western Muslim communities, that far from being an accident, British intelligence had murdered Diana to prevent her impending marriage to Dodi Fayed, an Arab Muslim. Apparently, this meant her conversion was imminent, if indeed it had not already happened. These are rumours that persist to this day.

Two years later, when EgyptAir Flight 990 crashed, killing 271 people, some Arab commentators portrayed this, of course without any evidence, as a Mossad sabotage aimed at crippling Egypt's tourism industry.

And of course, two years later again, came the terrorist attacks of September 11, 2001. If ever an event was made for conspiracy theorists, this was it. Literally thousands of websites are devoted to uncovering the hidden 'truth' behind September 11, attempting to disprove the conventional wisdom that it was the work of Osama bin Laden's al-Qa'ida network. A Pew Global Attitudes survey in July 2006 found majorities in several Muslim countries – including a whopping 65 per cent in Indonesia – do not believe Arabs carried out the attacks. Among British Muslims, the figure is 56 per cent. This is, of course, despite bin Laden's own praise for the atrocity, and subsequent, triumphant video confession released in the lead-up to the 2004 US election. That alone would be sufficient evidence to establish a preliminary case against bin Laden. But his confession is calmly dismissed as a forgery simply because this is the only way a conspiracy theorist can account for it. Naturally, none of the evidence presented by the 9/11 Commission in its report to the US government is of any consequence. Nor is the fact that a French-born Muslim named Zacarias Moussaoui has pleaded guilty in court to conspiring with bin Laden to execute the attack, and was sentenced to life in prison with no parole. All this is merely part of the machine covering up the 'truth'. This in spite of the fact that the 9/11 Commission has also made findings, such as denying any link between the Iraqi government and September 11, that were inconvenient to the Bush administration.

The rich irony in all this is that no one seems more upset by the September 11 conspiracy theory than al-Qa'ida itself, who told Al-Jazeera journalist Yosri Fouda that because of these conspiratorial doubts, 'the brothers' were being denied their due credit. So frustrated were they that the main perpetrators of September 11, Khalid Sheikh Mohammed and Ramzi bin al-Shibh, invited Fouda to spend 48 hours with them when they would reveal the details of what they called 'the Holy Tuesday operations'. Following the first anniversary of the attacks, the details were broadcast on Al-Jazeera from their own mouths.

It should be said that vast numbers of September 11 conspiracy theorists are not Muslims. Most of the books, pamphlets and websites offering a conspiratorial version of events have non-Muslim authors. Mark Steyn tells us that a third of Germans under 30 believe the US government was responsible for the attacks. Nevertheless, surrounded by a conspiratorial environment, many Muslims all around the world did not hesitate to act on cue. Hezbollah circulated the fabricated story that 4000 New York Jews all conveniently stayed home from work that morning, a myth that naturally formed the basis of the theory that this, too, was a Mossad plot. Not only is this theory ridiculous in the complete absence of any evidence outside of Hezbollah propaganda; it also assumes, quite absurdly, that all Jews are aligned, completely without division or dissent, as an international, monolithic force, generally for evil.

Similar assumptions underpin famously discredited and bigoted propaganda tracts such as the Tsarist forgery, *The Protocols of the Elders of Zion* and Henry Ford's *The International Jew*, which retain an inexcusably large level of popularity in Islamic bookstores. Anyone who has observed the near-farcical fragility of Israeli politics knows the idea of a unified, invincible, international Jewish political force, as advanced in these tracts, must surely be nonsense. That, of course, says nothing of the significant number of fiercely anti-Zionist Jews, or Zionist Jews with major moral disagreements with the conduct of the Israeli government. Most instructively, it is the very kind of fictional, sinister monolith that Crusading Christian propaganda promulgated about Muslims centuries earlier.

But while the Zionist conspiracies remain popular, none is quite so prevalent in connection with the September 11 attacks as the theory that they were orchestrated internally by the Bush administration, intelligence agencies, or someone within the US government. It is a stunning allegation to make, especially without convincing, unequivocal evidence, but that did not seem to deter figures such as Melbourne's Sheikh Mohammed Omran from telling *60 Minutes* that 'there is a mastermind behind these things and the mastermind, 100 percent he is from the US Government'.

What is most staggering is that, very often, the very same people alleging all manner of conspiratorial crime against Western governments are very vocal in arguing that the root cause of terrorist behaviour lies exclusively in the oppressive, anti-Muslim foreign policies of those governments, whether it be imperialist action in Iraq or near unconditional support for Israel. But few seem even to perceive the contradiction. If terrorist activity does not, in fact, come from the Muslim world, but is instead a theatrical fraud executed by Western governments, how can terrorism be the recompense of oppressive foreign policy? If you wish to argue that Muslims didn't do it, you cannot argue simultaneously that it is the response of an oppressed Muslim world. It is an extraordinary case of doublethink.

But Mohammed Omran gave a glimpse of the real driving force behind this conspiratorial thought in an interview with ABC's *Lateline* in mid-2005, when he said:

> Again, I don't believe that even September 11 – from the beginning, I don't believe that it has [been] done by any Muslim at all, or any other activities... This has happened in evil hands for an evil action, and first

target was the Muslims for that. How could I believe any Muslim could think to hurt his own religion by doing an evil act like this?

It would seem that Omran, and probably most other Muslims seduced by the conspiratorial siren, is simply not prepared to face the unsettling prospect that there are Muslims capable of committing acts of mass terrorism against the innocent. Apparently this is too painful a reality to confront, and refuge is sought in the sanctuary of quixotic denial. Quite clearly, this view has little to do with dispassionate assessment, and is more an emotive confusion.

While conspiracy theorists tend to concoct theories that lay blame at the feet of the superpowers, some Muslim theorists are not so fussy. Some held that the attacks on Washington on September 11 never really happened at all, and others that the whole operation was Japanese revenge for World War II. The conspiratorial culprit is, in some senses, irrelevant. What matters is that blame is laid entirely elsewhere. If it is possible to accuse a political foe, such as Israel or the United States (or in decades past, Freemasons), that is a welcome bonus.

And it certainly makes the theory far more attractive. It is why, often, the only basis needed for the conspiracy is an argument that the event in question somehow furthers the supposed aims of the conspirators. Thus, September 11 was executed either by Israel because it allowed Israelis to step up their persecution of the Palestinians, or by the United States because it provided a pretext for its own imperial agenda. Whenever something occurs that attributes evil to Muslims, it must be the plot of another who has something to gain from Muslims' tarnished image.

Naturally, all of this reeks of a massively overdeveloped sense of self-importance. As the Qur'an says at 63:4: 'They think that every shout is against themselves.' Conspiracy theorists, particularly those who habitually claim the role of victim in the conspiracies, create more than unsubstantiated theories. They create an alternative world that seems to exist for the sole purpose of plotting their destruction. There is a desperate conceit to all this. As Abdal Hakim Murad noted:

> ... it requires an apparently unbearable humility for the Islamist conspiracy theorist to recognise that until very recently Muslims have seldom been perceived by the United States as a noteworthy enemy. For most of its history, America has opposed and feared and stereotyped Englishmen, Rebels, Red Indians, Spaniards, Huns, Reds or Gooks. The current preoccupation with Muslims is shallow in the US memory, if we discount the brief and long-forgotten enthusiasms of the Decatur episode.

My feeling is that such theories, with their attendant narcissism, are useful in rehabilitating the shattered self-confidence of Muslims who wish to identify with a great civilisation, but in fact identify with a humiliated people in a repugnant condition. Denial becomes a source of redemption. Perhaps it is too painful to recognise that the world has simply moved on.

Unfortunately, this emotional balm has its side effects. It entrenches a hostile attitude towards the rest of the conspiring world, and especially towards the most powerful. This is not to deny the very real, legitimate grievances one might harbour towards, for example, US foreign policy. It is perfectly legitimate to argue that much of that policy is characterised by rank hypocrisy. The problem arises when a hysterical, conspiratorial orientation causes these objections to become so exaggerated that any relationship is likely to become utterly dysfunctional. Hence, some Muslims develop what can appear to be an irrational hatred of all things Western.

It also creates a crisis of credibility. It means some Muslims find themselves naturally, naively allied to the most extreme non-Muslim elements available, whether from the so-called hard left or far right. It is therefore lamentable, but not surprising, to read reports in *The Australian* that the peak Australian Muslim body, the Australian Federation of Islamic Councils, made donations to the Citizens Electoral Council, known to be a group of far right-wing, anti-Semitic lunacy. Muslims, in complete ignorance of such groups' philosophical stance, are seduced by their conspiratorial muck surrounding events such as September 11.

Perhaps more worryingly, it prevents many from confronting their own shortcomings and assessing in what ways we might be responsible for our own sorry condition. This is no doubt comforting, but it is also disempowering. Ordinary Muslim folk internalise feelings of helplessness in the face of the imaginary machine that is designed to devour them. This leaves no option but to turn to insularity. In this environment, any relationship between the Islamic and Western civilisations heads rapidly towards new depths of dysfunction.

When Amir Butler, an Australian Muslim commentator, made similar arguments to the above in a piece for his web magazine *A True Word*, rather than acknowledge that he had written the blindingly obvious, some Muslims responded with outrage. One began circulating an email stating that: 'My self [sic] and other Muslims found this article to be offencive [sic] to Muslim teachings ... Further to this, the website is suddenly getting a lot of exposure in the national press, is this the type of garbage we want people to read about Muslims?'

Another fumed: 'This seems to be another case of attacking Muslims – under the guise of over-intellectualized good will.' And it continued on internet forums:

> ... this writer has chosen to label and belittle Muslims in full view of an already hostile non Muslim world (as the result of September 11 and other alleged conspiracies perpetuated by Muslims). This is a very dangerous and divisive mind set, which inspires

Muslims to blame other Muslims for the current state of the world. And encourages non Muslims to do the same.

These responses are every bit as revealing as the conspiracy theories that set the discussion in motion. The tone is sanctimonious, the accusation of betrayal. It poses no meaningful counter-argument, but notes the damage the argument supposedly does to Muslims. At the heart of the response is the very same condition that inspires conspiracy theories in the first place: an outright refusal to admit Muslim culpability.

This is the epitome of defensiveness, and it cannot simply be dismissed on the ground that it is the irrelevant chatter of cyberspace. It is true that the internet tends to attract the most extreme voices in disproportionate measure, but in my experience, this discourse is genuinely representative of a significant sector of the Muslim West.

If anything, I have seen the spirit of Islam's golden age alive in many Christians and other non-Muslims I have met who have demonstrated considerable openness. They are the kinds of people who invite Muslims to speak at their own churches, not for the sake of argument, but for their own intellectual enrichment. They are clearly confident enough in their own faith not to feel threatened by this. Learning about other religions, even in their own places of worship, is not something considered risky or unnecessary.

In a political context, the lack of genuine Muslim confidence has resulted in what is almost a refusal to be understood for the sake of not being apologetic. Hence, the seemingly incurable tendency, with several notable exceptions, for Muslim condemnations of terrorism to be expressed in conditional language. Certainly terrorism is condemned, but not without using the opportunity to make a political point or two about the war in Iraq. To be honest, I sympathise with the frustration that causes this. The very strong (and entirely justified) feeling is that the loss of innocent Muslim life is rarely if ever mourned – in fact, it is rationalised – but the loss of innocent Western lives is a tragedy that changes the world. The determination of Western politicians to quarantine discussions of terrorism from those of foreign policy is indeed hopelessly artificial and worthy of challenge. But none of this alters the despicable moral character of terrorism, and it is certainly no reason for any Muslim to rationalise in reverse. Muslim spokespeople who pursue this discourse only hours after a terrorist attack, in the raw aftermath of the killing, are blissfully unaware of how their words sound to their audience. It sounds like hedging. As though Western foreign policy somehow excuses a terrorist response. At a time of such tragedy, people need to know clearly where you stand on the narrow issue of the tragedy at hand. At that moment, it simply won't do to say, 'We condemn terrorism, but . . .'

The result is deep miscommunication. That should be of major concern to Muslim spokespeople. Even if only for selfish reasons, the immediate aftermath of a terrorist incident is not a time to be misunderstood. It is necessary to make your position known as plainly, and without qualification, as possible – not to please others, but to make clear who you are. That is not weak apologia. It is, in fact, a firm assertion of identity.

But for some sectors of Western Muslim communities, this renders you a sell-out. Any alternative view is dismissed as the feeble appeasement of non-Muslims. We would rather err on the side of aggression and pride than be apologetic. If that means we come across as equivocating on even the most obvious of moral judgments, then so be it. If that only leads to greater social tension and misunderstanding, then that is not our problem. At least we were not appeasing anyone. We have preserved our faux-pride. I call this 'humiliated arrogance'.

The more insular the outlook, the more manifest this becomes. That is why you get exchanges such as this one on ABC Radio National with Wassim Dourehi, a spokesman for the Muslim political group Hizb ut-Tahrir:

INTERVIEWER: In 2002 on the British website of Hizb ut-Tahrir, they posted a passage from the Qur'an saying 'kill them wherever you find them' followed by material arguing that the Jews are a people of slander, a treacherous people, they fabricate lies and twist words from their places.

. . .

'For Jews are a people of slander'. Do you agree with that? 'A treacherous people'?

DOUREIHI: I'll agree with whatever Islam espouses.

INTERVIEWER: And what does Islam espouse when it comes to the Jews, according to you?

DOUREIHI: The issue here is bigger than the Jews. When you put it in the context of what we are trying to achieve . . .

INTERVIEWER: Well it can be the issue because . . . Hizb ut-Tahrir has been accused of being an anti-Semitic organisation. Is it an anti-Semitic organisation?

DOUREIHI: Well we have been accused of a lot of things. Our literature speaks for itself and our actions and our history speaks for itself.

INTERVIEWER: Well how about you speak for yourself and tell me whether you are an anti-Semitic organisation?

DOUREIHI: Well when we engage in the work to create the change, that change occurs for intellectual and political means. We're not about killing this person or that person. We are directly, directly aligned to the work to move the hearts and minds through discussion and debate.

INTERVIEWER: Okay, the simple question again. Are you anti-Semitic?

DOUREIHI: This is a matter that concerns the group itself. Now when you talk about the broader issues, about the Islamic viewpoint towards the Jews or towards any peoples, and clearly this is an issue that is beyond the Hizb itself.

INTERVIEWER: I'm sorry I'm going to ask you the question again. Is Hizb ut-Tahrir an anti-Semitic organisation?

DOUREIHI: Well let me ask you, what exactly does anti-Semitic mean?

INTERVIEWER: Well I would have thought that the passage which I quoted before, 'the Jews are a people of slander, a treacherous people who fabricate lies and twist words' would fall pretty squarely into the category of anti-Semitic.

Do you accept those words or do you reject them?

DOUREIHI: Well I accept what the Islamic position is in respect of this point. Now, I don't hide any passage of the Qur'an and I don't apologise for any passage of the Qur'an.

We have to be very clear about this point, but at the same time we have to be clear about what, how we interpret this passage of the Qur'an and the context in which it applies.

> It's not a blanket statement. It's not an official position in respect of how we should deal with certain people in all times at all places. It came down in a specific context, was applied in a specific context and most definitely should be implemented in its given context.

Never mind that Doureihi was unable to say he was not anti-Semitic. At least he didn't kowtow.

In December 2005, riots broke out on the beaches of Sydney. A drunken mob of 5000 mostly Anglo-Australians, some draped in Australian flags, others wearing T-shirts bearing the words 'Ethnic Cleansing Division' and singing Australia's national anthem as though it were a war cry, descended with flying fists upon anyone they deemed to be of Lebanese extraction, even if they were Bangladeshi. It was, ostensibly, an uprising against the antisocial behaviour of groups of young Lebanese-Australian men who had made their unwelcome presence felt on the beaches in preceding years by harassing women, making racist provocations, and assaulting security guards and locals. In fact, anger against these Lebanese-Australian gangs had been rising in Sydney for many years following dozens of shootings and murders, hundreds of sexual assaults, violence at sporting events and, most infamously, gang rapes of white women that had unmistakable racist overtones. Nevertheless, the beach mob's behaviour was unspeakably thuggish, and shocked and shamed a nation that is often engaged in internal debate about the existence of racist undercurrents in its society.

About two days later, a brick was thrown through the front window of the Islamic Council of Victoria's offices in Melbourne. It was, in fact, the second time in a month this had happened. The first brick was deposited only a few weeks prior in the wake of a series of counter-terrorism raids in Sydney and Melbourne that led to the arrest of seventeen men. Mainstream media around the country showed intense interest in the story, perhaps as an attempt to suggest that the riots of Sydney were on their way to Melbourne.

Immediately, the Islamic Council of Victoria was inundated with phone calls and emails of support. Most significantly for the purposes of this chapter, many of them saw fit to apologise for the vandalism:

> I would like to express my absolute disgust at the behaviour I have seen in the last few days towards those in our communities who are of the Islamic faith.
>
> I apologise as a fair-minded Australian and thought that I would never see the day when people in this country would treat their fellow citizens with such racist behaviour.

Representatives of Pax Christi Australia wrote: 'Please accept our apology, our support, our prayers and solidarity'; while an ordinary, unaffiliated citizen said:

> Please know that my thoughts are with you, and that I wish an apology from me would mean something more; as I do not wish to be in any way aligned with those that perpetrated this crime and insult. But I apologise just the same.

You could easily argue that there was no need for these people to apologise at all. It was not they who vandalised the Islamic Council's premises. Moreover, we do not even know if the culprits were associated with them in any way, because we don't know who did it. But here were a range of ordinary Australians who felt the need to apologise nonetheless. They were not waiting for proof identifying the guilty, or concocting conspiracy theories about the Islamic Council smashing its own windows. For them, this was all immaterial. They sensed a need for solidarity, and a need to distance themselves from this vandalism. They saw the social benefit in apologising proactively when no such sentiment was required of them. Their thoughts were not with themselves, but the vandalised. They felt no need to make a point about terrorism perpetrated by Muslims, or the damage Lebanese-Australian gangs have done in recent years. This was about reclaiming their society, our society, from a cycle of blame and reciprocal harm. So, they apologised. And they did it without the slightest hint of self-flagellation.

Why is it so difficult for many Western Muslims in similar circumstances to do the same? It is difficult enough for us to state unequivocal condemnation, let alone apologise. Why are we so resistant to the idea of apologising for the actions done by those with whom we are unavoidably, if involuntarily, associated? Why is it difficult for us to reflect the best examples of grace others have shown us?

Partly this is because of a fear that an apology would constitute an admission of guilt. Many Muslims feel as though they are blamed enough for the crimes that have nothing to do with them, without appearing to legitimise that blame by apologising. This is entirely understandable. But ultimately, this only underscores that this reticence is a function of social weakness. Ultimately, we do not even contemplate apologising because we lack the self-confidence to do so. We are too insecure to be generous in this way because we have an absurd perception that it diminishes us – as though an apology is an admission of moral defeat when, in truth, it is usually the opposite. Perhaps we do not perceive how weak it is to be incapable of grace, how pathetic it is to be so instinctively defensive.

This same defensiveness also underlies the common anxiety in Western Muslim communities to present a unified front. It is as though the situation is one of rival tribes, where unity is a show of strength, and any hint of division is death. What is less often understood is just how dangerous this fake veneer of unity is in the present environment. We live in an age where, fairly or unfairly, the dominant images surrounding Islam and Muslim populations are manifestly ugly. A rigid determination to appear united (which usually ends up meaning homogeneous) does little more than unify masses of Muslims with that ugliness. Moreover, it is simply untrue. Western Muslim populations, in particular, tend to possess such tremendous diversity that it is difficult, even for those within them, to grasp its extent fully. What those who desire such false homogeneity don't seem to understand is that diversity and disagreement within Muslim populations is, and would be perceived as, a sign of considerable social strength and health. 'If two men agree on everything, you may be sure that one of them is doing the thinking,' said former US president Lyndon Johnson. How much truer is this of entire communities? That many Muslims are so desperate to fit within this unhealthy category for the sake of some phoney 'strength', particularly when the reality is exactly the opposite, is evidence of a thoroughly defensive posture.

Contemporary hatred of Islam within Western societies tends, obviously, to feed off this posture. This voice demands not only that Muslims condemn practices such as honour killings or terrorism, but that they condemn Islam along with them. The bigoted dismiss any Muslim who distances Islam from this barbarism as being defensive. Meanwhile, a significant portion of the Muslim population derides as apologetic any admission that the Muslim world, even if not exclusively, has serious oppressive practices to confront. And so the circle is complete: contrarian defensiveness (or denial) in the face of Muslim terrorism breeds bigotry towards Islam and Muslims, which breeds further contrarian defensiveness. The dynamic is so thoroughly, tragically symbiotic.

And so, we are left with a conflict perpetuated by complex, deeply entrenched psychology. In this context, the surest sign of just conduct is that sworn enemies agree to despise you. In a world that dysfunctional, how can there be any understanding?

Yet, perhaps there is cause for hope. If the Danish cartoons furore provides a snapshot of our dysfunction, we should take heart that at its height, on 5 February 2006, a peaceful demonstration of 3000 Muslims and non-Muslims for peace, dialogue and understanding took place in Copenhagen. On reflection, we can recognise that the cartoon controversy was really the work of the most rabid extremes. Flashpoints usually provide a stage for such elements. In some sense, they deserve each other.

Meanwhile, a silent core, which I prefer to believe is a majority, watch on in depressed bewilderment. If the above explains how we got here, it is these people who will take us elsewhere.

3

Don't call me a moderate!

When the phones stop ringing and the chatter of popular journalism recedes into the background, when the pointless and spectacularly ignorant arguments of a thousand internet forums leave me in peace, when the clutter of my mind is swept aside and I find some precious mental space, I often find myself, almost involuntarily, peering silently into the debates of Islamic history.

On such rare opportunities, I do not see 'moderates' and 'fundamentalists'. I see vibrancy, diversity and passion. I see a subtlety I will never master; a richness and an open curiosity that is simultaneously inspiring and paralysing. To be sure, I see elements that discomfort and even disturb me. I see some conclusions that are products of environments alien to mine. But what I definitely do not see is a simple binary world. I see a world far too complex and sophisticated to be stuffed into two linguistic boxes labelled 'fundamentalist' and 'moderate'.

In *Nineteen Eighty-Four*, George Orwell wrote of a fictional totalitarian world in which Newspeak replaced standard English as the official language of the region known as Oceania. Newspeak was a language designed specifically to meet the ideological needs of Oceania's government, the Party, and its ideology, 'Ingsoc'. Orwell explained:

> The purpose of Newspeak was not only to provide a medium of expression for the world-view and mental habits proper to the devotees of Ingsoc, but to make all other thoughts impossible. It was intended that when Newspeak had been adopted once and for all . . . a heretical thought – that is, a thought diverging from the principles of Ingsoc – should be literally unthinkable, at least so far as thought is dependent on words. Its vocabulary was so constructed as to give exact and often very subtle expression to every meaning that a Party member could properly wish to express, while excluding all other meanings and also the possibility of arriving at them by indirect methods . . . Newspeak was designed not to extend but to *diminish* the range of thought . . .

Orwell's Party recognised the fundamental role language plays in shaping our thoughts. This is a matter of practical, and not merely theoretical, significance. Ideas that cannot find a home in our language, and cannot be expressed in words, are unsustainable. If they exist at all, they cannot spread, and accordingly, they very easily die. The career of Malcolm X as a black activist began in prison when he studied the dictionary. He had learned that words are power, and that to control them is to control thought.

Sometimes, when I contemplate the words popularly used in describing, or rather examining, Islam and Muslims, I feel like a similar phenomenon is at work. Of course, we do not live in an Orwellian world. Our public language is not as brilliantly manipulative and ideologically potent as Newspeak. But it is true that elements of it serve only to create barriers to understanding. We flirt regularly with linguistically entrenched nonsense. If Newspeak was designed to make it impossible to have a heretical thought, our language almost makes it impossible to have a meaningful one.

This has been particularly true since September 11, when Muslims became considerably less human in the public consciousness, instead being reduced to little more than the raw material from which public debate was processed. The debate was then, and largely is now, a conversation *about* Muslims – not with them. Muslims are variously accused, convicted and exonerated as though they are not even in the room. As a friend put it to me, just after September 11 it was 'like we were some species of ant'.

Often, that species has been considered monolithic. Of course, nothing could be further from the truth. The Australian Muslim communities alone span about 70 different national backgrounds, countless languages and cultures, the full range of the political spectrum and a staggering array of religious (and irreligious) views. There is, in fact, no singularly coherent Muslim community, but dozens and dozens of communities that happen to be made up of people who identify, to varying degrees, as Muslims. It is for this reason that I have argued elsewhere that the Muslims in Australia are as diverse as the world. The same diversity is observable in most migrant-based Muslim communities. Yet, if I mention anything of this diversity in the course of a speech, surprised listeners advise me with staggering regularity that they had no idea any diversity even existed. I am sure this is reflective of the way in which Muslims have been publicly portrayed for so long.

This is changing slowly, but not necessarily satisfactorily. Muslims may no longer be a monolith, but they are now a binary. Our language seems to require that every ant must be classified either as a 'fundamentalist' or a 'moderate'. I freely and frankly admit that I find the fundamentalist/moderate dichotomy utterly contemptible. But for present purposes, my objection is that it is meaningless. It is an example of how our public language plays a significant role as an inhibitor to meaningful understanding.

Perhaps it was inevitable that the Western conversation on Muslims would never encompass any great subtlety or accuracy. To some extent, public discourse never does. We lose much by having most of our public debate in sound bytes. In the cut-and-thrust world of political journalism, everything must have a label, even if it consequently has no meaning. Every argument must be simple, even if that means it is simplistic. Public debate is consumed, not conducted. It is entertaining before it is informative.

'Fundamentalism', for its part, is a slippery label. Historically, it was a movement that began in late nineteenth-century American Christianity and took root in the 1920s with the publication of *The Fundamentals*, a book that set out to re-establish the incontestability of certain core Christian doctrines. This movement arose as a reaction to modernism, which sought to integrate Christian thought with contemporary understandings of history and the sciences. It was a battle against the forces of rationalism and biblical criticism.

Its defining characteristic was not literalism, as is often imagined, but a belief in the inerrancy of the Bible. Indeed, sometimes, to maintain that the Bible was free from error, a fundamentalist reading would be forced to be non-literal. 'Fundamentalism' is, therefore, a term with a wholly Christian lineage, that arose in response to a very Christian phenomenon. If we seek to apply this label to Islam, we are therefore making an implicit assumption that certain circumstances from Christian history are readily transferable to Islamic thought and society.

Often, they are not. At least not in the way we might think. The war of faith against science that roared in Christendom was largely unknown in the Islamic world. In fact, the opposite was predominantly true: many Islamic theologians and scholars were also prominent scientists. Science was viewed simply as another available tool for making sense of the universe. Indeed, it revealed and explained the wonders of God's creation and, to that extent, was considered a form of worship. The elliptical nature of the Qur'anic text meant Muslim scientists faced no crisis of faith in examining and embracing new scientific theories. When Charles Darwin developed his evolutionary thesis in the nineteenth century, he was slammed as a heretic in Europe. Yet, some 600 years earlier, Shiite theologian, philosopher and scientist Naṣir al-Dīn al-Ṭūsī proposed an almost identical theory without the slightest recrimination.

Of course, this does not mean that the Muslim world upheld pure rationalism. Rationalist schools of thought flourished at various periods in Islamic history, the most famous of which were the Muʿtazilites, and several of their views came to be rejected by the majority. The Muslim world spent much time discussing the limits of human reason, and its reliability in discerning truth. And indeed, anti-intellectual approaches to Islam have long been part of the Muslim landscape, and continue to be. But it is also true that such views were traditionally marginal; even the brilliant Abū Ḥāmid al-Ghazālī, himself an opponent of Aristotelian philosophy and one of Islamic history's most strident critics of overreliance on human reasoning, likened revelation to the sun, and the intellect to the eye, which is a necessary and vital tool in perceiving sunlight. As contemporary scholar Tahir Jabir al-Alwani summarised it: revelation is reason from without, and reason is revelation from within. It remains that the mainstream of traditional Islamic thought was highly engaged in rational criticism in determining Islamic theology, law and philosophy.

Thus, the Muslim world never experienced any definitive conflict between faith and reason to anywhere near the extent Christendom did. By and large, Islamic thought did not fear new knowledge and new ways of looking at the world. Even reports attributed to the prophet Muhammad were tested against established human knowledge as a tool to determine their authenticity. Qur'anic exegesis, too, responded to such developments. Yet, traditional Islam saw no need to alter Islamic theology and doctrine in the manner of Christian modernists. Thus, the dynamics that led both to modernism, and its fundamentalist reaction in Christianity, were largely absent from Islamic societies. The concept of fundamentalism, therefore, as it evolved from Christianity, is essentially meaningless in the Islamic historical context. But it is precisely the language that is now used in connection with Islam more than any other faith.

In truth, fundamentalism has now become a vague term even as applied to Christian groups. For example, it is liberally applied to Pentecostal Christianity, a defining feature of which from the 1970s until recently was the belief that baptism by the Holy Spirit was evidenced by speaking in tongues. In some Pentecostal congregations, this meant that those who did not speak in tongues would be excluded from positions of leadership. This idea is nowhere found in the thought of the original fundamentalists.

If fundamentalism is misapplied in its homeland of Christianity, how much more nebulous must it become when applied to the very different dynamics of Islam? There is a very real argument that 'fundamentalism', as a term, has lost all substantial meaning. This is a major concern, because it is a term we use so often to frame our apprehension of Muslim societies. We are in danger of talking in a world of total fiction.

These nuances of our language are simply ignored, except by academics working in the area. If fundamentalism is ever defined in more popular discourse, it tends to be erroneously equated with literalism. But even that level of definition is rare. More commonly it is a label attached to anything of which the person using it disapproves. That which is ugly, offensive, isolationist or dogmatic is all now termed 'fundamentalist'. Even more worrying, it is often equated with being devout. This bears no relation to the term's original meaning. It is, in truth, a brand-new term that has never been defined, and is used far more frequently than it is understood.

The incoherence of this label, and its utter foreignness to the Muslims it purports to describe, means Muslims often find themselves supplying their own definition of fundamentalism in order to make sense of what is said about them. Here we can see a profound misunderstanding form before our very eyes. I will never forget hearing a prominent Melbourne imam tell a national Australian television audience that a fundamentalist was simply someone who followed their religion properly. He was trying to say that there is nothing disturbing about someone being devout. He was attempting to draw a distinction between piety and extremism or radicalism.

I understand his intent, but within the parameters of the public conversation, many will have understood him to be saying that the proper practice of Islam is necessarily fundamentalist, with all the ugly images that carries. He will have implied that it is only those who do not practise Islam properly that are not fundamentalists. And in the process, he may have implied that fundamentalism is equated with devoutness. Given that fundamentalism is nasty, this has the disastrous consequence of equating nastiness with devoutness. The only Muslims who are not of concern are those who are not religious. And it is precisely because of the meaninglessness of this popular term that the sheikh would have been blissfully unaware of how his comments sounded to his audience. And so we place layer upon layer of mutual confusion and misunderstanding.

The sheikh's articulation of fundamentalism is very common among Muslims, very few of whom will have recognised the need to know the term's origins. Partly this is because it is often translated into Arabic as *'uṣūlī'*, which connotes an emphasis on the basics or fundamentals. Thus, Muslims often talk of the term as though it refers to someone who believes in, practises and holds to the fundamentals of their religion. In the public space, this places Muslims in a quandary: to deny one is a fundamentalist becomes to deny one takes Islam seriously, yet fundamentalists are clearly understood to be unsavoury people.

If we must keep this term, the solution to this meaningless mess is simply to state explicitly what we mean by it. And in searching for meaning, it is helpful to return to consider the original fundamentalists. They purported to be defending the idea that the biblical text was true, and therefore rejected all interpretations of the Bible that contradicted that truth. The twist is that, as a singular proposition, this would be untroubling for a great many diverse Christian schools. For example, many could argue they are doing precisely that when interpreting the Book of Genesis to conform with evolutionary theory. By rejecting Christian creationism, they could easily argue they are rejecting an interpretation of the Bible that contradicts truth.

This reveals that the fundamentalist claim was not simply a matter of asserting the Bible's enduring truth. It is one thing to interpret the Bible by whatever approach will avoid 'error'. It is another not to recognise when 'error' is defined by one's own social outlook and predetermined views on what the 'truth' is. Those subjective, preconceived ideas of 'truth' and 'error' are rarely, if ever, examined. Rather, though this is never explicitly stated, they are the assumed starting point. So, if one has assumed a creationist view of the world to be true, it becomes instant heresy to suggest an alternative reading of the Bible without ever examining one's own assumptions, or indeed, the possibilities for the text to be interpreted alternatively, but still faithfully.

This allows for a deeper definition of fundamentalism that genuinely could span religious and ideological borders. The asserted inerrancy of a text or a philosophy is often more deeply a belief in the inerrancy of the self. We can therefore define as a fundamentalist one who holds his or her own view to be incontestable, however progressive or conservative those views are. Most often, this will be implicit, or even denied: few people will admit to considering their views incontestable. They will simply not tolerate any such contestation in practice.

Fundamentalism, then, is not a set of beliefs, but a state of mind. It is about dogma of the most arrogant sort: a kind that is inherently exclusive to one's own subjectivities, and worse, that considers those subjectivities to be supremely objective. As such, it is well known within the bounds of all religious communities, but is clearly far broader than a religious classification. Just as there are Muslim fundamentalists by this definition, so too are there secular fundamentalists as well as fundamentalist atheists or even democrats.

This is not to say that relativism is the only alternative to fundamentalism. One can believe in the existence of absolute moral, religious or political truth without taking the fundamentalist position of assuming that one has an infallible monopoly on that truth. One is not required to stand for nothing, but merely to recognise the presence of subjectivity in one's own worldview, and to accept, therefore, the possibility of error.

This state of mind that I call 'fundamentalism' has a profound social impact. Coming from the powerless, it necessarily tends towards isolationism. Coming from the powerful, it necessarily tends towards authoritarianism. In either case, it is an inherently divisive attitude, and if it is backed by military force, can be devastating. Defining fundamentalism in this way would have the advantage of being historically consistent and, most importantly, socially meaningful. We would at long last be describing something real and coherent. We might then have some hope of talking sense.

And, at least in the case of Islam, it would make clear the difference between devout traditionalism and fundamentalism. Indeed, there is a strong argument to say that traditional Islamic thought was compulsively non-fundamentalist. The starting point is the central concept of self-reproach and introspection: 'God does not change a condition of a people until they change what is within themselves,' counsels the Qur'an, making it plain that people must look within to find the cause of their maladies. This represents a total repudiation of spiritual arrogance. The classical Islamic vision would repudiate the idea that Muslims, or indeed anyone, are entitled to claim a status as God's people. People are not left merely to say they believe. They must work.

From that foundation, classical Islam takes on a thoroughly non-fundamentalist hue. If fundamentalism is ultimately a form of self-adoration, of a belief in the inerrancy of the self, then the self-reproaching attitude of classical Islam strikes at the root of the fundamentalist weed. Its starting point acknowledges, as a central tenet, the fallibility of human beings. Its starting assumption, then, is that there is an important distinction between absolute truth, as embodied in the Qur'anic text, and one's interpretation of it. Hence, as the great Imām al-Ḥaramayn al-Juwaynī contended: 'The most a *mujtahid* [distinguished jurist] would claim is a preponderance of belief and the balancing of evidence. However, certainty was never claimed by any of [the early jurists].' Even when Muslims assumed the dominant position of conqueror, eighth-century jurist Muḥammad ibn al-Ḥasan al-Shaybānī insisted that the enemy should not surrender on the basis of God's judgment 'since you do not know what God's judgment is'. Any pledge should be taken, not in God's name, but in the conqueror's. A significant difference is assumed.

This assumption was profoundly at work in a fascinating debate in Islamic history about whether or not, for every question, there was one true answer – the answer God would give. On the one hand, Muslims agreed that the Qur'an embodied the divine message, and is therefore pure and infallible. On the other hand, as 'Alī ibn Abī Ṭālib, the prophet Muhammad's cousin and fourth Caliph of Islamic history, observed: 'The Qur'an is written in straight lines between two covers. It does not speak by itself. It needs interpreters, and the interpreters are human beings.' It is humans, with all their attendant fallibility, that are charged with deciphering the divine message. This process is often called *ijtihād*: the expending of intellectual effort to render the sacred texts intelligible, and make them speak to new and changing circumstances. The one who does this is called the *mujtahid*.

This process of human interpretation surely introduces the prospect of error. Yet, according to a well-known narration, the prophet Muhammad had stated that 'every *mujtahid* is correct'. This sent Islamic scholars into a frenzy. How can every *mujtahid* be correct when they reach different, even conflicting, conclusions? Did this mean there was no uniquely true answer to every Islamic legal question? An impressive volume of classical Islamic scholarship from an impressive rollcall of Islamic jurists was devoted to such enquiries. The complexity of the debate gave birth to two schools of Islamic thought on the issue.

The first held that every conceivable legal question had a pre-determined solution, set by God, and that the theologian's task was one of discovery. This group understood the Prophet's statement to convey that Islamic jurists could not be considered sinful merely because they reach different conclusions. Jurists who ultimately settled upon an incorrect interpretation of the Qur'an would be excused for this provided their search was diligent, honest, and done in good faith with integrity. In this sense, every *mujtahid* is correct: their efforts are commendable, but their conclusions are not equally valid. The Prophet had said every *mujtahid* is correct; not that every conclusion is correct.

It followed that although there is one uniquely True answer to every Islamic question, we may not be able to say with certainty what it is. Only God knows the True answer to every question until it is revealed to us in the next life. This school came to be known to history as the *mukhaṭṭi'ah*, and included such notable scholars as Ibn Kathīr, Ibn Ḥajar al-Haytamī and Aḥmad ibn Taymiyya.

The other school concluded that there was no uniquely correct answer to every legal problem. Had God wanted us to discover the specific, correct answer to every question, they argued, the sacred texts would have been conclusive and unequivocally clear. For this group, it was senseless to say that God has given us the task of discovering the correct answer, but denied us the unarguable, objective means of discovering it. Accordingly, humanity's duty was to make a sincere effort to draw guidance from the sacred texts, but not to discover some abstract 'correct' result. If humans were charged with finding this result, they would not have been forgiven for failing to find it. Humans were not burdened with this obligation because such a result does not exist for every legal question, which is how it is possible that 'every *mujtahid* is correct'. This, of course, does not justify any and every reading of the sacred texts: any attempt at answering a legal question must be done diligently, in good faith, and with moral and intellectual integrity. This school came to be known as the *muṣawwibah*. Its adherents featured such other giants of medieval Islamic thought as al-Ghazālī, Fakhr al-Dīn al-Rāzī and, later, Jalāl al-Dīn al-Suyūṭī.

For the *mukhaṭṭi'ah*, such an approach was redundant. They argued that if conflicting responses can be equally valid, if we cannot aspire to finding the 'true' answer because it does not exist, then our discussions are for naught. They are rendered a nonsense. The *mukhaṭṭi'ah* insisted that debates are useful precisely because they help us get closer to the truth. Perhaps we will not always get there. Perhaps we cannot be certain we have succeeded even when we have. But it is still the goal of our intellectual efforts; our intended destination.

The *muṣawwibah* countered by arguing that the process of debate and discussion was beneficial in its own right. In this vision, ambiguity in the divine message is a gift because it forces us to spend our lives thoroughly engaged with the message; immersed in its unending riches; forever uncovering new depths and nuances; continuously exploring its possibilities and plumbing its mysteries; but never finishing the process. This is as much a spiritual experience as an intellectual one. By demanding a perpetual engagement with the sacred texts, God is giving us an eternal means of connection.

The debate between the *mukhaṭṭi'ah* and the *muṣawwibah* is far richer and more complex than this summary might illustrate. For present purposes, however, I mention it in simplified form to highlight that within this classical debate, both schools ultimately concede that, even if the absolute Truth exists on every legal question, they do not have access to it. At least, not knowingly.

Neither school took the fundamentalist position of declaring, or implying, that its legal conclusions were absolutely true. Of course, there were limits to this. Scholars in both camps accepted that there were certain core, defining issues where the Islamic position was clear and determinate – although they proceeded to disagree on what those issues were, perhaps highlighting the correctness of their original admissions that the absolute Truth is distinct from their own understandings.

In any event, the dynamics of classical Islamic thought created by such debates became one where the focus was not exclusively on specific conclusions (as it is for fundamentalists), but on the integrity and erudition of one's method of interpretation. The science of legal theory, or *uṣūl al-fiqh*, which concerns not legal rulings themselves, but the deeper questions of how such rulings are derived, became perhaps the most esteemed field of Islamic knowledge: *tāj al-'ulūm* – the crown of the Islamic sciences. Jurists developed diverse legal theories, which inevitably led to diverse legal conclusions. The result was a corpus of Islamic thought of rich subtlety, dizzying diversity and endless debate.

There is an inherent comfort with ambiguity in all this. To the classical mind, it is clear that the divine message is too vast, too rich, too endowed and teeming with meaning to be encompassed by a singular human reading. Abū al-Ḥasan al-Māwardī's eleventh-century Qur'anic commentary regularly lists four or five differing interpretations for a given Qur'anic verse. Certainly, the classicist shows interest in reaching a conclusion, but is compelled to accept a legitimate plurality of doctrinal views. Thus, the master jurist al-Shāfi'ī asserted that he considered his opinions correct with the possibility of them being incorrect, while the reverse was true of contrasting views. Fundamentalism, therefore, far from being associated with traditional Islamic practice, is actually profoundly untraditional.

This is important to note, because all too often, traditional Islamic practices are summarily derided as fundamentalist. Hence, a report in *The Sydney Morning Herald* in July 2005 describes a class of Sheikh Shady al-Suleiman, imam of Sydney's Lakemba Mosque, in which he is outlining the details of the ritual ablution a Muslim performs before prayer. We read about the minutiae: the hands are washed first, then the face and head, arms and feet; right limbs before left.

We read about al-Suleiman's warning against gazing licentiously at women, and his counselling against thinking ill of other Muslims based on hearsay. We read about details of Islamic dietary law, and in particular, methods of slaughter that apparently mitigate against the risk of bacterial infection. About the most foreign thing we read is al-Suleiman's response to a questioner that a Muslim woman should not pluck her eyebrows.

Then we read that the sheikh 'is equally strident in condemning terrorism and sexual assault. Islam's Prophet Muhammad, he says, led a life of scrupulous honesty and lived harmoniously with Jews and pagan tribes in Medina.'

Apparently, this is meant to show that 'it's a long way from fundamentalism to terrorism'. Certainly, this distinction is a welcome moment of sense, but I wonder precisely what it is that renders al-Suleiman fundamentalist. That allegation may well be true, but nothing mentioned here demonstrates it. Many of the views attributed to al-Suleiman are drawn to some degree from traditional Islamic teachings. Muslims have been performing ritual ablutions with high attention to detail for over 1400 years. Al-Suleiman's opposition to licentious gazing at women and making character judgments on the strength of gossip might perhaps be described as conservative, but has little to do with fundamentalism. Indeed, fundamentalism could only be relevant here if it is equated with such conservative traditionalism. At this point, 'fundamentalism' loses all meaning.

Meanwhile, in *The Australian*, Daniel Pipes praises France's ban on the hijab in public schools as a fight against 'radical Islam'. Pipes presumably would regard as prophetic French philosopher André Glucksmann who, more than a decade earlier, encouraged such a ban in *Le Monde*, screaming that 'The Islamic scarf is a terrorist emblem', that 'the veil is an instrument of terror'. Something about this inanimate piece of cloth terrifies these people. For them, it is the quintessence of radicalism and fundamentalism. Of course, for many who actually wear it, it is merely a manifestation of traditionalism. For others, it is a cultural practice. The reasons women have for wearing it vary widely, just like the opinions and attitudes among them. All of this underscores the fact that the hijab ultimately says very little about one's state of mind. As an indicator of radicalism, extremism and fundamentalism, the hijab is no more reliable than linen trousers. It is because we are yet to understand what we mean by 'fundamentalism' that we are prone to conflate it with traditional practice, and fear it accordingly. If ever those who have argued that the war on terror is simply a war on Islam needed supporting evidence, Pipes and Glucksmann have most unfortunately provided it.

So, in the absence of redefinition, 'fundamentalism' is a terribly confused term. Unfortunately, its polar opposite, 'moderate', is even worse. In my experiences and many conversations with a broad range of Muslims, it is rare to encounter anyone who has enthusiastically embraced this term or who understands what it means. Most intuit that it is externally concocted, and is likely to be used to manipulate the public perception of Muslims.

I cringe every time the 'moderate' label is applied to me. I understand it is probably meant to be a compliment, but the truth is that it is offensive in the way it would be to be called a 'moderate intellect'. It carries the connotation that one's faith is somehow diluted. It implies, condescendingly, that it is socially acceptable to be a Muslim, as long as you are not *too* Muslim.

But my own sensitivities aside, the greater problem is that 'moderate' is an explicitly political term, and not a religious one. We might describe moderates within the Republican Party or the Liberal Party. But I cannot remember ever hearing anyone talk of a moderate Christian. Why not? Christians have political opinions. Their involvement and interest in politics is growing substantially and continuously, to the point where many have begun to ask if we are seeing the Australian emergence of a Religious Right. This is a concept drawn from the experience of the United States, where Christian involvement in politics is famously intense. Indeed, at a domestic level, Christian communities in the West are far more politically active than Muslim communities. They also represent a range of political views, some quite extreme and some, particularly in the United States, quite violent. Why, then, are there no Christian moderates?

Ultimately, it is because we still recognise Christian communities as religious ones. That being so, we do not use the term 'moderate' to describe them, because it has no religious meaning. We understand different congregations may be associated with different political positions, but we are happy to accommodate them within our mainstream political discourse without feeling the need to create a separate political category. But with the creation of the moderate Muslim, we are seeing the elimination of Muslims as a faith community and their re-creation as nothing more than a political entity.

This is why, increasingly, the definition of 'moderate' ultimately depends on little more than the politics of the person using the word. When employed by a Western political leader, it describes only allies. Thus, we see George W. Bush applying this label to King Abdullah of Jordan, King Muhammad of Morocco, or even President Hosni Mobarek of Egypt. These are, of course, rulers whose countries have appalling human rights records and whose citizens and political opponents are habitually repressed and censored. Suddenly that doesn't sound so moderate. Certainly their subjects, who generally view them as corrupt, are unlikely to be comforted by the label. Islam is scarcely enhanced by such moderates.

The fact remains that you are far more likely to be a moderate Muslim if you are not anti-American and if you support – or are muted in your opposition to – the war on Iraq or US support for Israel. The 'litmus test of morality [and] moderation' declares

Melanie Phillips in *Londonistan*, is 'the issue of Israel'. Phillips' analysis soon makes clear that a 'truly moderate' Muslim is one who embraces the prevailing neoconservative orthodoxy on the Middle East conflict: namely that Israel is its principal victim, and the Palestinians their oppressors. It is difficult to imagine a more nakedly political formulation, or indeed a narrower one. Yet this is precisely how this term's meaninglessness can be abused. Since it is neoconservative ideologues who are most devoted to 'exposing' as extremist those widely considered to be moderate, and since most Muslims do not subscribe to neoconservative politics, we encounter the farcical situation observed by Mark Steyn that the 'most prominent "moderate Muslims" would seem to be more accurately designated as apostate or ex-Muslims'.

Clearly then, the term has nothing to do with one's theology and approach to religious practice. It is possible to be called a moderate, even if one is, theologically speaking, among the most extreme voices in the Muslim landscape. This is our Newspeak: where language obscures meaning and prevents Muslims from having a public existence beyond our political horizons.

But even when describing purely political ideas, our language can fall into meaninglessness. Often, this is because our words have in-built assumptions we fail to recognise. Within individual cultures this often has minimal impact because the assumptions of our language are more likely to hold. But in an intercivilisational space, we require the translation not merely of words, but of concepts. This makes it crucially important to identify the assumptions implicit in our language – a difficult task if they are invisible to us. Many examples could be provided in this connection, but one of the most central and potent is a concept that has come to define Western polities: secularism.

4

Save our secular souls

Secularism is, to use a grossly inappropriate phrase, a broad church. It takes many different forms across the world and encompasses many different ways of thinking of government. Indeed, it is difficult to come up with a definition of it that accurately accounts for all nations we would describe as secular. Yet, in spite of its obvious ambiguity, few ideas are as central to Western political identity.

It is with considerable irony that in much conventional Western political wisdom, secularism is a non-negotiable article of faith. In societies of immense political diversity, no political attitude seems to bind free Western democracies like this pervasive, staunch allegiance to it.

Secularism – not just as a concept, but as a value – is therefore destined to play a role in the public conversation on Islam and the West. Because the civilisational interface is now so inherently political, rather than human, so much of the conversation is about political identity that it is inevitable for secularism to become a major reference point. If it is a fundamental part of who 'we' are, the next logical step is to consider if it is who 'they' are not. But do we really understand it?

It is one thing to say that secularism is about freeing the State from the influence of religious institutions, and conversely, freeing religious institutions from governmental interference. But the reality is that such a clean separation is highly artificial. Religious institutions, if they are not in charge of the State, must still live under the laws and policies of the government. Similarly, where religious thought or institutions are part of the fabric of a society, the State can never avoid religious influence.

So, in Australia, the Constitution prohibits the State from making 'any law for establishing any religion, or for imposing any religious observance', yet, even though Australian society is comparatively irreligious, the State funds religious schools and provides tax benefits for religious institutions, while the Australian Parliament has held prayers before each sitting day for over a century.

The US Constitution similarly prohibits Congress from making any 'law respecting an establishment of religion, or prohibiting the free exercise thereof', and guards the separation of Church and State in a manner that would be considered absurd in Australia. Nativity scenes on public land have been found to be unconstitutional, as has an artistic rendering of the Ten Commandments in a courtroom. Yet, as the pledge of allegiance puts it, the United States is 'one nation, under God', and its currency declares proudly: 'In God We Trust'. Religion is a major driving force in US politics. Presidential and other political candidates are often overtly religious and may even quote scripture to garner support. It is difficult to remember a president who has not been overtly Christian (almost always Protestant), although George W. Bush has clearly taken public presidential Christianity to another level.

Meanwhile, across the Atlantic, France is altogether a different story. Its jealously guarded principle of *laïcité* represents a strict exclusion of religion from the public sphere. While US politicians sometimes give the impression they are pretending to be more religious than they really are, in France quite the opposite applies: it is politically perilous to bring one's religious beliefs to the French political table. Public servants are expected to be as religiously neutral as they are politically, and may be prohibited from wearing any visible religious identifiers.

In Germany, the State has given the churches special privileges under tax laws that allow them to levy taxes on members, which the State even collects on their behalf. Contrast this with Mexico, where members of the clergy are compelled to have a completely apolitical existence. They are barred from advocating partisan political views or supporting political candidates. They cannot hold public office, or even oppose the laws or institutions of the State.

Then, of course, there is Turkey, which went through what some might call quite a radical process of secularisation after World War I under Ataturk. The preamble to its Constitution provides that: 'There shall be no interference whatsoever of the sacred religious feelings in State affairs and politics.' But that does not prevent the Turkish government controlling religious organisations. It provides religious education in schools, pays the wages of imams, and even authorises and arranges for Turkish imams to preach in other countries.

There are many more variations on the secularist theme, but the above sufficiently demonstrates that it is difficult to grasp precisely what secularism is meant to be about. Secular states range from those that find themselves supporting religious institutions financially, to those that are downright hostile towards the clergy, and deny religious institutions freedom by controlling them. This is to say nothing of the governments of the old communist bloc, who took a decidedly aggressive approach to religious practice, essentially seeking to stamp it out. In the five years between 1917 and 1922, the Soviet Union executed 28 Orthodox bishops and over 1000 priests.

It is impossible to draw a line through this. All you can do is look to the historical development of secularism to get a feel for what secularism is meant to mean. The secular story really has its roots in the history of medieval monarchs. Kings did not simply rule their domain, but claimed an almost prophetic divine authority to do so. In pagan civilisations, such as ancient Egypt and Rome, rulers went a step further, not only claiming divine imprimatur for their authority, but usually claiming to be gods themselves. It was a theory given more modest expression in the Christian era, but the basic idea was the same: God was deemed to have selected the royal family for its task. This often meant that, aside from political power, the monarch, as a divine appointee, claimed religious authority as well.

That was never going to please the pope. He, too, claimed God's authority, leading to the assertion that ultimate authority, even over the State, was rightfully his. By the fifth century, political authorities in Western Europe other than the Church were weak, leaving the Church with no genuine rival for political power. Statehood simply became one of the Church's functions.

But power corrupts. The Church was now a direct player in the imperial realm, and had the machinery of state at its disposal. Commanding armies, and with absolute control over the justice system, the Church fell into authoritarian temptation. War was routinely declared on those deemed to be the enemies of God. Sometimes, as in the Crusades, these enemies would be Muslims and Jews, but the Church also showed frightening competence in persecuting Christians it regarded as heretics, as Christian Europe plunged into the Dark Ages. That part of history scarcely needs retelling. It has left a deep scar on the Western psyche, and formal apologies from modern-day popes stand as testament to how well this oppression is remembered.

As the Church's dominions expanded, nearby kingdoms were also rising to power and harbouring similar imperial aspirations. These two immovable institutions of Western society, the State and the Church, were once again on a collision course on the question of authority. Importantly, this power struggle was not replicated in Eastern Europe. The Eastern Church continued to administer the Byzantine Empire without challenge until it ultimately fell to the Ottomans in the fifteenth century. This is probably why Greece continues in this theocratic vein today.

But in the West, and in countries of the New World such as the United States, Canada, Australia and New Zealand that would inherit the Western tradition, this power struggle would be determined decisively in favour of the State. Through the Reformation, some Protestant denominations, notably the Baptist Church, in fact passionately and forcefully demanded that Church and State be separated for the good of both. As Europe progressed through the Enlightenment, and the influence of religion began to decline, the fate of theocratic Western government was largely sealed.

Finally, after centuries of Church-led persecution and strife, Western civilisation had erected an inviolable separation between Church and State. Christianity, once a powerful imperial force in its own right, now rendered such things unto Caesar. One of the many effects of this was to allow religious communities to practise their respective faiths. Religious doctrine would play no conceptual role in government, which was to be freed from the bounds of religious law. It was a development that appealed to Western populations with special resonance, given Western civilisation's dark historical experiences with oppressive theocracies.

Largely because of these historical experiences, the virtues of secularism became an axiom of Western political thought. As Terry Lane, a radio broadcaster and columnist for *The Sunday Age* in Melbourne, put it: 'the history of every advanced European nation is the story of progress achieved by the separation of church and state. Governments have no right turning religious scruples into law.' Lane overstates the position, unless he considers Finland, Norway and Denmark, which still conflate Church and State, not to be advanced nations. But his point remains a valid one that is deeply entrenched in the Western political psyche: that Western Europe's experience holds the separation of Church and State to be a fundamental prerequisite for the creation of a free and just society.

So, what does all this teach us about secularism? It seems to me that the history highlights that secularism developed as a response to medieval political power struggles between two mighty institutions and the authoritarian abuses that occurred under church-states. It was not a contest of religious and non-religious ideas, and it was certainly not anti-religious; indeed, some of its most vocal advocates were churches. Ultimately, secularism is really about kings and popes. It is all about *institutional* power.

The Western world clearly has much to lose in revisiting the darkness of its theocratic age. Accordingly, Western societies tend to be pointedly vigilant about preserving the secular nature of their governments. It is a point of concern for everyone I have met who has more than a passing interest in politics.

On this occasion it is a speaking engagement. I find myself in a wide-ranging panel discussion. The audience is a small group of bright, young future (or current) leaders from across Australia. They are intelligent and incisive. They press the panel on how Muslims in Western countries might negotiate any tensions that exist between their religious requirements and the prevailing cultural norms of society. They force the panel to explore the critical differences between Muslims in Australia and Muslims in Europe or the United States. These are all questions with a destination; questions worth asking, and worth answering.

Next to speak is a young woman at the back of the room. She is immediately warm, genuine, likeable. She is articulate, intelligent, and clearly knows her history. She is also interested in politics, and has a troubled look on her face; a kind of polite earnestness as she speaks.

'I consider the separation of Church and State an absolute fundamental,' she begins. My immediate thought is that I understand exactly why she would say this, and why she would be far from alone in holding this to be such a fundamental principle.

But already I can sense an unease growing within myself; a feeling that an overwhelmingly complicated conversation should now begin, but that any answer would have to be packaged into a few minutes. I listen as she continues politely.

'I'm increasingly concerned about how politicians are bringing their religious beliefs to bear on their public office. The rise of the Christian Right in the United States in recent years frightens me, and I can see signs that it is happening in Australia. But their religious beliefs should be kept out of politics. They don't belong there.'

She pauses, and looks down at her hands, as if gathering herself and her thoughts. It looks to me as though she wants to be precise, and I respect that immediately. Too many of our conversations already suffer much from a lack of precision. She looks back up and fixes her assertive but respectful gaze upon the panel.

'I'd be interested in hearing how a Muslim would handle the same issue in Australia. To what extent would a Muslim seek to impose their religious beliefs on others through Parliament?'

Her face is thoroughly engaged and her words are heartfelt. To be honest, I can understand her concern, flowing as it does from the rising Religious Right in the United States, for whose views I have no great fondness. There is something genuinely scary about the thought of the president of the world's superpower openly declaring he invaded Iraq because he believed God told him to do so. As a distant observer, the Religious Right seems to have the same short-sightedness of much unthinking religious neoconservatism, where the only morality of apparent relevance is sexual and reproductive. There is scarcely any moral engagement beyond abortion and homosexuality. Economic injustice, for example, is not on the radar. Who cares if countless (usually black) American families are caught in a vicious poverty trap with all the social ills that creates? Who cares if thousands of innocent Iraqi women and children are killed as 'collateral damage' in a senseless military invasion? In the universe of the Religious Right, these are not issues of moral concern.

Very rarely do I feel myself becoming uncomfortable having to answer a question. But on this occasion, despite my understanding of her position, my concern that this required an involved, protracted conversation, which was simply not now possible, had been realised. How could I possibly answer?

There were so many assumptions in the question. How could there conceivably be a singular Muslim way of formulating policy, any more than there could be a Christian one? Australia's most vocal Muslim member of Parliament is on record saying he serves as a member of his party, not as a Muslim community representative. Most Muslims I have encountered thoroughly despise his politics. It is not as though Muslims in any part of the world are some undifferentiated mass of gelatinous consistency. Surely this all depends on the individual.

But I am most intrigued by the questioner's sincere concern that a politician's religious beliefs might inform his or her policymaking. Not because her concerns are rare, but precisely because they are not. I am immediately reminded of Pamela Bone, a columnist with a fanatical hostility towards religion, who argued in *The Age* in May 2005 that:

> What many of those imbued with religious certainty fail to understand is that a significant proportion of the population do not share their basic belief that God exists, leave alone wanting to get into arguments about what God wants or doesn't want. For something like 30 per cent of Australians it is irrelevant to bring God into public debate.
>
> ...
>
> Yet increasingly this is what is happening. Many members of the Howard Government are devout Christians. Some months ago Treasurer Peter Costello urged Australians to follow the Ten Commandments. Health Minister Tony Abbott has tried to get a new argument about abortion going, has intervened in

debates about stem cell research, and more recently has criticised a recommendation by the Victorian Law Reform Commission to extend access to reproductive technology to lesbians and single mothers.

...

These issues are complex and difficult and surrounded by many shades of grey. They do need to be debated, but politicians are wrong to bring their own religious beliefs into public discourse.

The separation of church and state needs to be jealously guarded, and the Government should be very careful not to be seen to impose church teachings on the rest of the country. Apart from any other consideration, it is poor politics to risk alienating a third of the electorate.

I must confess, I have never been able to make any sense of this argument. If a politician is democratically elected, why should it matter if they bring their religious beliefs to their public office?

Of course, Bone might argue that it is unacceptable, at least in Australia, because a majority of voters do not share the politician's religious conviction. What I don't understand is why that should matter. A (probably tiny) minority of voters would identify as greenies, too. You could not say the majority of Australians are socialists, or liberals, or conservatives, or feminists. And if you drill down into any of these labels, you would unleash further shades of disagreement. I cannot think of any single philosophy, social theory, ideology or moral code that enjoys majority support in Australia. But no one would ever suggest that secularism forbids a politician from advocating policies informed by his or her commitment to, for example, feminist ideals. If I were a conservative, it is likely I would despise those who bring a radical socialist agendum to their public office. But I could never credibly claim that a politician should not be tolerated for doing this. The most I could say is that they are out of touch with the voting mainstream, and that they will be punished at election.

Isn't that ultimately the point? I can understand demanding (albeit pointlessly) that a dictator reflects the prevailing worldview of the people (in the unlikely event there is one), but in a democracy, ideas compete for the popular vote, at least in theory. If a politician wants to push a moral barrow that is rejected by most voters, is that not the politician's risk to take? If his or her religious beliefs are so hideous to the electorate, is not recompense only a ballot box away?

Politicians cannot, and should not, be moral vacuums. They bring their own moral codes to their work. Those moral codes will inevitably shape their policy decisions. Their morality may well derive from entirely non-religious sources, but this does not prevent it from being a source of guidance for their political judgment.

I take a deep breath, and decide to take the plunge.

'I have to say I'm a little bemused by the whole secularism discussion,' I begin clumsily. 'As long as a politician is elected by the democratic process, why should it matter if they draw inspiration from religion in determining their policy positions? We seem to have no objection to any other moral or philosophical code forming the basis of policy. I just don't get why that suddenly becomes unacceptable when one's worldview is inspired by a religious tradition. Why should a religious outlook be less valid an inspiration than a non-religious one, simply because it is religious?'

'But,' she retorts, 'it's not right for someone to use their position in Parliament to force their religious beliefs on to society.' Heads around the room begin nodding in agreement.

'Why not?' I enquire in the politest tone I can find, trying desperately not to sound antagonistic. I am aware that merely to ask this question shocks many people, including, probably, several in the room. For some reason, I cannot think of another way to put it.

She continues completely unfazed: 'Because I don't share those beliefs. People should have the right to choose whatever religion, if any, they wish to follow.' Visible signs of agreement become more pronounced around the room. Heads nod with increased amplitude.

'How are they forcing their beliefs on to society?'

'Well, for instance, by making their religious beliefs official Australian policy or law. Take, for example, the standard position of devout Catholics on issues like abortion or marriage. I see no reason why the rest of the country should have to follow this religion on these issues.'

I pause. A torrent of thoughts runs through my head. I try to hold on to them, but they flood past and I let go. There are too many issues to discuss. I search for some kind of coherent response.

'And what if the elected politician is a secular humanist?' I ask finally. 'Is it acceptable for that politician to use their position to implement their own philosophical beliefs through policy?'

'What do you mean?'

'Well, I don't think I have ever heard anyone object, as a matter of principle, to a politician bringing a secular humanist outlook to their policy-making.'

'True enough.'

'But surely the same criticisms made of religious politicians could be applied to secular humanists. I'm not a secular humanist myself. I do not share that worldview. I should be allowed to subscribe to whatever worldview I wish. By this reasoning, isn't it unacceptable for a politician to force their secular humanist outlook on me? Don't I have a right to demand they keep their own moral codes to themselves?'

The room becomes more animated. Another young woman raises her hand and interjects all in the one motion. She seems nervous, or perhaps just intense. Her face has taken on a reddish hue. I try to gauge whether or not that is anger on her face but cannot get a reading. Whatever the case, as she speaks it is clear she is passionate about the topic.

'But you see, this shouldn't be about morality,' she says sharply. 'That's the whole problem with religion. You talk of moral codes, but that is not what other philosophies and social theories are. They're just theories on how the world works. There is not a moral value attached to them, which means they are not judgmental. You don't force them on others.'

'But what does it mean to say these theories have no moral value attached to them? What does it mean to say they are not moral codes?'

Growing in confidence, she adds: 'It means they are morally neutral. That's the whole point of secularism.'

'But how can a governmental policy be morally neutral?' I reply, my speech becoming involuntarily quicker. 'When the Australian government decided to put asylum seekers arriving unauthorised on Australian shores into mandatory detention in harsh conditions in the desert, many people screamed about how cruel and unjust – which is to say immoral – that policy was. Certainly, you or I might disagree. You might argue this policy was either justified or abhorrent, but surely it's impossible to argue that it's morally neutral. It involves intensely moral considerations.

'When a US-led coalition decided to invade Iraq, millions of people across the world marched in protest because they thought that the war was unjust and perhaps illegal. Others felt the war was necessary for our security, or that it was wrong not to depose a tyrant like Saddam Hussein when you had the means to do so. Whatever position appeals to you, these were moral arguments. A decision to go to war is not morally neutral, whether it is made on the basis of free-market economics or theology.

'Or when a government restructures the welfare system, or makes changes to employment law, or family law, or punishes companies for misleading advertising, these all return, ultimately, to morality. One of the most common ways of attacking a government's policy is to say it is unjust. Justice is the very foundation of morality. There is nothing morally neutral about it, even if we might disagree on when and whether morality is being fulfilled.'

I felt I had spoken too much, but for some reason, I couldn't stop. For so long I had found myself frustrated by the popular conversation on secularism. For so long I had wondered if perhaps it was just me who didn't understand. In trying to make sense of the secularist discourse, I had been thinking about these questions for a long time. Now it was just all pouring out.

'Moreover, I'm not sure I agree that non-religious theories are not judgmental. Anything that purports to identify a just and proper outcome necessarily implies the existence of unjust and improper alternatives. Theories have to make judgments if they are to say anything. That's the nature of politics. And because no policy is morally neutral, it will always be morally judgmental to some degree.'

Clearly, none of this is of any reassurance to her. Her face grows more determined, as she continues: 'Maybe, but the difference is that religions are so intolerant. Religious people are so convinced they are right that they think they can force their beliefs on to you.'

'Yes. That's certainly true of many religious people. But then, that's true of many non-religious people. I've come across plenty of atheists that are stauncher in their lack of belief than most religious people are in their belief. Some of the most dogmatic, arrogant, intolerant people I've met are anti-religious. I call such people "atheist missionaries". If it is the goal of some religious people to convert the world to their faith, it is no less the goal of these people to convert the world to atheism.

'But when we're talking about government, isn't the whole issue of forcing beliefs on to people a bit of a red herring, anyway? No one is forcing people to adopt certain personal beliefs. But forcing beliefs on to people, in the sense of implementing one's own policies, is exactly what politicians do. Surely that has nothing to do with whether or not the inspiration for those policies is religious. A politician who believes stridently in globalisation will act accordingly. Their beliefs will affect people all over the world. If you agree with this politician's view, that's good for you. If not, then not. Either way, you have no choice. All you can do is vote against them next time you have a chance and encourage others to do the same.'

'But there are some places government shouldn't go that religious politicians do,' she counters. 'Abortion is a classic example. The government has no right to legislate on that issue, yet some religious politicians keep pushing to interfere.'

'Surely, though, that isn't a question of religion, but of authoritarianism,' I ponder aloud. 'That's really a question of the legitimate scope of governmental action, isn't it? Exactly what should be considered simply a personal matter and the level to which government should interfere in such affairs is a matter of contention in any system of government. There have been plenty of secular governments that are authoritarian. The thing about democracy is that it's meant to give the people the final say on how much interference on what issues they are prepared to tolerate. I might argue that the government has every right to decide on what your children's names will be, and you might disagree. Indeed, everyone else in the world might disagree with me. Presumably, if a democratic government tried to take away our ability to name our children, it would be political suicide. That's exactly the point.'

At the back of the room, the young woman whose question started this whole discussion has been observing with interested engagement, yet impressive calmness. Her expression is open, but she is clearly interested in pursuing the possibilities of her own train of thought.

'Are you forgetting the crimes of the Church?' she enquires. 'Has the persecution it perpetrated slipped your mind? There is something about religion that simply causes conflict. It is inherently combustible. It is not conducive to freedom and harmony that it even gets a whiff of political power. That's what the separation of Church and State was all about. Western civilisation went through a lot of pain to realise that. We don't need to go through that pain again to arrive at the same conclusion.'

'Yes,' I say, in genuine sympathy. 'I definitely understand. And I haven't forgotten Christendom's experience with Church rule. But I also know there are plenty of examples of non-religious governments that have wrought comparable havoc. It seems to me this is just what people in power often do. The crimes of the Church while it governed are evidence of the evils, not of religion, but of people in power. And all the horrors of medieval Church history came back ultimately to authoritarianism; to the crushing of ideas that did not have the Church's sanction.

'Church–State separation was meant to give all ideas the right to contend. For that reason, I think it is fundamentally anti-secular, that it runs fundamentally against the very principles of Church–State separation, to say religious ideas cannot form the basis of policy. In fact, this only re-creates the very oppression secularism was meant to remove. Just like its infamous theocratic predecessor, this approach says certain worldviews are simply not approved for public consumption.'

A silence.

Instantly my mind wanders off to France, where I cannot help but feel secularism has completely lost the plot. In truth, the French have always had an aggressive brand of secularism. The history that produced this, spanning centuries of bitter and destructive religious conflict, is complex and episodic. Most recently, the persecution of religious populations, especially Protestants, in favour of Catholics in Vichy France during World War II only entrenched the connection between religion and authoritarian oppression in the French consciousness. Like the rest of the Western world, it responded by booting the Church out of politics, but the French response was particularly emphatic. It resulted in what could scarcely be called the separation of Church and State, but rather the annihilation of Church, by State. In the process, perversely, the French have pursued a policy of vigorous assimilation towards minorities, effectively amounting to an enforced but artificial French monoculture. This is really nothing more than the replacement of one Church with another. Standing where once the Catholic Church stood is the Church of French Secularism.

The highest-profile, recent example of this is the infamous law prohibiting conspicuous religious symbols in public schools that came into operation in mid-2004. In theory, this law applies to all religious symbols, whether it be Sikh turbans, Jewish yarmulkes or Christian crosses. But no one seriously doubts it was aimed primarily at the headscarves worn by Muslim women.

When French president Jacques Chirac first supported the idea in late 2003, many French religious leaders protested angrily. Secularists should have been even angrier. The law might have had a more direct effect on religious communities in its operation, but at a philosophical level, it was a complete wreck job on liberal secular thought. This was secularism waging war on itself.

The whole point of secularism was to avoid the authoritarian evil of an ideological dictatorship, to allow religious and other minorities to live free from repression without having to conform to, and live in accordance with, a worldview to which they do not subscribe. The whole point is that it is a freedom-enhancing theory.

The French law, though, is the exact opposite. It denies freedom. It creates an aggressively anti-religious symbolism that says if religious beliefs are to exist at all, it is best they exist where they cannot be seen. The tragic irony of this is that this approach effectively moulds all people into an artificially created, authoritarian homogeneity. The State has expressed, publicly, hostility towards modes of religious expression that in no way impact upon governmental administration. The rhetorical effect of this is the creation of dominant, governmentally approved norms to which one must adhere at points of public intersection. Conform. That sounds eerily like the theocracies from which many secularists seek refuge. It does not leave Church and State to operate in their respective spheres. This does not even respect the separation of Church and State, much less fortify it. If this deserves to be called secularism at all, it represents the point at which secularism becomes the very oppression it purports to remedy.

Clearly, such confusions are not confined within French borders. This kind of authoritarianism is echoed in Singapore, where a similar ban applies and politicians are not permitted to talk about religion. It is the same confusion, it seems to me, that causes commentators in Australia to go wild at the first signs of public religiosity in our politicians. Yet, in the United States, a much more religious society, public religiosity in presidential candidates is not simply tolerated, but almost demanded. I am unable to avoid the impression that a lot of what parades as upholding secularism is in reality motivated by contempt for religion. It is far more anti-religious than it is pro-secular.

I find myself wondering if perhaps this kind of approach to secularism is just how we approach it now. Maybe we have all agreed to transform secularism from a governmental framework into an ideology of its own that is no more immune from authoritarianism and totalitarianism than any other. Or maybe it is just me who has the problem. Maybe I don't understand secularism at all. If so, I have much less respect for it than I thought I did.

'You're more optimistic than me,' comes the voice of a third woman, suddenly, perhaps unexpectedly, piercing a hole through the silence and reminding me that I'm in a conversation. She has a calm resignation about her demeanour that flows through her words. She appears a little older than the two others, and has a slightly darker complexion. Her face conveys an experienced cynicism, in stark contrast to the others' unmistakable passion.

'The Australian government has led us into a war on false pretences, lied to and misled its people, and now it is pushing its right-wing Christian agenda. None of that stopped them being re-elected in the 2004 election.'

I struggle to remember where I was in the conversation. Once more I was lost, selfishly, in my thoughts.

'Well, I'm not sure the Australian government's agenda can best be described as being right-wing Christianity,' I stutter. 'But I think I see your point. I guess what I'm saying is that I don't see how that demonstrates that politicians should not be allowed to draw on religious traditions for their political ideas. Even if we assume this really was a right-wing Christian government, the fact that it was re-elected would just mean the public either supported its religious orientation, or didn't know or care enough about it to remove the government at election. Other concerns clearly outweighed objections to any religious affiliation.'

The focus returns to the second woman, whose face is less reddish than before, but who still seems passionate and nervous. 'But look at the rise of the Religious Right in the United States,' she says. 'Their views are just so narrow-minded and bigoted. Their foreign policy is so gung-ho and misguided. Their increasing power and influence is worrying. And in Australia, with the Family First party's links to Pentecostal churches, and the increasingly public religious beliefs of senior politicians, it seems to be growing here in a similar way.'

'Look, I also object to the political agenda of the Religious Right in the United States. I see a lot of hatred and backwardness in it, and as a Muslim, I probably see more of it directed at me than most. But the fact is my objection to this lobby has nothing really to do with its religiosity. If they renamed themselves Atheists for Family Values, I would be equally troubled. I have a problem with what I consider to be bad policy. I will happily criticise policies I deplore, and I will often do so on moral or ethical grounds. But whether or not those policies are in any way religious is beside the point. I found nothing redeeming in the persecution of vast populations under Soviet communism. I took no solace from the fact that you could at least say this persecution did not come from a religious regime.

'Isn't it time we moved beyond being blinded by the religious label? We should simply recognise that all public policy comes from one worldview or another. It's very unlikely a majority of people will agree with the worldview in question, but that alone isn't sufficient grounds for complaint in a democratic system. It seems to me that we should simply look at the policy in question and assess it on its merits. I guess I'd just prefer to play the ball and not the man.'

These ideas had been building in my mind for so long that as they emptied from me cathartically, I had stopped being conscious of my surroundings. I survey the audience and realise I have not even broached the question of how, if at all, a Muslim might give expression to his or her religious convictions in Parliament. There is so much to say, but time is up. The moderator closes the session.

Churning loudly in the background to this conversation is a broader one about what role secularism does, or should, play within the Muslim world. The conversation frustrates me no end. If, as appears to be the case, we have inconsistencies and contradictions in the way we think about secularism in our own societies, how can we even hope to make any sense when we apply it to Islam and the Muslim world? It strikes me immediately that we can't, and we don't.

Nevertheless, Western civilisation's faithful devotion to secularism means that many Western conversations about Islam and the future of the Muslim world raise secularism as the golden standard. It explains everything that is wrong with the Muslim world, and everything that is right anywhere else. As Terry Lane wrote in *The Sunday Age* in November 2005 after the arrests of seventeen terror suspects in Melbourne and Sydney:

> Putting a few ratbags behind bars will not solve the problem of an unsettling alien presence in the nation. The most urgent requirement is the assimilation of Muslims and the secularisation of Islam. The Man

of Steel [John Howard] should tell us what he has in mind along those lines. We need an Ataturk.

To place this in context, it should be said that Lane does not seem to have much time for religious people, though he apparently has even less time for religious Muslims. For Lane, public religiosity is a social curse, and the world can only ever resemble decency when it enters into a deeply entrenched secularism. Eighteen months earlier, he lamented that:

> Sadly, even in an almost perfect democracy such as ours, the Catholic Church has wielded undue influence and has been able to force craven politicians to turn its peculiar scruples into law, but its influence is waning.
>
> . . .
>
> . . . the Commonwealth has no opinion on religion. That is not just a wise decision for local administration, it is fundamental to the wellbeing of any society that the bigoted, irrational and superstitious not get their hands on the levers of power.

Apparently we are meant to believe it is only the religious who are bigoted, irrational and superstitious.

It is fair to say that Lane's devotion to secularism is more dogmatic than most. Nevertheless, far from being marginal and extreme, his line of argument is common. That is why much is often made of the assertion that Islam, unlike Christianity, recognises no separation between Church and State. While the New Testament Jesus rendered much unto Caesar, Islam is allegedly incapable of doing the same. There is, of course, a great irony in the fact that it was Christianity's own experience with church-run states that led to secularism. Perhaps paradoxically, if Christianity was so unequivocally, inherently secular, the very history that brought secularism about could never have happened.

But more than ironic, the whole conversation about secularism and Islam simply makes no sense. It is deeply incoherent.

As we have seen, the very concept of secularism arose out of the struggle between two entities: the Church and the State. Accordingly, the second we speak about secularism, we assume the existence of these two institutions. They simply must exist if we are to separate them. And that is precisely where the language of secularism breaks down when applied to the Islamic tradition.

Islam, at least in its majority Sunni stream, has no institutional form. It has no theologically ordained hierarchy. Beyond the authority of the prophet Muhammad himself, there is no incontestable authority. Theologians are not appointed to official, structured positions of theological gravity. They do not gain prominence through titles and appointments so much as they do through a process of natural selection. The biographies of Islamic history's greatest scholars are full of stories of religious teachers whose classes and lectures became popular, and whose reputations grew through engaging in discussions and debates with other scholars. To put it shortly, there is no Church in Islam.

This seems to me to be the natural consequence of Islam's strictly held position that there is no intermediary between God and humanity. The role of the priest, particularly in the Catholic tradition, is at odds with the Islamic idea that any human may communicate directly with his or her Creator. In that doctrinal environment, an official structure such as the Church would have no meaning, or worse, would be blasphemous.

How coherent is it, then, to argue that Islam does not recognise any separation of Church and State when Islam does not recognise a Church in the first place? Without a theological institution to rival the State, the whole discourse of secularism collapses. The assertion raised above becomes utterly meaningless because it has false assumptions built into it. Islam and its history are not, for all relevant purposes, equivalent to Christianity and its history.

To identify that Islam, unlike Christianity, has no Church, is not merely to point to a trivial, semantic difference. It is, in fact, to highlight a distinction of crucial importance so far as it relates to the idea of secularism. Because Islam is not institutionalised, there is no officialdom, and accordingly, there can be no official position or policy on a given issue. Certainly Muslims can, and do, reach consensus on a range of issues, but no one can claim the authority to articulate official Islam on behalf of God. As we saw in the previous chapter, Muslim scholars have always recognised the inviolable distinction between their own interpretations of the Islamic texts and the absolute Truth those texts embody. Put another way, Muslims have traditionally recognised that the Qur'an is absolute Truth, but one's understanding and interpretation of it is not. This is why traditional Islamic jurists, when asked to respond to legal questions, have always concluded their analysis with the phrase 'and God knows best'. It is an acknowledgment that the ultimate answer to any question is not within their knowledge, but is known only to God.

This means that, in theory, debate within Islam is perpetually open. In practice, it would only close once everyone was persuaded nothing more could be said on a particular issue. This makes it very difficult to silence anyone, except through weight of popular support. The resultant dynamic is, in some ways, democratic. The closest analogy available in modern Western societies might be that of academia, though arguably Islamic scholarship had greater grassroots penetration.

This is fundamentally different from the case of an organised, official hierarchy. In the case of a church, official doctrine is simply stated, as opposed to the more negotiative and less controlled process of debate and consensus that developed in Islam. The views of Muslim scholars, therefore, were exposed to contest in a way that Church doctrine, in large part, could not be. 'Anarchy' is too strong a word, but in comparison with the structured authority of the Church, the dynamics of Islamic thought could fairly be considered 'intellectual chaos'. This was a tremendous advantage in Islam's early period, as the incessant contest of ideas nurtured rapid, profound intellectual development. Conversely, it also means it is more difficult to quash dangerous thought. There is no Church to crush terrorist ideologies definitively, for example.

This basic structural difference between Islam and Christianity meant religion interacted very differently with government in their respective histories. For about the first 30 years after the prophet Muhammad's death, the political leaders of the Muslims happened also to be among the community's most respected Muslim theologians. However, almost immediately after that brief period, the Muslim world experienced a clear conceptual split between religious thought and political action. Naturally, one could observe tremendous diversity among the different Islamic civilisations, but in many traditional Muslim societies, most religious scholars were independent of government, while those who were not often lost their prestige. Of course, most of the work of an Islamic jurist concerns purely private and personal matters, but the jurist's public role was to be a voice of Islamic conscience and commentary. You could say this role was quite similar to the one played in free, modern societies by media.

The jurists would perform their work largely at a theoretical level, assessing the actions of government and seeking to explain the limits of acceptable governmental action. But they had no power to implement their rulings unless the ruler delegated such power to them. Thus, Islamic jurisprudence developed, in one sense, independently of the actions of Islamic governments. The actions of the caliph, and the judgments of his courts, are not cited as precedents in Islamic legal thought. The theoretical works of jurists were, and remain, vastly more influential. To the extent that caliphs appear in these works, they are usually in the position of seeking advice from the jurists. In this way, Islamic doctrines as derived by scholars could often differ from what Islamic governments did. This is different from the Church becoming the State, where doctrine and political action were one.

So, whereas in medieval Christendom one had a choice between official, Church-sanctioned orthodoxy and heresy,

Islamic history features far more manoeuvring for supremacy between different schools of thought. Different schools managed to get political support at different times, and it is true there were examples where this led to sectarian persecution, but the reality was that there could be no unimpeachable, exclusive claim to the ownership of Islamic doctrine, even from the ruling class. Any enforcement of a religious or sectarian view was not a function of theology, but of political power in much the same way one finds in any system of government. Even then, it invariably failed precisely because it could not make an authentic claim to religious authority.

The most infamous example here is the inquisition (known as the *miḥna*) led by the Abbasid Caliph al-Ma'mūn in the ninth century. This concerned the esoteric Islamic theological debate about whether the Qur'an was created or uncreated. Al-Ma'mūn wanted a consensus that the Qur'an was created, and set about banning, imprisoning, or even torturing and killing theologians who insisted otherwise. The majority acquiesced. The most famous dissenter was Aḥmad ibn Ḥanbal, who insisted that the caliph had no authority to make such doctrinal demands of the scholars. Ibn Ḥanbal was imprisoned and publicly beaten. The result was popular unrest, which brought about the end of the inquisition. Al-Ma'mūn's campaign was, at its heart, not so much a fight over doctrine as it was over religious authority. It was an attempt to assert his power to define Islamic theology over the conscience of the theologians. It failed miserably, and through ibn Ḥanbal's steadfastness, the independence of the theologians survived.

This ultimately meant that Islamic governments were able to be held accountable to some degree. They were at all times fallible and carried little inherent theological meaning. While the Church was the final and ultimate doctrinal authority, it was entirely possible that an Islamic government could be overthrown if the people were persuaded of the religious criticism from independent scholars. Traditionally speaking, the role of theologians was a liberal one: to warn against the creeping authoritarianism that is often the nature of government.

In using the language of separating Church and State, we tend to assume that the only alternatives are a secular government or a theocracy. Either religious scholars play no role in government, or they *are* government. The Islamic approach, though, seems traditionally to have been a kind of hybrid. It is definitely not a theocracy, because ultimately the government is sovereign over the Islamic scholars. Most scholars' power would be rhetorical, but not political. The government still had the power to ignore them if it wished. However, I cannot comfortably call it secular either. Governments usually sought to promote themselves as Islamic, attempted to justify their actions Islamically, and appointed Islamic jurists as judges in the courts (which, like our courts, were usually independent).

It is possible to say this arrangement falls somewhere in between, but it is probably more accurate to say that the whole concept of secularism just does not make sense in an Islamic context where no Church structure exists. This is why, when I am asked if Islam is compatible with secularism, I am lost for an honest answer. Whether 'yes', or 'no', my answer will be misleading. The most honest answer I could give is to say I do not know what the question means. As the conversation is currently proceeding, we are simply talking across each other.

Some Shiites, though, unlike the Sunnis, have a far more analogous theoretical structure to the Church. In the largest Shiite school, religious and political authority resides with specified imams appointed by God. Their position is effectively papal. In the Shiite context, then, it might be possible to speak coherently of secularism and theocracy. But even here, the chosen imams are spread throughout history rather than existing in perpetual succession, and there has not been one since the ninth century. Modern-day Iran, with substantial political powers placed directly in the hands of fallible theologians, is something of an anomaly even in Shiite history. But it is very rare that popular commentators would recognise this sort of nuance before launching into a discussion of secularism and Islam. We tend just to plough on, unthinkingly, with the discussion.

At the heart of this senselessness is the human tendency to project ourselves on to others. I think we do this as a kind of short cut. It is often too laborious to go to the trouble of learning about foreign cultures, countries, religions or ideologies. It is much easier to take our own template and squeeze whatever we encounter into it. In taking this approach to understanding the unfamiliar, we tend to identify rough approximations with our own experiences and assume identical similarity. There is little engagement beyond this superficial exercise. It is no wonder we tend to miss significant differences that may have massive consequences for our analysis.

This same phenomenon of projection is present in much of our commentary on issues of foreign policy, not to mention the policies themselves. Of course, the textbook example of our times is the US-led invasion of Iraq that began in 2003, and the discourse surrounding it. To be fair, it is difficult to figure out exactly what the justification for this war really is. It began as a war of security: a pre-emptive strike against a dictator with biological and perhaps nuclear weapons, who, we were told, could effectively destroy the Earth within 45 minutes. When it turned out these weapons did not exist, an alternative pretext was sought. Suddenly, this was a war of liberation. It was about bringing the wonders of democracy to a people that had been under the thumb of tyranny for half a century. Iraqis would be free of Saddam Hussein, and be given the freedom to flourish in a newly built nation: kind of like the United States in the Middle East.

It is here that the projection starts. The United States took no time to remove Saddam Hussein, but as it set about rebuilding the country's government, it rapidly took the posture of a biblical deity seeking to create in its own image. Of particular relevance to this chapter, this meant that Iraq would be a secular democracy. Our man in Baghdad would be Ahmed Chalibi, a staunch secularist who lost favour only after he was alleged to have passed on classified information about American troop movements in Iraq and other top-secret information to Iran's Ministry of Intelligence and Security. The United States would hold a veto power over Iraq's interim constitution, and it said in no uncertain terms that it would use it to ensure that Islam played no constitutional role in Iraq. After all, the only road to civilisation was, and is, *our* road.

The initial pretext for war may have been bunkum, but at least it dealt only with a simple matter of security: bomb Iraq before it bombs us. The minute we started trying to recast Iraq, and even the entire Middle East, in accordance with the lessons of *our* history, we projected ourselves on to them and began to think of ourselves as the universal humans.

Several commentators followed suit, although once more, Terry Lane of *The Sunday Age* provides the best example. In May 2004, it dawned on him that the people of Iraq might not vote for a secular party. This mortified Lane, who retorted staggeringly that 'Saddam Hussein may be a bad man, but at least before 1990 he was a secularist and an emancipator of women'. He then surprised even himself when he concluded that a Singaporean-style secular autocracy might be a better fit for Iraq's political future than democracy, because Iraqis would probably elect a religious government. Apparently, if you do not choose secularism, you are not fit to choose. So much for choice.

Not to be outdone, John Keegan, military historian and defence editor of *The Daily Telegraph* in London, went so far as to conclude: 'better a Baathist Iraq than an Islamic one. Let us hope it is not too late.' Keegan's broader argument is more nuanced than Lane's, but appears to embrace similar assumptions: that Saddam Hussein's Baathist regime, though brutally repressive, was at least secular, unlike those nasty Islamic parties, which are increasingly gaining popular support. Apparently, popular support only matters when it delivers a result we like.

A people who decide otherwise apparently do not deserve self-determination.

There are many reasons why these kinds of analyses are dangerously wrongheaded. At the simplest level, they are breathtakingly arrogant and Eurocentric. These are examples of analysis that is deeply rooted in the Western historical experience. This brings with it certain limitations because that historical experience is not universal. The solutions Europe generated in its own development are not necessarily transferable to other parts of the world. Yet, in the above examples, we can see a complete failure to recognise these limitations. It is an act of extraordinary arrogance to assume one's own experiences are absolute and universal.

Of course, Iraq is not in Europe. Like most of the Muslim world, it has a very different sociopolitical history to that of the medieval Church that so inevitably led to the secularism adopted in the West. In discussing Iraq's postwar future, Lane and Keegan should have recognised that the lessons of European history might provide only limited guidance.

As it happens, a sketch of Islamic history is, roughly speaking, the inverse of Western history. Christendom progressed through the Dark Ages to Reformation and Enlightenment. Yet, for the Muslims, enlightenment has *preceded* darkness and ignorance. Self-described Islamic governments presided over periods of relative tolerance, social justice and profound intellectual growth that were beyond imagination in Christian Europe at the time, plunged as it was in its Dark Ages. Of course, there was discrimination, but compared with those under Christian rule, religious minorities prospered. Jews, in particular, would often seek refuge under Islamic governments, and flourished most notably in Andalusia. Muslim women in the eighth century occupied esteemed positions of scholarship and had rights, such as the right to own property, only known to their Western sisters in the last century or so. Certainly, pre-modern Islamic governments were not perfect – far from it – and there is naturally much in their history that would horrify us were it to occur today, but they must be understood in their historical context. So understood, it is clear why Muslims justifiably locate their golden age within these centuries.

Whereas Christendom struggled through the medieval period, valiantly shedding its past to discover a new future, the Muslim world has much to admire in its past and would do well to recapture its essence. The contrast with the Muslim world's present condition barely requires articulation. In the very places where some of humanity's great civilisations once stood, there are now low literacy rates, almost no intellectual freedom, little modern intellectual contribution, misogyny, and a string of oppressive and dictatorial regimes. Anyone who has travelled in the Muslim world or spoken to those who have lived there can tell you just how widely despised these regimes are by the people they govern.

But here is the tricky part: while rulers presiding over Islam's proudest moments at least claimed religious inspiration, the majority of the contemporary Muslim world's despised regimes claim to be secular. Worse, they have often enjoyed Western support at some point. Indeed, Saddam Hussein's Iraq itself was a potent case in point.

Muslims are sharply aware of their current, disastrous political condition, and of the glory, albeit often exaggerated, of their history. Moreover, many Muslims are becoming increasingly convinced, rightly or wrongly, of a correlation between their condition and the role of Islam in their public lives in almost exactly the opposite way the Western world came to associate Church government with darkness. Accordingly, there is a natural desire in the Muslim world for Islam to re-enter the public square.

Recent election results in Muslim-majority countries reinforce my hunch. In 1991, the ruling military brutally prevented the impending victory of the Islamic party in Algeria. In 2002 alone, Islamic parties scored victories or sharp increases in support in elections in Turkey, Pakistan, Morocco and Bahrain. In late 2005, Islamic political parties in Egypt tripled their vote in spite of the obstacles put before them by the ruling party. And of course, in the case of Iraq, religious, particularly Shiite, coalitions have emphatically and consistently outpolled secular alliances since elections resumed in 2004.

Each of these cases is unique, but these events underscore an increasing trend: clearly there are significant and increasing numbers in the Muslim world who want their governments to rule with reference to Islamic imperatives. A Gallup poll in January 2007 of 10,000 people from ten Muslim-majority countries collectively constituting 80 per cent of the global Muslim population only confirmed this. The survey found that while there is clear majority support for democracy in the Muslim world, a mean of 79 per cent across the ten countries support Islam being at least one source of law. It is clear that these respondents saw this as a means of safeguarding – not limiting – their freedom: vast majorities also supported freedoms of speech, religion and assembly. Over 90 per cent in Egypt and Iran believe freedom of speech should be constitutionally enshrined. These are nations long deprived of free political expression.

It would be unwise to ignore this social dynamic. Yet, by failing even to contemplate the sociopolitical histories of the Muslim world and universalising the Western experience, this is precisely what Lane and Keegan, not to mention the US-led coalition in Iraq, have done.

We are all, to some degree, products of our histories. That is exactly why we should not pretend our aversion to religious government in the West is some inherent, absolute, universal truth. Like much human thought, it is heavily influenced by our subjective experiences. What we must come to understand is that the inverse history of the Muslim world very likely leads to an opposite conclusion. Those who have been tyrannised by secular rulers are likely to crave a government bound by the strictures of religion. A moral code, particularly one generally shared with the population, is likely to be received as a desperately welcome brake on unaccountable and corrupt power and authority. In this context, and with a glance to a proud religious history, religion becomes, not the means by which governments can oppress, but the very means by which they can be held accountable. To use a crude analogy, you can think of religion in that context as a kind of bill of rights. It stands to reason that the repulsion inspired by the thought of religious government in the West will be equally matched by many in the Muslim world forced to contemplate yet more secular governance.

When it comes to Iraq, then, we should consider the likely consequences had Lane and Keegan's advice been taken. Or, indeed, the likely consequences had the United States executed its original plan of planting power in the hands of a staunch secularist such as Ahmed Chalibi and vetoing any quasi-religious constitution. We should be asking how positively we could expect the Muslim world to react to the implementation of yet another secular government established as a consequence of Western interference.

But, of course, one cannot deny the ghastly modern attempts at so-called Islamic government in the Muslim world either. Iran has been a mess economically and socially. Afghanistan under the Taliban was insufferable. Saudi Arabia has scarcely been a beacon of light. I do not pretend, as Islamic resistance movements often do, that one can put an Islamic stamp on a regime, cloak it in Islamic platitudes, and all will be well.

But we have to recognise that the existence of Iran and Afghanistan's regimes was rooted very heavily in revolutionary sentiment. They were the product of disillusionment and anger. The Iranian revolution followed decades of oppressive, US-backed rule and, in any event, only became 'Islamic' after its completion. The Taliban took power with an iron fist to restore order to a society in anarchy, where no one was safe and violent crime was rife; then they themselves became an oppressive force. These were not regimes borne of considered reflection and careful development. For them to be enlightened would have been a miracle.

Modern-day Saudi Arabia was not a result of revolution but sprang from ongoing tribal and sectarian conflict ultimately won by an alliance of a moneyed family and a puritanical religious strand.

By contrast, Islam's more inspiring eras were the product of a confident, empowered people. They were enlightened for their age because they were intellectually curious and open to the wisdom of others. Theirs was not a worldview that grew out of revolution or conflict. Their orientation was far more optimistic, and their societies could accommodate cultural and intellectual diversity and evolve organically. They were constructive, not reactionary. It should come as no surprise that it is usually those who feel empowered, rather than those who react to disempowerment, who are far more likely to manifest enlightenment.

That is why few things would be more likely to create more fertile ground for an uprising of regressive, and probably repressive Islamic resistances, than imposing some messianic vision for the Muslim world that takes its cues from European history, and none from the history of Muslims themselves. Unfortunately, surprisingly few of our commentators seem to appreciate this. We seem implicitly to think that deep inside everyone in the Muslim world dwells a little American just busting to get out, and hoping we will free them.

It is this failure to recognise our own egocentricity that has led to the incessant, senseless questioning about whether or not Islam is capable of secularisation. No one seems to care whether or not Muslims want to, or even should, secularise. That seems a foregone conclusion. No one even asks what secularism is supposed to mean in an Islamic context. The question is simply one of identifying the roadblocks to the secularisation so that we can propose ways of overcoming them or bemoan their stubbornness.

It is now later on the evening of the panel discussion where all this began. A dinner has been organised for the participants, and the panellists are invited to attend. Embarrassed by my earlier rudeness, I approach the young woman who asked the first question and apologise for any offence I had inadvertently caused. The conversation continues informally but, initially, covers little new ground. That is not surprising. The sharing of new perspectives often gives rise to circular discussions at first as we grapple with the unfamiliar.

I share with her my thoughts about the meaninglessness of secularism as a concept in the Church-less context of Islam. I explain to her my thoughts on the phenomenon of projection, and how there is so little consideration of Muslim history before we attempt to save the Muslim world with the products of our own. Now the conversation is moving, which is enough.

I do not pretend she agrees with everything I say. She says this is the first time she has encountered this analysis, and that the discussion encourages her to think outside her square. Nothing will be resolved tonight. On the contrary, we will each walk away with more questions. But for each of us, new doors are opening.

This is not an exercise in political conversion, but a genuine exchange of ideas. It is about honest and sincere engagement. My daughter, now restless and tired, cries in a manner that tells me it is bedtime, and we head home. So much remains to be said in this conversation, but its sincerity gives me hope.

5

Women as a battlefield

Way off in the distance, obscured by horizontal blinds, the silhouette is faint but unmistakable. Even from here, the minarets rise majestically into the air, and imply the piercing, haunting call of the muezzin, summoning the faithful to prayer. But here, it provides only the subtlest of allusions.

Considerably more noticeable is the Arabesque window through which it appears. The window's top third is covered with intricate latticework, presumably wooden. To its right is a large stuccoed archway, then a smaller one made from bricks of alternating light and dark colours. It looks an obvious reference to the iconic arches of the *Mezquita*, the grand mosque of Cordoba.

The room is tiled and, aside from the Eastern flourishes, clinical. Typically elaborate rugs provide an intermittent contrast. In the foreground sits an elderly, dark-skinned man. His head sports a large, white turban; his face, a flowing white beard. His chair has almost disappeared beneath his obese body. In his right hand is a clipboard. Around his neck is a stethoscope.

At this moment, the doctor is looking over his left shoulder.

A small pair of spectacles rests on his bulging nose. His head is tilted down; his eyes looking up, peering over his glasses in the manner of an old-fashioned schoolmaster. But, ever so subtly, his face hints at a smirk, a glimpse of dirty anticipation.

His gaze is fixed upon a latticework screen, again presumably wood. From our vantage point, we can see the woman on the other side. Her dark eyes are looking anxiously around the barrier. At her feet rest her shoes and clothes. She is the quintessential sex symbol: impossibly shapely, voluptuous and naked.

Almost. Her face from the eyes down is covered by a white veil.

The cartoon is from the November 1967 edition of *Playboy*. It is reproduced in *The Veil Unveiled* by Faegheh Shirazi, a compelling study of the ways in which the image of the veiled Muslim woman has been used in modern cultures around the world. And as Shirazi notes in her chapter titled 'Veiled Images in American Erotica', the veiled Muslim woman has often been an exotic symbol of erotic mystique. She evokes the largely imaginary prurience of the sultan's harem: silent, secluded, sexually ravenous. Shirazi references several *Playboy* and *Hustler* cartoons where the veil itself is used as a tent-like lair in which these women have their lustful way with men. Similarly, Malek Alloula's collection of Western photographs and postcards of Algerian women, *The Colonial Harem*, features typical colonial representations of Muslim femininity, including the now familiar images of women who are both veiled and bare-breasted; a fiction tailor-made to satiate the Western voyeur.

This phenomenon is not particularly new. In *Colonial Fantasies*, Meyda Yegenoglu argues that the stereotype of the licentious seductress whose veil serves her own lascivious ends featured prominently precisely when Europe was puritanical and viewed sex as anathema. The suggestion is that the image in the West of Muslim women has always been the antithesis of the prevailing perception of Western women. Thus, in the Western conversation, the face-veil or headscarf, or indeed any readily identifiable aspect of Muslim life, is to be constructed as the very opposite of the Western self-image. Our apprehensions are a polemical, fluid construct that say more about ourselves than anyone else.

The theory suggests that Western perceptions of the veil will vary over time as the West thinks differently about itself. And indeed, today, as the West views itself as free and liberated, yet in a struggle against the forces of terrorism, perceptions of the veil – the very same article of clothing – have developed accordingly. Now, it symbolises sexual and social oppression and imprisonment. It may even represent extremism and terrorism. The theory is strikingly incisive: these are surely some of the defining stereotypes of the contemporary West.

Quite simply, no article of clothing so controversially evokes hostility and revulsion in Western societies as the headscarf, or hijab, worn by many Muslim women. Sampling the vitriol of a thousand talkback radio callers, this cannot plausibly be denied. Any hijab-clad Western Muslim can confirm it by painful, personal experience. A report in 2004 published by Australia's Human Rights and Equal Opportunity Commission reported several distressing personal accounts from hijab-wearing women of the kind of abuse they had faced in the years since the terrorist attacks of September 11, 2001. Most commonly, these included physical assaults such as being spat at, having objects, such as eggs, bottles or rocks, thrown at them from moving cars, and having their hijabs pulled off. Other reports included people deliberately setting their dogs on Muslim women, punching them, attempting to drive them off the road or to hit them with a car, and threatening rape and extreme violence. Some of these events resulted in women being hospitalised. Often, these women reported that bystanders watched on, yet did nothing.

With these social dynamics in place, and with a long Western history of obsession with Muslim women's attire, the veil, whether the face-covering *niqāb* or the more common hijab, was always going to find its way into political discourse. And indeed, recent years have evidenced such political fixation.

The most famous example is the French law, first proposed in 2003 and passed in 2004, which bans students in state schools from wearing overt religious symbols. The ban is generic, but it was unquestionably directed at the Muslim girls who wear the hijab. Rationalisations of the law were always destined to be unsophisticated. Take, for example, the argument I heard while watching BBC World in January 2004 that, because the French government believed many Muslim girls were forced to wear veils, a law banning them in schools was a necessary response. Of course, even assuming the dress code of French Muslim girls is imposed upon them, forcing them not to wear veils is precisely the same oppression – it is just the opposite manifestation.

In Australia, more than a year before the French government seriously proposed the idea, the Reverend Fred Nile had made a similar suggestion in his role as a New South Wales parliamentarian. But unlike the French, Nile did not suggest, and quite clearly would not have countenanced, any corresponding prohibition of Christian symbols. Coming ostensibly from a man of religious observance, it was an overtly adversarial proposal.

By August 2005, Australian Federal Government MP Bronwyn Bishop had warmed to the idea, advocating a headscarf ban in Australian public schools. It was an especially provocative suggestion coming from a woman and a politician who, in other circumstances, is known to have a libertarian streak. Here, she was clearly coming from a place of hostility, as her comments made apparent. 'In an ideal society you don't ban anything,' she said. 'But this has really been forced on us because what we're really seeing in our country is a clash of cultures and indeed, the headscarf is being used as a sort of iconic item of defiance' by 'the sort of people who want to overturn our values'.

Subsequently, on radio, Bishop would say that hijab-wearing women were 'in a position of being a slave' and 'can't deal with the choices that freedom offers'. She was unable to 'accept someone who wants to be a little bit of a slave, or a little bit subservient'.

They were comments remarkable for their incoherence. Somehow, we were expected to believe in the image of a Muslim woman who was simultaneously cowed, deprived of choice and enslaved, yet defiant and provocatively iconic. This internal contradiction never seems to have occurred to Bishop. Indeed, when confronted with the thought that many of the women she considered enslaved actually feel entirely free, she responded with even more rabid incoherence: 'Nazis in Nazi Germany felt free and comfortable, but that's not the sort of standard that I can accept as being free.'

But this was not about intellectual consistency. It was about hostility, and a broader prejudice, a fact only reinforced subsequently when Bishop clarified that her invective was not applicable to other forms of visible religious distinction, such as Jewish yarmulkes. For Bishop, no such ban was necessary because Jews did not use the 'skull cap as a way of campaigning against the Australian culture, laws and way of life'. This was explicitly, specifically, about Islam.

The comments triggered a national debate that sought the views of almost everyone except headscarf-wearing Muslim women themselves. *The Age* in Melbourne ran a spate of opinion pieces on the topic over several days, but not one was from a woman who actually wears the hijab – despite the fact that such publishable pieces were submitted. This is a common feature of these discussions, and has been for centuries. Western politicians and commentators presume to tell us what the hijab symbolises and why women who wear it do so. Bishop has no hesitation in taking the arrogant position that, simply because they cover their hair, Muslim women are either too stupid or too feeble to cope with freedom. At no point in the public conversation is she rebuked specifically for such neocolonialist conceit.

Writing in *The Age*, Jewish feminist and ethicist Leslie Cannold states baldly that 'many of my lifelong identifications – as a member of a minority group, an opponent of racism and a feminist – steer me in opposing directions when it comes to the hijab'. Here, the possibility of a feminist argument for the hijab is dismissed summarily by implication. She acknowledges that 'some Muslim women maintain that the hijab liberates rather than oppresses them', but goes on to suspect that such comments come from 'the most disempowered of women who look to conformity with the rule of the Fathers'. Ultimately, Cannold concludes:

> My impression is that, rightly or wrongly, many Australians see the scarf as a symbol of the gender-based oppression women suffer in many non-Western countries, and thus a challenge to the credo of gender equity preached and largely practised in Australian public schools.
>
> Because equality of people and of opportunity is a critical value that Australian schools must – and must be seen to – uphold, the wearing of the hijab in public schools must be banned.

Cannold's argument requires Muslim women to be held captive by what she admits might be the mistaken apprehension of others. This, apparently, is preferable to confronting any such ignorance. Their decisions are subordinated to others' prejudices. It is a repulsively oppressive proposition; one that underscores how hijab-wearing women are the great un-people of our day: spoken about as though they could not possibly be part of the audience.

Alone, feminist academic Liz Conor seemed able to grasp the egocentricity many commentators brought to the discussion. With admirable restraint, she confesses:

> I'm not in a position to speculate on what it might mean to wear the hijab. I have not worn the veil as a religious observance and therefore have no understanding of its associations and experiences . . .
> . . .

As for my own responses to the hijab, they are certain to have their origin in longstanding and deeply held beliefs about women's public visibility and their associated freedoms, male sexuality and its refusal to take responsibility for itself, and, oh, until I'm listening to Muslim women, my responses have their origin in ignorance. Frankly, that ignorance should not be Muslim women's problem.

Only *The Sydney Morning Herald* published a single contribution from a hijab-wearing woman, Amal Awad. Her argument was clear, simple and sincere. 'I would ask Bishop how on earth she equates covering one's hair with a form of suffocated freedom,' she begins. 'I am not locked in a golden cage and I am especially thankful that I am not imprisoned by prejudices.' Awad's exasperation with the dehumanising debate is clear: 'Who cares that a headscarf does not preclude one from having interests and goals, and an intelligent mind to pursue them?'

Bishop's outburst was positively outrageous. But her boss, Prime Minister John Howard, mustered only a feeble response: 'I don't think it's practical to bring in such a prohibition. If you ban a headscarf you might, for consistency's sake, have to ban a yarmulke or a turban. And it does become rather difficult and rather impractical.' The primary problem here seems to be that non-Muslims might be affected. Never did Bishop's comments receive the stern admonition they deserved. The strongest Howard's response became was to note, almost as an afterthought, that in addition to finding Bishop's proposal impractical, he did not find it 'desirable'. Of course, in the same breath, he had said the same of covering oneself fully, including the face. Howard could 'understand why people might be affronted' by this dress code.

It was a theme to which the prime minister would return in February the following year, when, with no apparent reason for discussing it, he decided to volunteer his views once more on the dress of Australian Muslim women – as though it deserved to be a matter of political relevance. 'I don't believe that you should ban wearing headscarves, but I do think the full garb is confronting and that is how most people feel,' he opined on talkback radio. He even had the temerity to speak on behalf of Muslim women by claiming, without consulting them in any way, that they agreed. Naturally, this was 'not meant disrespectfully to Muslims because most Muslim women, a great majority of them in Australia, don't even wear headscarves and very few of them wear the full garb.' Presumably, then, this was meant disrespectfully to the few who do.

Howard found a British echo in the leader of the House of Commons, Jack Straw, who revealed in October 2006 that he 'would rather' Muslim women did not wear face veils, and that he asks female visitors to his office to remove them. Not being able to see a person's face makes Straw feel 'uncomfortable' and harms 'community relations'. The grassroots responses to Straw's comments hardly enhanced community relations either: the next day, a London man pulled the hijab off a young Muslim woman and threw it to the ground. Another threw a newspaper at her and shouted, 'Jack has told you to take off your veil.' A Glasgow imam was punched, kicked, then hit with a chair and a safe deposit box after the weekly Friday congregational prayers. A Turkish student was verbally abused in a Canterbury supermarket by a woman who told her she hated her presence in Britain and demanded that she leave. In Preston, bricks were thrown at cars parked at a mosque while Muslims were praying inside. A mosque in Falkirk was left gutted after being firebombed. The next day, a dairy owned by a Muslim family in Windsor was also firebombed and besieged by up to 30 people.

At a political level, Straw provoked more outrage than any Australian politician had faced for saying more. Sixty Muslims held a demonstration in which they labelled Straw a 'Christian fascist'. Fellow parliamentarian George Galloway called for Straw to resign for his 'offensive and disturbing' comments. Conservative policy director Oliver Letwin felt it would be a 'dangerous doctrine' to start telling people how to dress. Liberal Democrat party chairman Simon Hughes labelled the comments 'insensitive and surprising'.

But this only led to a counter-escalation. Tory politicians accused Muslim leaders of creating closed communities in a form of 'voluntary apartheid'. Shadow home secretary David Davis wrote in *The Sunday Telegraph* in support of Straw's stance. For him, Straw's comments pointed symbolically to 'the fundamental issue' of whether, in Britain, social and religious divisions will 'corrode the foundations' of society. Britain's race and faith minister, Phil Woolas, demanded the sacking of Aishah Azmi, a Muslim primary school teaching assistant who wore a face veil in class, asserting that it got in the way of her doing her job. Salman Rushdie's profound contribution was to inform us that 'veils suck'.

On one level, it seems the political fixation with Muslim female dress remains alive and well. But on another, it has little to do with dress code. The Muslim woman, in her varying degrees of cover, has become merely a symbol; a battleground for a much broader polemic. She is not a person with interests, aspirations, struggles and feelings. She is a concept. Bronwyn Bishop was most explicit on this point: 'What I was saying was not about headscarves *per se*, it's about a clash of cultures where there are extremist Muslim leaders who are calling for the overthrow of the laws that indeed give me my freedom and my equality as defined by the society in which I live.' Bishop did not identify which 'extremist Muslim leaders' so troubled her. What she had identified was a cultural battleground in which Muslim women are rhetorical pawns.

This is why, whenever John Howard seeks to evoke the spectre of Muslim incompatibility with Australian society, he is sure to place gender equality in the conversation. Speaking to *The Australian* in December 2005, Howard asserted that Muslim migration posed a social challenge to Australia unlike anything before it. 'You can't find any equivalent in Italian or Greek or [presumably non-Muslim] Lebanese or Chinese or Baltic immigration to Australia,' he insisted. The reasons for this were twofold: first, a 'fragment' of Australian Muslims apparently keep 'raving on about jihad'; second, some exhibit 'an attitude towards women which is out of line with the mainstream Australian attitude'. He would repeat these sentiments around the fifth anniversary of the September 11 attacks when he suggested on radio that some Muslims need to understand that Australia is 'contemporary and progressive' when it comes to 'the equality of men and women'.

The invocation of gender equality in Howard's commentary in this instance is revealing. It is difficult to recall even one occasion on which people's attitudes to women have concerned him in the slightest. As a conservative politician, he does not often celebrate a 'contemporary and progressive' Australia. His concern for women and what they wear seems exclusively reserved for Muslims. It is an appropriation for a cultural battle.

And it is a battle many preachers in the Muslim world are all too happy to join. It is one of the saddest facts of contemporary Islamic discourse that Muslim women are so often reduced to the same symbolic function that they are in the Western conversation. Here, too, they are not people. They are appropriated, usually by men, as symbols of Islamic identity, purity and resistance to Western cultural hegemony. And just as in the West, the hijab has become the central, obsessive fixation of the discourse.

A potent example is Amr Khalid, the populist Egyptian preacher with a pop star following among Arabic-speaking Muslims across the world. Khalid speaks on a diverse range of topics, and has found favour particularly with the British government for his ardent opposition to suicide bombing, whether in London or Tel Aviv. Yet, a large proportion of his preaching is focused on women. And such is the rhetorical environment in which he works, that it is possible for him to claim that 'the most important thing in a woman's life is the hijab', without earning so much as a raised eyebrow. Elsewhere, he elaborates further that for a woman to take it off is 'the biggest sin, the biggest sin, the biggest sin'.

Some hyperbole is inevitable in Khalid's televangelist style. But even so, this kind of discourse is deeply nonsensical. On no account is a failure to wear the hijab 'the biggest sin'. That title could more plausibly be reserved for idolatry, murder or even adultery. And just as the common Western fixation on the hijab demeans Muslim women by reducing their significance to nothing more than a cloth, so too is it deeply degrading for Khalid to assert that the hijab is 'the most important thing in a woman's life'. It is as though education, health, love, family and spirituality are mere footnotes to the primary function of women as living mannequins. This is what her life has become.

But on further inspection, it becomes clear that Khalid sees deeper issues at stake. 'When the enemy of Islam wants to destroy something, the first thing they look to destroy is the woman.' Here we get the sense that, for Khalid, this is a matter of cultural survival. Having assumed the hijab is necessarily about modesty, Khalid is in a position to construct it as a counterpoint to Western culture, which 'cannot even sell a box of matches without painting a half-naked woman on it'. He specifically rebukes those who refuse to wear the hijab because they 'want to follow the Westerners'. Like many Western critics of Muslim societies, Khalid's grasp of a foreign culture is little more than caricature, but the underlying message is unmistakable: this is about cultural resistance.

Similarly, Iran's supreme leader, the Ayatollah Sayyid Ali Khamenei, fields an online question from a woman: 'What is the duty of women nowadays in combating the cultural invasion of our Islamic society?' Khamenei's response is entirely predictable: 'The most important of women's duties is observing proper Islamic hijab, promoting it, and keeping away from wearing that which reflects the norms of the enemy's culture.' The most important of women's duties. The enemy's culture. The cultural antagonism is clear. And as is almost always the case, it is outsiders, whether men or non-Muslim women, who do the talking.

Such, lamentably, is the prevailing nature of contemporary Muslim apologetics. Because it imagines itself in an enduring struggle for religious and cultural preservation against the forces of an invading Western culture, it regularly adopts a defensive, even patronising stance. And because it almost never comes from the mouths of women, it invariably expresses an inherently male perspective – one that assumes women must dress to accommodate the frailties of men.

This finds its most contemptible expression in attempts to draw a connection between revealing clothing and rape:

> A victim of rape every minute somewhere in the world. Why? No-one to blame but herself. She displayed her beauty to the entire world . . . Strapless, backless, sleeveless, nothing but satanic skirts, slit skirts, translucent blouses, mini skirts, tight jeans: all these to tease man and appeal to his carnal nature.

The comments belong to Australia's Sheikh Feiz Mohammad, and unleashed a fierce outcry when they became public in May 2005. He earned a swift scolding from a broad range of Muslim organisations. Outraged Muslims swarmed talkback radio to register their anger for the public record. And rightly so. With little option, the sheikh attempted an apology, but only reinforced his objectionable message: 'Maybe I should have said it another way meaning they are attracting to themselves and are partly to blame but not fully to blame.' They remained 'eligible' for rape.

Mohammad's rhetoric finds a frightening echo in the work of Muhammad Saalih al-Munajjid, a popular Saudi imam whose website contains a bank of thousands of responses to questions submitted from around the world. Asked why it is necessary for Muslim women to cover themselves, he resorts to misogynist type:

> When women go out showing most of their bodies – as the questioner mentions – this is one of the greatest causes of crime and corruption of men's morals, and of the spread of immorality.
>
> ... What does a woman want when she shows her body and exposes her charms to onlookers? Does she just want them to look and stare, and what is the affect [sic] of that on rapists and the foolish? How are you going to stop them from getting what they want by attacking you and trying to rape you. Are you going to show some meat to the hungry and then try to stop them from eating it?

Suddenly, women are captive to the impulses of rapists. It is as if the rapist is the victim of the devious taunts of uncovered women. His behaviour is presented almost as the inevitable, even if foolish, response to sexual stimuli. As inevitable, at least, as a hungry person feeding on meat. We are invited to conclude it is unreasonable to expect men to resist raping uncovered women. In this way, rape is normalised, and it is women who must pay the price for such criminality by modifying their appearance and behaviour.

But it is also an intellectually ridiculous argument. It makes the ignorant and infantile assumption that rape is a sexual crime, when this is almost never the case. Rape is about power and violence. It is most commonly committed by people who know the victim; not strangers aroused by revealing clothing. Ninety-year-old women living in nursing homes get raped. Are we to believe this is a product of sexual enticement? Can we possibly be stupid enough to believe that a hijab would have made any difference? It certainly hasn't prevented the rape of countless women in the Muslim world.

Yet, this kind of argument is not as rare as it should be. It was almost precisely replicated by Australia's Sheikh Taj al-Din al-Hilali in an infamous sermon that exploded into international scandal in October 2006. After asserting that, in the case of adultery, 'the responsibility falls 90 per cent of the time with women' because they possess 'the weapon of seduction', al-Hilali indicated that such seduction could end in rape:

> She is the one wearing a short dress, lifting it up, lowering it down, then a look, then a smile, then a word, then a greeting, then a chat, then a date, then a meeting, then a crime, then Long Bay Jail, then comes a merciless judge who gives you 65 years.[1]

But the whole disaster, who started it? The scholar Al-Rafi'ī says in one of his literary works . . .: If I come across a crime of rape – kidnap and violation of honour – I would discipline the man and teach him a lesson in morals, and I would order the woman be arrested and jailed for life.

Why, Rafi'ī? He says, because if she hadn't left the meat uncovered, the cat wouldn't have snatched it. If you take a kilo of meat, and you don't put it in the fridge, or in the pot, or in the kitchen, but you put it on a plate and placed it outside in the yard. Then you have a fight with the neighbour because his cats ate the meat . . . Right or not?

If one puts uncovered meat out in the street, or on the footpath, or in the garden, or in the park, or in the backyard without a cover, then the cats come and eat it, is it the fault of the cat or the uncovered meat? The uncovered meat is the problem! If it was covered the cat wouldn't have. It would have circled around it and circled around it, then given up and gone.

If she was in her room, in her house, wearing her hijab, being chaste, the disasters wouldn't have happened.

---

1 This is a reference to the conviction of Bilal Skaf for a series of gang rapes in Sydney in 2000 that have been popularly dubbed the 'Lebanese Gang Rapes' because of their racial overtones. Skaf was originally sentenced to 55 years' imprisonment, a sentence that was reduced on appeal to 31 years.

Of the above examples, perhaps the rhetoric of Sheikh Feiz Mohammad is the most explicit. It is easy to recognise in it a knee-jerk response to a perceived cultural threat: a broad campaign in the West to crush Islam by stripping Muslims, particularly Muslim women, of religious observance. It aims to fight the rhetoric of freedom and gender equality that underpins this threat, and the most natural weapon is a discourse of security and superiority. Hence, the righteous, well-dressed Muslim woman is protected, while the scantily clad rape victim has 'no one to blame but herself', even if only 'partly'.

A by-product is that the hijab is seen purely in sexual terms. Immediately, this transports us to a male universe, where the primary nature of women's appearance is sexual. In that environment, the only relevant consideration is what impact the hijab has on *men*. This merely reinforces the common Western perception that Muslim women wear the hijab to satisfy male imperatives. Here, we must surely note al-Munajjid's comment above, that the true evil of uncovered women is what they do to 'men's morals'. Entirely absent from such apologia is a consideration of what the hijab might mean for women. In this way, these Muslim preachers replicate the arrogance of Western polemicists who determine the meaning of the hijab on behalf of those who wear it, without giving any weight to their views.

Not surprisingly, such a discourse is notably at odds with the messages that tend to come from Muslim women on the rare occasions their view is sought. In the midst of the storm surrounding al-Hilali's remarks, several female Muslim voices managed to find their way into the public space in protest. Saara Sabbagh, a youth and cross-cultural community worker who has studied Islam formally in Syria, remarked that al-Hilali's comments demonstrated he was 'truly out of touch with . . . the reason we wear a head dress'. Sabbagh insisted it 'has nothing to do with conservatively dressing to prevent men from targeting [women]'. Sherene Hassan, speaking as a board member of the Islamic Council of Victoria, insisted that 'men do not enter the equations. I don't [wear the hijab] to hide from men.' Her hijab was primarily about her 'devotion to God'. Maha Abdo, of the Muslim Women's Association in Sydney, reiterated the point: 'The hijab is not a tool to be a deterrent for sexual assault or any assault, or physical assault, for that matter. It is a spiritual connection between myself and God.'

These attitudes reflect the findings of a September 2006 study published by the Konrad Adenauer Foundation, which examined the reasons why hijab-wearing Muslim women in Germany choose to dress as they do. The survey of 135 religious women of Turkish extraction elicited an emphatic response: 97 per cent said they wore the hijab as a religious matter – not as a matter of cultural resistance or to protect themselves from rape. Ninety per cent said they felt the hijab gives them self-confidence. Most said their decision to take to the hijab was purely a personal one, not influenced by their father, husband or brothers. Indeed, the study found that female role models in the family more often provided the inspiration.

Obviously, one should not read too much into this. It is only one study with a small sample of a Western Muslim population with a single ethnic background. It is unlikely to tell us a great deal about the reason women in Pakistan, Saudi Arabia or Uzbekistan wear the hijab. But the point is that while a flood of outsiders are keen to speak unflatteringly on their behalf, few people seem eager to ask Muslim women. We might be surprised at the responses if we did.

Take Rachel Woodlock. Rachel is a sixth-generation Anglo-Australian who converted to Islam from the Baha'i faith in her mid-twenties. She has since completed a Masters degree in Islamic studies and describes herself as a Muslim feminist. She knows all the arguments that surround the hijab, and can rattle them off effortlessly and authoritatively. She surveys the nuances of classical Islamic discourses on female dress – which she says are intriguing because they tended to focus principally on the appropriate attire for prayer – before canvassing more modern arguments to do with identity politics and the desexualisation of the public space. She notes the spiritual dimensions to veiling that she feels are often ignored, but is careful to point out the oppressive ends to which dress codes can be deployed as well. But it is when she speaks of her own experience as a hijab-wearing woman, rather than in dispassionate academic tones, that she is at her most personal and compelling.

'Even if various preachers give hijab a meaning, it's not my meaning; that's not my veil,' she says without fuss. 'I never really bought into the argument that it would protect me from the sexual advances of others.'

Rachel confesses to having always had a fondness for veils. 'I always thought, even before I was Muslim, that it looked very feminine and beautiful. When I was a little girl, I used to wrap myself up in my mother's bedsheets and flow down the hall in them,' she says, without any hint that she understands why. 'The odd time I would catch sight of a veiled Muslim woman, I was always fascinated.

'I never got the message that it symbolised inequality. So I took to the veil very quickly, once I converted.' Before that, Rachel used to spend time trying to unlock the mystery of how Muslim women put them on. 'I noticed that Turkish women wore it in a distinctive style, for example. I kept staring at Muslim women on trains and in shopping centres! I figured out some of the tricks to it, but every time I tried to put a scarf on, I looked like a Russian grandmother.'

Of course, people's reasons for their behaviour change over time. At first, Rachel wore the hijab as a means of expressing her new religious identity. 'I liked being visible as a Muslim woman. People could recognise me, and I liked them knowing that. Before September 11, I was very confident about it.' September 11 naturally altered the landscape. Within a week, Rachel found the venomous looks and cutting remarks too intense, and for the first time considered abandoning the hijab. 'I felt so conspicuous wearing it. I went out wearing a baseball cap, and I felt naked, which was quite unusual because before I was a Muslim I didn't wear hijab.'

It didn't last. 'I didn't like it at all,' she recalls. 'I came back home and thought, "What am I doing? This is stupid." I shouldn't have to change because of the prejudice of others, and this is me.'

Over time, it seems Rachel's own reasons for veiling have become richer, deeper and more layered. She still maintains that wearing the hijab 'demonstrates my identity as a Muslim – not in a way that means I am rejecting society or casting aspersions on other people's choices – I'm simply saying I'm a Muslim and that's not a bad thing.' But it is clear from speaking to her that she finds an intensely spiritual dimension to it as well.

'In some Sufi mystical traditions, for both men and women, one of the rituals is to wrap yourself in a loose, flowing garment when you pray – over and above your normal clothes. This is seen as part of the ritual of prayer. I *really* like that. I love that sense of quiet separateness; the creation of a sacred space. Hijab is a bit like that. It is your portable private space. It's like you're wearing your portable privacy.'

Hereabouts, Rachel's feminist instincts find expression. 'I also wear it because I do have a problem with the focus of Western society on women's sexuality. I'm disturbed by the emphasis on body image and the unattainable ideal. It really bothers me when you open up a women's magazine, and you see advertisements for plastic surgery, alongside advertisements for miracle creams and fad diets or selling clothes that are incredibly expensive using anorexic models. You open up these magazines and you're bombarded with it. The use of women's bodies to sell food. I do believe that if you wear clothes that do not buy into that beauty myth, that you're making a feminist statement.'

Historian and philosopher Michel Foucault theorised that the ideal prison was one in which prisoners felt they were constantly being watched, even if they weren't. This, he argued, would cause them to regulate themselves. The theory rested on the idea that the gaze of an observer disempowers the observed. By analogy,

Rachel sees that the hijab can become a means of empowerment through reclaiming the female body from the public gaze, and determining what may be observed. In this vision, the hijab is for women's benefit, not men's. After all, the imperative to uncover is often a male one. 'To stand and say I don't want you to see me is quite a rebellious act,' Rachel suggests, but not in the way Bronwyn Bishop might suppose. 'She thinks we're rebelling against the West, and democracy and freedom. What she doesn't understand is that we're rebelling against having these anorexic models shoved down our throats.'

Even so, Rachel is realistic enough to know that the hijab can be exploited, too. Its emergence as a cultural battlefield clearly irritates her. 'I do see that it has become an identity symbol. I don't like the fact that it has been co-opted by secularists, neoconservatives and Islamists alike to assert either that Muslim women are oppressed, or that they are the pearl in the oyster that is the salve to cure all of society's ills,' she urges with clear frustration. 'The symbol isn't one of oppression or liberation. It is that I am a Muslim. These other identity meanings are meanings I don't give it. And that annoys me. I don't like that it has been co-opted by both ends of the spectrum. What was a relatively inconsequential part of the religion, really, has become a sixth pillar,[2] and it never was that.'

Rachel's is just one perspective. In my conversations with hijab-wearing women, I encounter a startling diversity of motivations for their dress. Some echo their German sisters in viewing it purely as a private religious matter with no deliberate social meaning. For others it is nothing more than a cultural practice. A few consider it an important part of their identity. Most draw on a combination of reasons, which might change over time. None tell me they wear it to avoid rape. None tell me they wear it on

---

[2] The prophet Muhammad described Islam as being built on five pillars: the declaration of one's faith, ritual prayer five times daily, the annual donation of a portion of one's wealth to charity, fasting in the month of Ramadan, and the pilgrimage to Mecca. Muslims will sometimes talk of something being a 'sixth pillar' when it is being falsely elevated in importance.

the instruction of men. In fact, it is far more common for their husbands and fathers to put pressure on women, not to wear the hijab, but to *remove* it. Such perspectives go missing when outsiders monopolise the conversation, speaking for Muslim women they would apparently prefer to remain voiceless.

In purely Qur'anic terms, there is little justification for popular sexualised rationalisations of the hijab. It is true that the verse widely considered to mandate the hijab explains that it is for women's protection; so they are 'not harassed'. But it also explains that the prescribed dress code is designed so that Muslim women will be 'known'. This indicates that the Islamic modes of dress were introduced as a means of identification.

And in its historical context, this makes perfect sense: many classical exegetes explain that the relevant verse appeared at a time when a group of men in Medina were harassing women at night. However, perhaps out of cowardice, they would not attack free Muslim women. By asking free Muslim women to dress in an identifiable way, the Qur'an was seeking their protection. As the Qur'anic verse expresses it, they would be 'known and not harassed'.

There is nothing inherently sexual about this. Indeed, to construct the hijab as a sexual measure sits uncomfortably with it as a means of identification; of being 'known'. Moreover, there would be no justification for the fact that, according to many classical jurists who wrote during periods in which slavery existed, slave women, even if Muslims, were not to wear the hijab. Presumably, slave women can be just as sexually alluring as free women, and if the primary purpose of the hijab is to prevent seduction, it must surely apply universally.

In truth, the sexualisation of the hijab is more male than divine. It is a product of its male appropriation in a struggle for identity. Muslim thinkers who promote such apologia have far more in common with hijab-fixated Western commentators than either cares to realise or admit. Both take a simple piece of cloth, and transform it into an apocalyptic cultural struggle. Both use it to assert the superiority of their cultures. Each, in the process, shockingly simplifies the culture of the other and even themselves. Both dehumanise the women they have appropriated as symbols by presuming to reveal to the world the single true meaning and significance of the hijab on behalf of those who wear it. Both are deeply entrenched in nonsense.

This is bad enough when confined to the level of cultural polemic. It is positively disastrous when it seeps into the realm of public policy.

A week after his moment of French prophecy, the Reverend Fred Nile went a leap further, suggesting that Muslim women should be prohibited from wearing their loose-fitting religious dress in public. This was necessary, he argued, on security grounds: he was convinced there was a danger Muslim women could hide weapons beneath their concealing garments.

This suggestion, and the assumptions on which it was based, were obviously preposterous. If taken seriously, it would also have implied the prohibition of winter coats or barristers' robes. But then, weapons could equally be hidden in shoes or bags. The logical extreme of Nile's absurd proposal was enforced public nudity – at least for Muslims.

It all made quirky fodder for the talkback radio machine. In the course of an interview, a Sydney talkback host quite predictably sought the prime minister's response. The machine was about to be thrown into overdrive. Howard said he did not 'have a clear response' to Nile's suggestion. He was, however, careful to appear open to it by pointing out that public security came before religious beliefs. In an attempt to persuade us that Islam was not unique in being so subordinated, Howard cited the example of the children of Jehovah's Witnesses who, owing to public interest, may be given a blood transfusion despite the religious beliefs of their parents. It was a feeble analogy. Until it is demonstrated that merely wearing loose clothing will cause certain death to others, it will remain so.

'To lead the people, walk behind them,' said the Chinese

Taoist philosopher Lao Tzu. Perhaps Howard was merely showing ancient wisdom; he certainly was not leading Australians from the front. Several hours later, when his comments met with public disbelief, Howard ruled out support for Nile's proposal.

And so the progression was complete. The veiled Muslim woman had already moved from a seductress of loose moral virtue, to the embodiment of sexual and social repression. Now she had become a security threat. This is why Daniel Pipes can talk of France's headscarf ban as though it were a counterterrorism measure. In *The Australian* a few weeks after the 2005 London bombings, Pipes argued that Britain, in stark contrast to France, was 'hapless' in the war against 'terrorism and radical Islam', in part because British law had recently reaffirmed the rights of students to wear religious clothing in schools. Pipes was merely echoing the French government, which also promoted its law as a necessary part of France's fight against extremist ideology. The clear assumption was that wearing a headscarf is the exclusive domain of extremists, and that forced changes in clothing would necessarily inculcate a moderate outlook. Apparently, extremist ideology is something you wear on your sleeve – or perhaps more precisely, your head. Headscarves are about 'radical Islam', which becomes terrorism. That is a lot to read into a piece of cloth.

By his discourse, Nile had merely tapped into the West's ancient, anxious preoccupation, perhaps fetish, with veiled Muslim women, and politicised it. But just as Muslim women can become the symbolic target of much political venom, so too can they suddenly find themselves at the centre of self-described political benevolence. Indeed, if we are to believe the rhetoric of Western political leaders, they are so concerned by the plight of Muslim women, in particular, that it shapes their foreign policy. They are prepared to go to war to liberate them if necessary.

In a statement for Women's Equality Day in August 2002, US president George W. Bush claimed credit for 'restoring fundamental human rights to Afghan women' by toppling the Taliban, who 'used violence and fear to deny Afghan women access to education, health care, mobility and the right to vote'. Some nine months earlier, just after coalition forces had invaded Afghanistan, President Bush relinquished a regular radio spot reserved for an address to the nation, handing it instead to his wife, Laura. It is safe to assume she was acting on her husband's request when she used this forum to:

> ... kick off a world-wide effort to focus on the brutality against women and children by the al-Qa'ida terrorist network and the regime it supports in Afghanistan, the Taliban ... Afghan women know, through hard experience, what the rest of the world is discovering: The brutal oppression of women is a central goal of the terrorists.
> ...
> ... The plight of women and children in Afghanistan is a matter of deliberate human cruelty, carried out by those who seek to intimidate and control.

Three days later, Cherie Blair, wife of British prime minister Tony Blair, reinforced the first lady's sentiments, telling *The Guardian* that 'the women of Afghanistan have a spirit that belies their unfair, downtrodden image. We need to help them free that spirit and give them their voice back.'

Around the same time, but almost certainly not coincidentally, the US Department of State issued a *Report on the Taliban's War Against Women*. Written in a highly editorialised style, it briefly describes the horror of life as a woman under the Taliban, relaying stories of women who were beaten or shot for being alone in public. That said, the content of the report is unsurprising: the misogynist brutality of the Taliban is well known and beyond question. But the report is remarkable for its existence. The US Department of State does not often publish such passionate assessments of women's rights.

As Australian social scientist Shakira Hussein notes in this context, typically, gender justice issues are either confined to the domestic political arena, or as is often the case for conservative politicians, excluded from the political conversation altogether. Indeed, it is fair to say that neither Blair nor, especially, Bush have strong reputations as champions of women's rights. Yet, suddenly these rights had risen to political prominence. For the first time in living memory, gender justice had made its way on to the foreign policy agenda. 'Because of our recent military gains in much of Afghanistan, women are no longer imprisoned in their homes,' said Laura Bush in her radio address. Making the foreign policy link explicit, she continued: 'The fight against terrorism is also a fight for the rights and dignity of women.' Around the same time, US secretary of state Colin Powell promised that: 'The rights of women in Afghanistan will not be negotiable.' Not only were women's rights a concern; they could be invoked as part of a legitimate pretext for going to war. Western politics had managed to get in touch with its feminist side.

Afghan women were entitled to wonder what they did to deserve such special magnanimity. After all, people in search of a women's rights cause are hardly bereft of options. The world is tragically full of them. As new converts to feminism, Western politicians could well have declared a war on child sex slavery in Thailand, dowry burnings in India, or the selective abortion of females that occurs throughout the world, but especially in India and China. Yet, there was no activist foreign policy to eradicate female genital mutilation in sub-Saharan Africa. Nor have we heard a word against breast ironing – a horrific practice particularly common among Christian and animist communities in the south of Cameroon, where a fire-heated stone is pressed hard on the chests of young girls to stunt breast growth as a way of making them less sexually attractive and protecting them from sexual harassment. It can cause severe pain and abscesses, infections, breast cancer, and even the complete disappearance of one or both breasts. As many as a quarter of Cameroon's teenage girls suffer from this practice.

I can only ask forgiveness for my cynicism, but the whiff of political convenience is overpowering here. While the US Department of State was rightly lashing the Taliban, it finds only praise for Saudi Arabia where 'more than half the university student body is female'. This, observes Hussein, is a nation in which, by law, women can neither drive nor vote. It enforces a dress code not significantly different from that of the Taliban, which the report saw fit to criticise. And it was the Saudi religious police who, in 2002, drove fifteen women back into a burning school, and to their scorching deaths, because they were not sufficiently covered to appear in public. But Saudi Arabia is an ally of the United States. The rights of its women are not of political concern.

Central in the Afghan war, once more, was Muslim women's dress. The burqa, an all-covering garment with a mesh patch over the eyes to allow for vision, became the defining image of the downtrodden Afghan woman and, by extension, the war. The US Department of State's report told stories of women 'donning the tent-like burqa'. Hussein recalls that, in the United States, the Feminist Majority Foundation cut burqas into blue squares, and sold them for US$5 for people to wear as a 'symbol of remembrance for Afghan women'. Remembrance! Burqas found their way into feminist theatre, such as *The Vagina Monologues*, where Oprah Winfrey lifted the garment off an Afghan woman to reveal her face to the world. The symbolism is discomforting. The Afghan woman's rescue would be performed, not by her own will, but by her American saviour.

So, it would be war with Afghanistan. A war, among other things, for the liberation of women. This despite the fact that war almost always has a disproportionate impact upon women. In Vietnam, US soldiers were photographed gang raping a local peasant woman. Forty years later, some of their successors have been discovered raping Iraqi women. In July 2006, *The Washington Post* reported one particularly vile example of US soldiers from the 502nd Infantry Regiment raping fifteen-year-old Abeer

Qasim Hamza before shooting her and four of her family members, and attempting to set her dead body on fire.

But this is not uniquely an American military trait. Rape has so often accompanied war that the more meaningful challenge is to identify a major invading army in history that did not do it. The Old Testament records it happening. The ancient Greeks and Romans did it. English invaders raped Scottish women in the Battle of Culloden Moor. During World War II, Japanese soldiers raped Chinese women, and Russians raped Germans. In the 1990s, Serbian forces infamously employed rape as a weapon of war in the Balkans conflict. Iraqi soldiers raped thousands of Kuwaiti women during Iraq's invasion. Hutu troops raped Tutsi women as part of the Rwandan genocide. Women suffered similarly in recent conflicts from Bangladesh, Uganda, Somalia and Cambodia, to Cyprus and Haiti. The list could continue apparently to infinity. This is to say nothing of the unknown number of women killed or maimed, and presented facelessly to the world as 'collateral damage'.

And once more, Muslim women are reduced to mere spectators in the conversation. Few organisations had been as courageously vocal and active in response to the atrocities against Afghan women perpetrated by the Taliban as the Revolutionary Association of the Women of Afghanistan (RAWA). Long before Western politicians, or even their wives, raised an eyebrow over their plight, members of RAWA were risking their lives by concealing video cameras under their all-covering burqas in order to film Taliban beatings and executions, and distribute the horrific images to international media. Yet, despite the fact that its own people were directly, tragically suffering under Taliban rule, RAWA was a vocal opponent of the US-led war to oust the Taliban, calling it 'a vast aggression on our country' that only assists in 'sharpening the dagger of the "Northern Alliance"'.

Put simply, RAWA understood what newly zealous champions of Afghan female liberation did not: that their condition was a complex product of a nation ravaged by decades of war, and could not simply be sheeted home to a singular villainous organism called the Taliban. On women's rights, as in so many other areas, the Northern Alliance, of which the West was suddenly enamoured, were no better. The US Department of State's report may have claimed that '[p]rior to the rise of the Taliban, women in Afghanistan were protected under law and increasingly afforded rights in Afghan society', which was characterised by 'a mood of tolerance and openness'. But RAWA, whose members lived through this, is emphatic that women were 'crushed and brutalized, first under the chains and atrocities of the "Northern Alliance" fundamentalists', whose rule preceded the Taliban's. And so it has proven since.

The extent to which the lot of Afghan women has improved since the Taliban's demise is dubious. It is true there have been some success stories, especially the province of Bamiyan, which appointed Afghanistan's first female governor. But life may even have deteriorated for many others. Writing some sixteen months after the US-led invasion, Mariam Rawi, a member of RAWA, wrote in *New Internationalist* under a pseudonym that:

> In truth, the situation of women in Afghanistan remains appalling. Though girls and women in Kabul, and some other cities, are free to go to school and have jobs, this is not the case in most parts of the country. In the western province of Herat, the warlord Ismail Khan imposes Taliban-like decrees. Many women have no access to education and are banned from working in foreign NGOs or UN offices, and there are hardly any women in government offices. Women cannot take a taxi or walk unless accompanied by a close male relative. If seen with men who are not close relatives, women can be arrested by the 'special police' and forced to undergo a hospital examination to see if they have recently had sexual intercourse. Because of this continued oppression,

every month a large number of girls commit suicide – many more than under the Taliban.

Women's rights fare no better in northern and southern Afghanistan, which are under the control of the Northern Alliance. One international NGO worker told Amnesty International: 'During the Taliban era, if a woman went to market and showed an inch of flesh she would have been flogged; now she's raped.'

As much was predictable to those who cared to familiarise themselves with the recent history of Afghanistan. The Northern Alliance had killed some 50,000 civilians during its rule in the 1990s. Before the Taliban seized power, the country was ruled by ruthless warlords and, according to Rawi, it was during these warlords' 'reign of terror throughout Afghanistan' that '[t]housands of women and girls were systematically raped by armed thugs, and many committed suicide to avoid being sexually assaulted by them'. Indeed, the Taliban's arrival, with the stated goal of crushing the warlords and restoring law and order, was initially welcomed by many Afghans, including women, who hoped they could save them from the Northern Alliance's barbarity.

As Taliban religion minister Al-Haj Maulwi Qalamuddin rhetorically asked *The New York Times* before the invasion: 'Why is there such concern about women? Bread costs too much. There is no work. Even boys are not going to school. And yet all I hear about are women. Where was the world when men here were violating any woman they wanted?' I detested his regime, but his point remains piercingly correct.

Yet, the Northern Alliance was the West's proxy in Afghanistan. These were the people fighting our war. Suddenly, their crimes against women were forgotten. The only ones that mattered were those of the Taliban. Only this explains the pervasive stupidity that asserted the removal of the Taliban would restore Afghan women's rights.

This is where the tears of certain Western politicians and feminist groups for the women of Afghanistan are exposed for their simplistic selectivity. This was most pronounced in the United States where Hollywood celebrities jumped aboard the Feminist Majority Foundation's 'Stop Gender Apartheid in Afghanistan' campaign. While Afghan women spoke clearly about the Northern Alliance's abuses of women, few, if any, of their champions in the West were listening. From Oprah Winfrey to the Feminist Majority Foundation, only the abuses of the Taliban were deemed worthy of attention.

None of this is to suggest that Western outrage at the Taliban's treatment of women was unjustified. There can be no denying the Taliban's oppressiveness in this regard. This was a regime that prohibited women from leaving their homes without a male relative, and allowed them to conduct businesses only if they could do so without leaving their houses. Women with children were not permitted to do any work at all. UNESCO reported that levels of female education had dropped massively under the Taliban's rule, and an endless stream of interviews with Afghan women since its fall tell stories of women being arrested and punished for establishing schools to educate themselves. Those punishments could be infamously brutal. The Taliban's religious police quickly earned a reputation for infamy as a result of the regular beatings they administered to women they considered inappropriately dressed, or who were discovered unaccompanied in public.

In that context, the forced wearing of burqas on its own, while grotesque, seems perfectly mundane. It is true that a few, mainly urbanised, educated women, objected to the burqa in principle. But, notes Hussein, poorer Afghan women often objected on economic grounds: that the burden of buying another garment was too great. Others rejected the burqa specifically, but not veiling generally, preferring instead to wear the common hijab, or other styles of traditional Persian dress. Western activists were apparently unfamiliar with this level of nuance. Accordingly, they were shocked to find that while some women removed their burqas after the Taliban's fall, many didn't, while others resorted to their preferred form of veiling. It seems attire was of far less symbolic significance for many Afghan women than it was for their Western saviours.

Meanwhile, the women of Afghanistan, with whom we were once so agonisingly concerned, have dropped off the political radar. The US-led political narrative is simple: it begins with the Taliban's brutal oppression of women and ends with the West's war to liberate them. It does not acknowledge the lengthy prequels and sequels to this ghastly story because such acknowledgment is not politically useful. Nor are the continuing cries of Afghan women. They are henceforth irrelevant to the political classes. By the time Sima Samar, Afghanistan's women's affairs minister and one of only two women ministers in the US-backed Karzai government, was forced to abandon her job as a result of death threats, Western polities had well and truly lost their feminist zeal.

Of course, Western forces did not enter Afghanistan simply as a militant form of women's rights campaigning. The dominant pretext was that the war was a matter of security: a strike at the Taliban, which had harboured Osama bin Laden, whose organisation had just executed terrorist attacks on the United States. Its primary purpose was to dismantle terrorist networks and remove their state support. But it was clearly disingenuous to trade on the suffering of Afghan women for political capital. These women were used for the political imperatives of the United States and some of its allies.

In this way, the women of Afghanistan are symbolic of their Muslim sisters more generally. Muslim women have been reduced to a battlefield on which an intercivilisational war of politics, ideas and identity is being waged. That is their reality.

And most contemptibly, it is not a one-sided battle. Hussein argues that since at least the time of the Afghan jihad of the late 1970s against the Soviets, Muslim reformist movements have established their Islamic credentials primarily by making women suffer. Soon after coming to power in Iran, the Ayatollah Khomeini reduced the official female age of marriage from eighteen to thirteen, fired all female judges, and punished unveiled women by public flogging. Nearly 30 years later, in April 2007, with inflation estimated to reach 24 per cent, unemployment soaring and poverty increasing, Iranian police commenced a hijab blitz, arresting hundreds of women deemed to be wearing loose headscarves and tight overcoats. Dozens of shops selling such clothing were shut down. Taxi agencies received circulars warning them not to take passengers dressed inappropriately.

In Pakistan, General Zia ul-Haq assumed control, and as president, purported to embark on a project of the Islamicisation of the country. He spoke effusively of building a model Islamic society, but his promises of delivering an interest-free economy and introducing Islamic banking went completely unfulfilled. In fact, Zia ul-Haq's reform agenda was little more than an exercise in patriarchal political populism. There was scarcely anything Islamic about it. Rather than following the prophet Muhammad's lead in confronting and dismantling the feudal and particularly tribal structures within Pakistani society that cause so much oppression, the president played to patriarchal powerbrokers by stripping women of their rights. This was the sum total of his so-called Islamic reform. Women's testimony became legally worth only half that of a man. Women were to cover up and be confined to their homes.

Meanwhile in Indonesia, as religious political parties begin to assert themselves, women are once more disproportionately the focus. In Tangerang, the local mayor, who is from an Islamic party, has introduced a new law prohibiting prostitution that empowers the Public Order Police to arrest women merely on the basis of suspicion. And it can be enough to arouse suspicion, leading to arrest, that a woman is out late at night unaccompanied. The effect is that women are subjected to a de facto curfew. Women waiting to catch a bus home at night after work have been arrested, accused of being sex workers.

Within a day, these women are put on trial outside the local mayor's office without legal representation and before a laughing, jeering crowd. Dozens are tried in one sitting, as though by a legal sausage factory. Judges take note of whether or not the accused has plucked eyebrows and ask to inspect their handbags. The most mundane discoveries, such as make-up, are used as evidence to convict women of prostitution. Predictably, a parade of guilty verdicts ensues, and the women are fined. Some cannot pay it and are imprisoned for three days.

The assumptions of feminine virtue embedded in this oppressive regime are clear: only the promiscuous wear make-up and are out late at night. And almost certainly, the promiscuous do not wear the hijab: those arrested are invariably such women. The trauma of this injustice has a significant impact. One such victim told *Dateline* that she, and many women she knows, are too scared to leave their homes and go to Tangerang now, even to do shopping.

Numerous other examples of misogynist oppression from parts of the Muslim world could be cited. Indeed, in Western media, they regularly are. And while it is true that often the most heinous injustices are hardly exclusive to Muslim societies, it is equally true that the Muslim world faces a misogynist crisis of which the Taliban is only the most extreme recent example.

It is not as if Western feminist ideals have never reached the Muslim world. On the contrary, Western voices calling for gender reform have been there for well over a century. Primarily, this took the form of denouncing local cultures and Islam as a religion, and demanding that they be replaced with a duplicate of Western civilisation.

This approach to women's rights advocacy found, and still finds, some reflection in local activists. Most commonly, this is said to have commenced with Hudā Shaʿrāwī in Egypt, who, returning to Cairo from a feminist conference in Rome in 1923, publicly removed her face veil. The Western origin of Shaʿrāwī's activism is explicit in her desire to 'follow in the footsteps of the women in Europe in the awakening of our women'. More recently, activists such as Doria Shafik, Nawal El-Saadawi, Fatima Mernissi and Taslima Nasreen have continued on this trajectory.

But it is instructive that misogynist dynamics are flourishing in the Muslim world so long after this intervention commenced. Clearly, this activism, which had strong support from the ruling class, failed to capture the popular Muslim consciousness. And frankly, it is not difficult to see why. Put simply, to the average Muslim ear, Western secular feminist discourse smacks of colonialist imperialism. It echoes a broader historical polemic between the Muslim world and the West in which Western prescriptions for Muslim reform were often perceived as egocentric and hypocritical. Western feminists may not agree with this perception, but it is vital for them to understand it. Here one must surely cite Lord Cromer again, who argued that the 'fatal obstacle' to the Egyptian's 'attainment of that elevation of thought and character which should accompany the introduction of Western civilisation' was the fact that Egyptian women wore veils. Cromer insisted that Egyptians should be persuaded or 'forced' to become 'civilised' by eschewing such clothing. But clearly, Cromer was no advocate for women's equality. While in Egypt, he actively raised school fees, which had the effect of making the education of girls more difficult, and discouraged women from training as doctors. Upon returning to Britain, he promptly founded the Men's League for Opposing Women's Suffrage and became its president. Cromer was a Victorian establishment male. His plan for Egypt was clearly more about Westernisation – or even Victorianisation – than women's rights.

In feminist circles, there was the International Alliance of Women, which left many Eastern feminists disillusioned in 1939 when it appealed for the release of a Czech member held by the Nazis, but refused to do the same for a Palestinian member imprisoned by the British. Feminism and imperialism seemed to have some kind of undisclosed memorandum of understanding.

This image problem was only exacerbated by the fact that secular feminism's most vocal advocates among Muslims almost always belonged to the elite upper classes, who distinguished themselves with their Western lifestyles and cordial relationships with the colonial masters so deeply resented by the majority.

Ultimately, Western secular feminism was doomed in the Muslim world for two very predictable and related reasons. First, it prescribed for Eastern women that they abandon their entire culture, and become mere duplicates of their Western sisters in order to be liberated. In so doing, Western feminists revealed a cultural double standard. As Leila Ahmed notes in *Women and Gender in Islam*, despite centuries of Western patriarchal oppression, Western feminists never called for 'the abandonment of the entire Western heritage and the wholesale adoption of some other culture as the only recourse for Western women'. Instead, they would 'engage critically and constructively with that heritage on its own terms'. It never seems to have occurred particularly to second-wave Western secular feminists that Muslim women might want the same opportunity to locate their liberation from within their own traditions. This is a pointed example of the problems caused by egocentricity; when we assume the solution to another's woes is simply that they become more like us.

This led inevitably to the second reason for failure: the refusal of secular feminist discourses to make religious arguments and express themselves in religious language in societies where the masses still identified strongly with a religious tradition. To the extent they pursued a religious discussion at all, it was usually limited to the belligerent criticism of Islam as a whole, and often made basic theological mistakes along the way. This was spectacularly counterproductive. Arguments seeking gender equality by prising Islam's fingers off social norms and constructing a society on secular foundations were, and for reasons discussed in the previous chapter remain, profoundly offensive to many in the Muslim world, where religion is still so central to identity. To attack Islam was not, as many secular feminists believed, to attack the tool of patriarchal oppressors; it was also to attack the identity of the oppressed. This is where Western discussions in general, and Western secular feminist discourses in particular, hit a mighty roadblock. Even among Muslims seriously committed to gender equality, Western secular feminism has often presented more of a hindrance than a help.

This perceived link with cultural hegemony continues to the present day. We have seen above how Western politicians can appropriate the plight of Muslim women to rationalise their foreign policies in Muslim-majority countries. And while many Muslims agreed passionately with Western feminist criticisms of the Taliban forcing Afghan women to wear the burqa, nary a squawk was heard from those same Western voices in opposition to laws in Turkey that denied women the choice to wear headscarves in educational and political institutions. Indeed, it is unimaginable that this would provoke even the mildest Western feminist outrage. It is far easier to imagine second-wave Western feminists cheering this on as some did in France and even in Australia when similar ideas were mooted. The deafening silence (or worse) leaves many Muslim women wondering whether their feminist sisters only defend a woman's right to choose when she chooses to renounce Islamic norms, but not when she chooses to adopt them. Being forced to abandon Islamic behaviour does not seem to matter.

The result has been a predictable, if excessive, backlash against feminism in the Muslim world. It quickly came to be imagined as a Trojan horse intended for the destruction of Islam. Its mere mention creates a kind of invincible paranoia that captures the resonance of colonialism and imperialism in the collective Muslim mind and paralyses it. Hence, women became symbols of cultural resistance, leading to some of the despicable Muslim rhetoric we have seen above. Most grievously, it became easier for the patriarchy to dismiss any women's rights discourse as the Western corruption of Muslim societies, implying that those who sympathise with this cause are traitors. In this way, valid objections can be derided and avoided, rather than engaged.

This response is as bullying and effective as it is intellectually crude. In it, feminism, which itself encompasses a very broad range of often divergent and competing ideas, becomes appallingly stereotyped and misunderstood; much in the same way secular feminism often stereotypes Islam. For the reactionary, anti-feminist Muslim, the feminist caricature is a woman who pretends men and women are indistinguishable, and wants herself to be a man. In so doing, she aims to promote division and animosity between the sexes, causing society to disintegrate while simultaneously destroying masculinity and femininity. 'Feminists assert the absolute and unqualified equality of men and women,' wrote Maryam Jameelah in *Islam and Western Society*. 'They demand the abolition of the institution of marriage, home and family, assert complete female sexual freedom and that the upbringing of children should be a public responsibility.' Accordingly, '[f]eminism is an unnatural, artificial and abnormal product of contemporary social disintegration which in turn is the inevitable result of the rejection of all transcendental, absolute moral and spiritual values.' In truth, Jameelah is describing only the most radical strand of second-wave feminism, and using it to attack feminism entirely. She was writing in the 1970s, so had not yet encountered third-wave feminism, but even so, she reduces the entirety of feminist thought to a singular, extreme, minority manifestation. This is only slightly less ridiculous than citing al-Qa'ida as evidence for the malevolence of the entire Islamic tradition. Yet, the assumptions that underpin Jameelah's description of feminism are rampantly popular among those dogmatically and compulsively opposed to the feminist bogeywoman.

Allow one Muslim internet forum to illustrate. In February 2005, an Australian trade union lobbied Toyota to provide female staff with twelve days' annual menstrual leave to accommodate those who suffer seriously during their monthly cycle. Vividly, I recall the internet discussion that ensued in response to the news. This, apparently, was a death blow to feminism, because women were admitting they were different from men, perhaps even physically weaker. Of course, this proceeds from the simplistic (indeed, bogus) equation of feminism with the idea that there are no differences between men and women. To be fair, this mindless stereotype is shared by many Western critics of feminism, such as Janet Albrechtsen, who, in *The Australian* in September 2006, invoked scientific evidence of the differences between the brains of men and women as proof that 'feminist orthodoxy' is dangerously misguided. Such arguments merely demolish straw (wo)men. The prevailing trend in contemporary feminist thought proceeds precisely on the basis that men and women *are* different. However one feels about the union's proposal for menstrual leave, it is not the destruction of feminism, and might be its very fulfilment because it is calling for the accommodation of a uniquely female need.

In light of the above, it is easy to understand how the more Western secular feminism speaks didactically and arrogantly about Muslim gender reform, the more it entrenches the misogynist response, and the more damage it does to the plight of Muslim women on the whole. It was a point well made in a public lecture at Stanford University in May 2006 by Asifa Quraishi, a Muslim feminist and professor at the Wisconsin-Madison Law School specialising in Islamic jurisprudence. Stressing that 'it's not just the thought that counts', Quraishi lamented what she considered the 'innate, often subconscious sense of superiority' Western secular feminists sometimes exude when talking to, or about, Muslim women. 'It is a situation of friends, but they are not having a conversation as equals.' For Quraishi, this inevitably transforms the conversation into one of 'Islam versus the West', which leaves Muslim women nowhere to go: a situation only exacerbated by the fact that 'Western feminists usually don't have a filter of what is Islam, so things get lumped all together . . . It is fundamentally assumed Islam is part of the problem so there is the attitude of why should we even bother looking into what they think about this issue.' Quraishi argues that it is harmful 'to have an approach that doesn't take nuances of Islamic law into account', and that arming Muslim women with arguments from within their own tradition is far more potent.

The good news is that in recent decades, some movements in Western feminist thought have learned from the culturally imperialist blunders of the past. Third-wave feminism, which is grossly underrepresented in popular media, tends quite deliberately to recognise the very real differences in the experiences and aspirations of women living in diverse societies around the world. It takes what is, in truth, a conservative view that social change is best achieved organically from within existing social and cultural frameworks; effective solutions are indigenous to the societies in which change is needed, and locate themselves within the dominant cultural paradigm. Where second-wave feminism tended to view Muslim women as silent, passive victims awaiting Western saviours, third-wave feminism is more inclined to seek to empower Muslim women to make their own choices, even if they are not the choices their Western sisters might make.

Particularly in societies where Islamic identity remains strong, women's rights activism that is impulsively hostile towards Islam will always be rejected as foreign by many and rendered largely irrelevant. Doubtless, it will have its rare achievements, but lasting, widespread change is unlikely. Far more effective will be those who view Islam, not as a servant of patriarchal oppressors, but as a weapon against them. The fight for gender justice will stand the best chance of success when it comes from within an Islamic framework.

It is therefore encouraging that this kind of advocacy is growing in the Muslim world. Some has emerged from surprisingly conservative quarters. The best-known example is the late Zaynab al-Ghazālī, who was a member of Hudā Shaʻrāwī's Egyptian Feminist Union before leaving to establish the Muslim Women's Association in 1936. Al-Ghazālī's outlook embraced the social conservatism of the Muslim Brotherhood, but she was nevertheless a vocal advocate of the right of women to play an active role in public social and political life. Al-Ghazālī's approach was emphatic. She insisted that Islam, properly understood, gave women such rights. And indeed, she had precedent on her side. Examples of Muslim female involvement in the political sphere can be found from the very earliest days of Islam, which in the thoroughly patriarchal environment of seventh-century Arabia was a somewhat miraculous feat. The oft-neglected fact is that Muslim women in history were often far more liberated and publicly active than either their Western contemporaries or their current-day Muslim sisters. Accordingly, there is a reservoir of compelling Islamic arguments against the most misogynist practices of the Muslim world from which to draw. This is crucially important, because while it is often claimed, and sometimes true, that the oppression faced by Muslim women is a product of culture and not religion, it must frankly be acknowledged that a considerable portion of this misogyny is perpetrated in Islam's very name. The battle of Islamic ideas is therefore central.

An example may be found in Tamil Nadu, India, where women were confronted with the fact that divorce cases were being determined in mosques that denied access to women. This meant that women who were party to the proceedings were unable to give evidence in their own divorce hearings. The women responded by establishing their own mosque, headed by a trained female theologian. On a similar theme, two predominantly female organisations in North America released a paper, endorsed by five of the largest Islamic organisations in the United States and Canada and several prominent, traditionalist male scholars, providing guidelines for the creation of 'Women Friendly Mosques and Community Centres'. The subtitle is telling: 'Working Together to Reclaim Our Heritage'. This was an indigenously Islamic response, not a secular feminist one.

This seems also to have been the aim of the American Society for Muslim Advancement which, in November 2006, gathered more than 100 Muslim women from 25 countries in New York with the aim of establishing a council of female Islamic scholars to project the voices of women on matters of Islamic law. The council would also provide scholarships for women in countries like Morocco, Egypt and Iran to create more qualified female scholars. Executive director Daisy Khan noted specifically the importance of expressing 'the principles of social justice within the framework of Islamic law'.

Today, the scene is probably most vibrant in Iran through publications such as *Zanaan*, a journal focused on Islamic law and Qur'anic exegesis with a view to challenging interpretations that marginalise women in society. In her book *In Search of Islamic Feminism: One Woman's Global Journey*, American feminist writer Elizabeth Fernea found, after a series of interviews throughout the Muslim world, that 'Islamic belief is also the stated basis of most behavior I felt to be feminist'. She explains this as follows:

> In Egypt, Kuwait, Turkey and the US, Islamic women begin with the assumption that the possibility for equality already exists in the Qur'an itself. The problem as they see it is malpractice, or misunderstanding of the sacred text. For these Muslim women, the first goal of a feminist movement is to re-understand and evaluate the sacred text and for women to be involved in the process, which historically has been reserved for men.

Other Muslim women's rights activists argue that the sacred Islamic texts bear several possible interpretations, some of which are more patriarchal than others. However, because human interpretations are necessarily fallible, this group of thinkers, such as Malaysia's Zainah Anwar or South Africa's Shamima Sheikh, assert that even popular patriarchal interpretations are not immune from challenge. Their discourse encourages conversations about the meanings of Islamic sacred texts to remain open, and that gender-equitable readings have an important role to play in this space. This is a more intellectually sophisticated argument than that of Zaynab al-Ghazālī, and it remains to be seen how successful it will be in the long run. Certainly, it is destined to sit uncomfortably with the theologically conservative, but that has not necessarily stopped ideas rising to prominence in the past.

In any event, the issue of women's rights has come to attract the attention even of more traditionalist, male Muslim scholars. Traditionalists such as Hamza Yusuf and Zaid Shakir in the United States and, to a lesser extent, Cambridge's Abdal Hakim Murad, have often been critical of oppressive practices against women in Muslim societies and regularly promote gender-equitable interpretations of Islamic law from a thoroughly traditional perspective. Khaled Abou el Fadl, professor of Islamic law at the University of California in Los Angeles, is perhaps one of the most passionate advocates of women's rights as a matter of Islamic justice in the world today. His methodology and thought is controversial in conservative circles, and certainly goes considerably further than Yusuf, Shakir or Murad, but he is also a self-described traditionalist, having been traditionally educated in Egypt and Kuwait, and is a staunch critic of any reform agenda that would dismantle traditional Islamic thought.

Meanwhile, activist groups such as Sisters in Islam in Malaysia, the Muslim Youth Movement and Call of Islam in South Africa, and Karamah (Muslim Women Lawyers for Human Rights) in the United States are turning thought into action. They are lobbying governments on questions of domestic violence, and acting as civil rights lawyers. Karamah, in particular, blends a range of people with expertise in American and Islamic law to bolster its advocacy.

The diversity in approach is plain – many of these thinkers and activists would disagree vehemently with one other. But the common thread is equally clear: a belief that the solution to gender injustice in Muslim societies can be found within the Islamic tradition itself.

Such movements and thinkers can properly be described as feminist in the sense that they assert the inherent equality of men and women and seek to improve women's lot. Most, however, would reject that label. Given the history, by now feminism has become the f-word, even in many reformist Muslim circles. Only a few Muslims would dare use it, and most positively shun it, preferring more indigenously Islamic nomenclature such as 'gender jihad'. It is true that such movements face an enormous task. Like all agents of change, they will be maligned. But because they speak the language of Islam, they cannot be ignored. They do not alienate men and women who are concerned about gender justice in Muslim societies, but also value their religious tradition. Accordingly, they will attract broader support. Let us hope that the Trojan horse has not yet bolted.

Of course, defeating gender injustice is not merely an intellectual exercise. Often, the most brutally misogynist practices arise only in regions of high illiteracy and intergenerational poverty. Accordingly, they are not confined to national or religious borders: honour killing, for example, where a woman is killed by her family members on suspicion of even the mildest form of sexual impropriety for bringing shame upon them, is found among Sikh and Hindu communities in the subcontinent, Christian communities in the Middle East, and even Greek and Italian migrant communities in Britain. These communities span a broad range of religions, but tend to have poverty and ghettoisation in common. Clearly, there is more to misogynist brutality than religious, cultural or ideological identification. It is a sociological phenomenon, too.

Certainly, though, the intellectual battle – call it a gender jihad, if you must – is indispensable for change. But it is a battle that must be won in the West as much as the East. Only when Muslim women are treated as human beings whose views matter and who are valued in their own right, will we have cause for optimism. As long as they remain symbols, and as long as those symbols are invoked by opposing sides in obnoxious rhetorical wars of culture, they will continue to be little more than a battlefield. Relentlessly discussed, never consulted, invariably exploited.

6

The war on jihad

There is nothing for me to do now but stare at the carnage. Naturally, the news crews arrived late. There was not meant to be a story here. That is the point. There is only some amateur video and some shots of the aftermath.

The chaos has now become familiar. Behind the superimposed newsroom graphics that dominate my screen is vision of the bloodied and the hysterical. Footage is scarce, so is constantly repeated. The same bloodied body is loaded on to the same stretcher and hurried to the same hospital hundreds of times over.

Police cars and ambulances swarm the area. Perhaps fire engines, too. I cannot recall because I am not absorbing even that level of detail. To be honest, I can scarcely claim I am watching. I am sitting in front of the television, staring at it, but I am not really watching. My state is too passive for me even to be considered a spectator.

Now comes the parade of commentators. All of them attempt to share information that is simply useless at a time like this. All of them respond to questions on who is responsible, or what this will mean politically, or what action emergency services will be taking. All of them do little more than conceal the fact that we really have nothing to say.

There is something so thoroughly vulgar about commentary at a time like this, but what option do we have? You cannot deal with such an event in a newsbreak. It demands constant, relentless coverage. It is the kind of news that means there can be nothing else to talk about, even if we have nothing meaningful to say. We must fill hours even if we only have enough information to fill minutes.

For all the words and images, the story hardly develops. Any meaningful development will take weeks, months, years – long after we have returned to normal programming. For now, we only get updates on the death toll. I acknowledge it is important information, but it still repulses me. It feels like we are updating some kind of scoreboard.

I want to stop watching, but find myself compelled to stay tuned. For me, this is really catharsis. I let the images wash over me like waves over rocks. Yet, they do not cleanse me. I decide to surrender emotionally, but this brings only an unfathomable feeling of simultaneous calm and agitation.

Babble, babble, babble. The vulgarity continues. It is an exercise in incoherence. The stream of words is as empty as those saying them must feel. In the back of my mind I recognise I have work to do. A press statement is in order. Then come the interviews. And so I will join the chorus of incoherence.

When terrorists bombed London in July 2005, my daughter, Aisha, was just over two years old. She had a toddler's fondness for trains and I recalled how excited she would get whenever she saw, or travelled on one. It struck me now as never before that she could just as easily have been killed in a bombing like this. Only a year before we had caught a train to Atocha station in Madrid – a month before bombs blew it apart. For the time being she skipped around our flat, singing to herself, blissfully unaware of what had happened.

But children will always surprise you. At two, Aisha was at that age of repeating everything she heard. Somewhere amid her singing and playing she had learned a new word: 'bomb'. So much for innocence.

There is a surreal madness about the immediate aftermath of a terrorist attack. It is a kind of hysteria that cannot be explained simply by the loss of life. In statistical terms, we have far more to fear from road accidents and natural disasters. Yet, natural disasters bring a sympathetic, compassionate response, and road accidents just bore us. Neither scares us into irrationality. Terrorism, though, is about drama. Its impact far outweighs its damage. Its legacy is not simply death, but senselessness.

Every now and then, an expression emerges from the babble to grab my vague attention. Someone always tries to claim responsibility for the act early on. Usually some tiny organisation of whom no one has ever heard, and who are not in any way capable of launching any kind of attack, but who want to cash in on the fear for their own cause. Claiming responsibility within the first few hours should be seen as an admission of innocence. I don't know why I listen, but I do.

Perhaps I am listening for that dreaded phrase. Despite my mental numbness, I recognise it is only a matter of time before some commentator or other rolls it out. 'Jihad against the West,' they will bellow. It is never too long in coming, for that is the preferred catch-all explanation of the political classes for contemporary terrorism directed at Western civilians.

It is at this point I routinely sigh and embrace my numbness. By all means, call this terrorism 'barbaric'. By all means call it 'depraved'. Certainly call it 'criminal', 'inhuman', 'evil', 'perverted'. Feel free to call it by the strongest known terms of condemnation and contempt. But please, don't call it 'jihad'.

I understand my request is an unrealistic fantasy. Terrorists themselves employ this label to describe their actions. They even use the word in their organisations' names. It is now an irreversible fact in the public conversation that as terrorism has come to dominate our public consciousness, it has taken jihad as its hostage. For all public intents and purposes now, terrorism is the evil act, jihad the evil doctrine. Accordingly, it must be condemned in toto.

Do people who make such blanket statements even understand what they are saying? It seems to me that few concepts generate so much heat and so little light as jihad. Few ideas are central to such intense debate, and few words are surrounded by so much senselessness.

Central to this confusion is the stubborn tendency to equate jihad with holy war. Holy war, though, like fundamentalism, is an indelibly Christian term. It comes from a specific doctrinal tradition in Christianity that is not common to Islam. Those who use 'jihad' interchangeably with 'holy war' usually do not know the meaning of one, or perhaps both, of these terms.

Consult any worthy Arabic–English dictionary and you will find that definitions of jihad spill over several pages. You will see that it is derived etymologically from the Arabic root word *juhd*, meaning 'effort'; that it conveys the process of struggling, striving, labouring, toiling, exerting effort or exerting one's utmost power in resistance to an object of disapproval for the sake of some goal. Linguistically, 'jihad' could refer to any kind of strenuous effort for any kind of goal. So, for example, the exertion of effort in order to provide aid after a natural disaster can properly be called a 'jihad'. As a linguistic term, it is absolutely neutral on violence: the relevant effort may be violent, or even positively pacifist.

By contrast, 'holy war' rendered in Arabic becomes *ḥarb muqaddasah*. No search of the Qur'anic text, or indeed of any of the Islamic sacred texts, will yield this term. The words are completely alien to the Islamic tradition. What we have, then, when we render 'jihad' as 'holy war', is not in fact a translation at all. We are instead interpreting an Islamic concept and passing it off as translation. This is problematic because, although translation is a subjective act, it has claims to a higher level of objectivity than interpretation; an objectivity that 'jihad' rendered as 'holy war' does not deserve.

As an interpretation, it isn't much good either. Merely assuming that jihad is the doctrinal equivalent of holy war negates any engagement at all with the Islamic tradition. Jihad merely becomes a copy-and-paste from medieval Christianity. Yet, unfortunately, these are merely unstated, and therefore often undetected, assumptions. As it happens, the Islamic concept of 'jihad' makes a very poor approximation of holy war. As a comprehensive concept, it actually has very little to do with the holy war doctrine.

To begin with, 'jihad' is not necessarily a military term. Within the Islamic sacred texts, we find a plurality of actions categorised as jihad. The Qur'an itself refers twice to parents who strive ('do jihad') to entice their children to engage in idolatry (29:8 and 31:15). That the parents' efforts here are not violent is obvious from the response mandated in the Qur'an: '... do not obey them, but keep company with them in this world kindly ...'. Here, the jihad in question is not only non-violent, but is in fact thoroughly anti-Islamic. Such is the breadth of jihad's linguistic compass, even as expressed in the Qur'an.

But the Qur'an also uses 'jihad' as an Islamic imperative. This, however, does not mean the actions falling within this imperative are significantly narrower in scope. Just as jihad's literal meaning encompasses a broad range of conduct, so too does the Qur'an contemplate similar breadth in demanding that Muslims engage in jihad.

Consider, for example, 25:52, which implores the Prophet: '... do not obey the disbelievers, and strive ['do jihad'] against them with it [the Qur'an], a mighty jihad.' Muslim theologians have unanimously interpreted the use of 'jihad' in this verse to refer to the Prophet's preaching of the Qur'an, in part because the verse dates to a time before the Muslims had engaged in any warfare. Here, the tool of jihad is the Qur'an, and not any military weaponry. It is clearly directing the prophet Muhammad to continue responding to the verbal attacks of the pagan Arabs with the Qur'anic text. Not only does this verbal conduct constitute jihad, but it is 'a mighty jihad'.

Consider also 29:69, which states: 'And [as for] those who strive ['do jihad'] for Us, We will certainly guide them to Our ways; and God is surely with the doers of good.' It is evident that the jihad contemplated here is non-violent because, like the previous verse, this verse appeared at a point in history well before Muslims engaged in any warfare.

But the most commonly invoked non-violent doctrine of jihad concerns the internal spiritual struggle to live a virtuous life. This concept is articulated in 22:78:

> And strive ['do jihad'] for God as you ought to strive ['do jihad'] . . . perform the ritual prayers, give the alms and hold fast to God. He is your Master; and what a blessed Master and a blessed Supporter.

This doctrine came to be known as *jihād al-nafs*: the jihad against the defects of one's own soul. In an age where jihad is regularly associated with violent barbarism, this doctrine has been promoted as its antidote. It is relentlessly emphasised by sympathetic comparative religionists and (largely Western) Muslim apologists whose aim is to make Islam look as innocuous and friendly to a Western audience as possible. Often in such discourses, the primacy of spiritual jihad is grossly overstated, but this does not mean the idea is fabricated for the benefit of Western sensibilities. Though polemicists against Islam often suggest otherwise, there is no doubt whatsoever that the concept of *jihād al-nafs* has abundant support in classical Islamic literature.

Indeed, for a host of classical Muslim writers, this was considered the 'greater jihad', in contradistinction to the 'lesser jihad' of physical fighting. This is most famously embodied in the following narration attributed to the prophet Muhammad:

> A number of fighters came to the Messenger of God, and he said: 'You have done well in coming from the "lesser jihad" to the "greater jihad".' They said: 'What is the "greater jihad"?' He said: 'For the servant [of God] to fight his passions.'

The 'greater jihad' concept rose to prominence from the early twelfth century, through the seminal masterpiece of Abū Ḥamid al-Ghazālī, *The Revival of the Religious Sciences*. Al-Ghazālī is a giant of Islamic thought, who to this day remains among the most influential thinkers of Islamic history. His treatment of the above narration, and the concept of 'spiritual jihad' against the self, became definitive of Islam's spiritual tradition. Subsequent mystic scholars such as Muḥyī al-Dīn ibn 'Arabī adopted and expanded upon al-Ghazālī's thought, ensuring that the concept of the 'greater jihad' was soon entrenched in Islamic discourse for good. Even scholars not immediately associated with Islamic mysticism echoed the idea: an example is Ibn al-Qayyim al-Jawziyya, who wrote:

> The jihad against the enemies of God with one's life is only a part of the struggle which a true servant of God carries on against his own self for the sake of the Lord. This striving against the evil tendencies which have dominated his mind and heart is more important than fighting against the enemies in the outside world.

As it happens, this famous 'greater jihad' report is of highly questionable historical authenticity. It does not appear in any of the most authoritative collections of narrations of the Prophet, and probably surfaced for the first time among ascetic movements just before al-Ghazālī's time. But even without the 'greater jihad' report, the doctrine of jihad as a spiritual struggle was widely accepted by Muslim scholars. From 'Abd Allāh ibn al-Mubārak in the eighth century, to al-Muḥāsibī and Ibn Abī al-Dunya in the ninth, as well as subsequent theologians like Abū Ṭālib al-Makkī, al-Qushayrī, al-Sulāmī and al-Ḥakim al-Tirmidhī, the concept of waging jihad against one's lower soul was widely accepted. None of these theorists relied on the 'greater jihad' report for their doctrine of spiritual jihad. This is principally because a plethora of other, more authentic narrations of the Prophet send a similar message: 'The *mujāhid* [that is, one who carries out jihad] is he who strives against himself for the sake of obeying God,' is but one.

In fact, the Islamic concept of jihad, at least as articulated by the Prophet, encompassed striking breadth. Authentic reports have the Prophet, for example, explaining that the greatest jihad is to speak the truth to a tyrant; a purely verbal act that is nevertheless an act of tremendous courage. Elsewhere we read of Muhammad telling his wife, 'Ā'isha, that 'the best jihad is a perfectly performed pilgrimage to Mecca'. Alternatively, there is the famous report of a young man who approached the Prophet asking for permission to join an imminent battle, but who had parents depending on his support. The Prophet denied the young man's request, sending him back to be in the service of his parents. 'Exert yourself ['perform jihad'] by serving them,' advised the Prophet.

In this way, the Prophet detailed diverse forms of jihad specifically in the context of an enquiry concerning a military expedition. This emphasises the fact that jihad cannot be reduced to a military matter. It is as if, by choosing such a context to make these comments, the Prophet sought to make a point of jihad's conceptual breadth.

By extension, the Islamic conception of martyrdom came to be similarly broad. Based on a profusion of statements of the Prophet, Muslim scholars concluded that people who died from a stomach complaint, drowning, or in a plague were martyrs. So, too, those killed in a building collapse or in a fire; a woman who dies giving birth to a child; a shop-owner who dies defending his goods; or a man who dies defending his family. The list continues, almost to infinity. Those who deem jihad and martyrdom in Islam to be absolute evils often fail to recognise just how wildly sweeping their judgments are.

Yet, it would be extremely dishonest to deny that jihad also encompasses a military expression. The simple fact is that while Muslim theologians recognised diverse modes of jihad, the word's primary meaning was reserved for armed struggle. This was often true, even of promoters of spiritual jihad. The two were often considered to share a relationship. Al-Muḥāsibī argued that fighting could be a spiritual activity because of the hardships associated with it. Conversely, al-Muḥāsibī acknowledged that warriors can also fall prey to arrogance and showing off, through which their souls are destroyed. Ibn al-Mubārak considered armed struggle to be a kind of asceticism, and therefore a thoroughly spiritual activity. Here, we see an awareness that spiritual and physical forms of jihad often accompany each other. Islamic history is replete with examples of warrior mystics, such as ibn al-Mubārak. In this view, armed jihad is not possible without first disciplining the soul. This implies that not every act of war can be considered a jihad.

But even if we confine our attention solely to military jihad, we cannot reasonably conclude that it is synonymous with, or even roughly approximated by, the medieval Christian doctrine of holy war. The above establishes nothing other than the fact that an Islamic theory of legitimate warfare exists. For the purpose of comparison with holy war, it is the contents of these Islamic doctrines that are relevant, and not their mere existence.

The doctrine of holy war was a late development in Christian thought. Opinion is divided on whether early Christianity was inherently pacifist, or merely ambivalent on war. It is true that early Christian converts were soldiers by profession, and remained so following their conversion, but it is equally true that pacifist movements had always existed within the early Christian Church.

Tertullian was most adamant when he wrote in the second century: 'If a catechumen or a baptised Christian wishes to become a soldier, let him be cast out. For he has despised God.' Athenagoras echoed this hard stance in declaring that even the pursuit of justice was not sufficient pretext for Christians to engage in violence. By contrast, their contemporary, Origen of Alexandria, encouraged Christians to pray on behalf of those who are fighting for a righteous cause and a righteous king, and for the destruction of the enemies of the righteous. Origen did not call Christians to fight, but recognised that war might be necessary to keep the peace.

Perhaps predictably, it was when Christianity met empire via the conversion of the Roman emperor Constantine that the Church developed a more positive official orientation towards warfare. As the Roman Empire, now a Christian empire, descended into violent maelstrom, and particularly given the threat of invaders from Germany, Christian theologians developed doctrines that justified Church-led wars. Heading this intellectual development was Augustine, the bishop of Hippo, who conceived of the doctrine of 'just war'. This held that war was to be condemned when it was unjust, but that in some circumstances, justice may demand it. War therefore became justified, broadly speaking, on the fulfilment of three conditions: it must be pursuant to a just cause, waged with due authority, and it must be waged with right intentions.

According to Augustine's doctrine, fault would lie in the 'wickedness of the opposing group, which compels the wise man to wage just wars'. A just war was one prosecuted to right wrongs and preserve the peace. Such warfare became a Christian duty. Augustine's ideas took root to the point where a mass held by local clergy would sometimes replace the king's pre-battle address to the soldiers.

Today, the just war tradition in Christian thought is a rich and immensely varied field. Some modern just war theorists, such as Elizabeth Anscombe, maintain that the determinative imperative in choosing to wage war is justice. For Paul Ramsey, war is justified only when Christian love demands it, such as in defence of the oppressed. Still others, often drawing on Aquinas, proceed from a presumption against violence, rather than justice or love. They hold violence to be an evil, but argue that passivity might, in some circumstances, be a greater one. Amid all the debate, Augustine's broad framework remains essentially intact.

But Christian thought also developed alternatives to 'just war' theory. Imagine a crowd of priests, bishops, monks and laymen gathered together in a field just outside the medieval French town of Clermont. The year is 1095, and Pope Urban II, now an old and frail figure, has summoned nobles from across Western Europe to hear his sermon. Many do not come, but he proceeds with the following famous proclamation:

> This royal city [Jerusalem] is now held captive by her enemies, and made pagan by those who know not God. She asks and longs to be liberated and does not cease to beg you to come to her aid. She asks aid especially from you because, as I have said, God has given more of the military spirit to you than to other nations. Set out on this journey and you will obtain the remission of your sins and be sure of the incorruptible glory of the kingdom of heaven.

The crowd roars in responsive unison: 'God wills it!' and so begins the First Crusade.

Urban II's speech was reflective of a radical philosophical shift that had developed in the tenth and eleventh centuries. By now, the Church had established its own armies, something unthinkable to its predecessors. The Church soon concluded that violence used for the purposes of advancing Christ's kingdom would be not a lesser evil, but an act of positive good. This doctrine became known as 'holy war'. Recapturing land once ruled by Christians became a major focus. The Church came to embrace offensive warfare enthusiastically, particularly against those, such as Muslims and Jews, they considered to be pagan.

There were, in fact, many varying theories and forms of holy war, but a defining feature of its dominant expression was that it legitimised war as a means of coercing conversion to Christianity. Doctrinal and theological differences alone could legitimately become the pretext for war. Thus, holy war was simply the prerogative of the true believer to be exercised against the infidel, whether Jewish, Muslim or even heretical Christian. Witness, for example, the Spanish Inquisition, which in 1568 sentenced the entire population of the Netherlands to death as heretics.

This doctrine, perhaps accompanied by eschatological fervour predicting the imminent return of Christ, was the theological driving force behind the Crusades: one of the darkest periods of Christian moral history, and one of which the overwhelming majority of current-day Christians are rightly critical. This recent description from British comparative religionist Karen Armstrong captures their horror:

> On July 15 1099, the crusaders from western Europe conquered Jerusalem, falling upon its Jewish and Muslim inhabitants like the avenging angels from the Apocalypse. In a massacre that makes September 11 look puny in comparison, some 40,000 people were slaughtered in two days. A thriving, populous city had been transformed into a stinking charnel house. Yet in Europe scholar monks hailed this crime against humanity as the greatest event in world history since the crucifixion of Christ.

Repulsed (and often victimised) by such excesses of the Church with all their attendant bloodshed, Western civilisation came ultimately to reject the holy war doctrine. Western philosophies of war retreated to a modernised just war theory. Unlike holy war, this theory denied legitimacy to doctrinal wars. Legitimate pretexts for war became limited to those that could be appreciated irrespective of creed. War purely for conversion or the advancement of religious doctrine, which is to say holy war, was no longer considered legitimate. As sixteenth-century Spanish Dominican theologian Franciscus de Victoria specifically proclaimed: 'Difference of religion is not a cause of just war.' When Grotius famously wrote *The Law of War and Peace* in 1625, he cited, among other things, the wars of the Church as examples of war waged for illegitimate reasons. This thought process was accelerated by the Church's increasing subordination to the State.

This does not necessarily mean that a religious war could never legitimately be fought. War for the defence of religion would still be acceptable, but only when this was a function of legitimate reasons of state. As the separation of Church and State became more entrenched in Western civilisation, and with the Church, as a result, not commanding vast armies as it once did, religious wars, too, receded more into the background. It would be sheer folly to suggest this necessarily made the world a more peaceful place: perhaps the bloodiest century of human history was the twentieth when the most devastating wars were fought between secular states. It does, however, mean that religious wars became relegated to the history books of Western civilisation, at least so far as their religious bases were to be officially recognised.

That may explain why holy war is so often conflated, incorrectly, with religious war in the Western public imagination. It now seems any act of war that has religious expression is deemed to be a resurrection of holy war, and condemned accordingly, irrespective of the motivations or justifications of the actors. The logical extension of this is that collectives with a religious identity can have no justifications for war; not even those available to secular states.

Perhaps, then, it is understandable that, confronted with the phenomenon of terrorism, the immediate reaction of contemporary Western commentators is to reach for the doctrine of holy war to explain it. Thus, events and currents of thought within Christian history become thoughtlessly and artificially superimposed on all things Islamic. As is so often the case, our interpretations of the Other reveal far more about ourselves. We habitually exhibit the tendency to look for the crudest approximation of our own experiences and whack our ill-fitting labels on to the sometimes very different traditions and histories of others. It is via this process of projection that jihad becomes rendered equivalent to holy war in much of the Western imagination. Holy war was the repugnant religious concept about war Christendom experienced, and given the claimed religious motivations of terrorists, we look for a corresponding religious concept that we assume contains similar repugnance and assume they are the same thing. It really is as simple as that.

Any distinction between military jihad and holy war is more than merely of semantic consequence. It is of vital and real importance because of the imagery that the term 'holy war' evokes in the Western imagination. Given the increasing tendency for the dominant voices in the Western public conversation to demand that Muslims renounce jihad just as Western civilisation rejected holy war, any differences need to be identified.

As with Christianity, Islam's pacifist phase coincided with the absence of a viable body politic. But whereas the Church took centuries to obtain governmental authority, Islam found a degree of governmental expression during the life of the prophet Muhammad, about a dozen or so years after his mission began. This meant that warfare was a fact of life for the early Muslims, and that Islamic doctrines regulating it were highly developed at an early stage.

The Qur'anic discourse on jihad is subtle, however. As we have seen, it uses the word in a wide variety of ways, and rarely uses it in an explicitly military sense. That much has to be inferred from the historical and textual context in which the term is used. Nevertheless, the ambiguous Qur'anic use of 'jihad' does underscore an important distinction that the Qur'an draws between the concept of jihad, and fighting.

Where the Qur'an explicitly commands Muslims on matters

relating to warfare, it does not generally use the term 'jihad'. It more often uses '*qitāl*', the Arabic word for 'fighting'. The distinction is important, because whereas all commands for Muslims to engage in jihad are absolute and unconditional, references to *qitāl* are heavily qualified. In the Qur'anic vision, the Islamic concept of jihad, like justice, is something of invariable nobility. By contrast, *qitāl*, fighting, of itself, is not. It follows, then, that not every war can legitimately be called a jihad. This is why political authorities often tried to label their military expeditions a jihad.

Sometimes, this was largely unsuccessful. The Persian wars against the Russians in the early nineteenth century and the Ottoman World War I campaign are examples where the authorities attempted to rally Muslim support by declaring their efforts to be jihads, only to find that most Muslims rejected their characterisation and failed to respond to the call. These were clearly examples of *qitāl*, but not necessarily jihad. Conversely, there is little evidence that the expansionist wars of Muslims in the seventh and eighth centuries were called jihads by those who perpetrated them, yet Sunni historians have retrospectively deemed them such – perhaps as a rationalisation. Several Shiite scholars, meanwhile, have suggested the wars were not sufficiently motivated by Qur'anic demands to earn the legitimacy of being labelled jihads.

Doctrinally speaking, the starting point is, of course, the Qur'an itself. Here, it is crucial to remember that the Qur'an did not emerge as a single book all at once. It consists of over 6000 verses that came to light gradually over 23 years. Verses often appeared in response to specific situations that the early Muslims confronted. For this reason, every Qur'anic verse brings with it a social and historical context which is imperative in understanding its meaning. This is not a fringe idea developed to give a liberal spin to the Qur'anic text. It has been a core principle of Qur'anic exegesis since the discipline began. Countless volumes of classical Islamic texts are devoted to the narrow task of identifying the particular historical event from which each Qur'anic verse emerged; what Qur'anic exegetes call the *sabab al-nuzūl*, the 'occasion of revelation'.

In the case of verses concerning warfare, this becomes of heightened importance. The first verses sanctioning war did not appear until thirteen years after the beginning of the Prophet's mission. During that time, Islam's message of monotheism had become highly controversial to the pagan Arabs, and because of its emphasis on the inherent equality of human beings, it was a major threat to the tribal structures of Arabian society. Consequently, the most powerful pagan tribes sought to exterminate Muhammad's fledgling movement, and tortured, killed and banished the earliest Muslims from Mecca. Throughout this period, the Muslims did not fight back. This was not from fear or a resignation to political weakness – indeed, many of them wanted to defend themselves physically – but because they had not yet been granted permission from God to do so. The Qur'an had certainly prescribed jihad for them, but not *qitāl*. This jihad was clearly non-violent.

When finally the Muslims were granted permission to defend themselves in war, the relevant Qur'anic verses (22:39–40) explained the justifications for fighting:

> Permission is given to those who fight because they are wronged; and indeed, God is capable of giving them victory. They are those who were driven out of their homes merely for their saying 'Our Lord is Allah' . . .

These verses explicitly predicate the permission to fight on the Muslims' position as victims of oppression. They refer specifically to the Muslims who had been driven out of Mecca solely on the basis of their beliefs, and forced to migrate some 400 kilometres to Medina, losing most of their worldly possessions in the process. Thus, the original conception of armed jihad was firmly rooted in notions of justice.

Various battles against the tribes of Arabia precipitated as a result, in which the Muslims fought for their existence as a community. Few historians, and even fewer Muslim theologians, argue that these wars were anything other than defensive. This is reflected in other Qur'anic verses, such as 2:190, which reads: 'Fight in the path of God those who fight you; but do not initiate hostilities, for God does not love the aggressors.' Similarly at 60:8, the Qur'an provides that 'God does not forbid you to be kind and equitable to those disbelievers who have not made war on your religion nor driven you from your homes. God loves those who are equitable.' Moreover, at 8:61 we read: 'If they [the enemy] incline towards peace, then you should so incline, and place your trust in God.' Here, peace is a divine favour that should be readily accepted.

For some Muslim thinkers, these principles set the philosophical and moral standard for armed jihad. The implication is that the legitimacy of fighting against non-Muslims is directly proportional to the physical threat they pose to the Muslims. Aggression against Muslims, or against non-Muslims living under the protection of Muslim rule, is a legitimate basis for war. That much was unanimously agreed. More contested was the idea that, in the absence of a threat, war was not justified and could not be called a jihad in the Islamic sense. This theory of defensive jihad became particularly popular among Muslim theologians living under Western colonial rule. Thus, in Egypt at the turn of the twentieth century, Rashīd Riḍā and Muḥammad 'Abduh argued that jihad was purely a defensive doctrine. A generation later, Hassan al-Banna, who founded the Muslim Brotherhood movement, did the same. Of course, there were classical precedents for these views, too, and al-Banna quotes from such classical scholars to support his argument.

Meanwhile, in India, reformist preacher Abul A'la Mawdudi articulated an almost Socialist approach to jihad. For him, jihad was a means of confronting illegitimate and tyrannical rulers; a tool of liberation, the attainment of equality, and the defence of the weak. The question for Mawdudi is not whether jihad is defensive or offensive. It could be either, provided it was in pursuit of justice. As we will see, this was in some ways a departure from the more imperial, classical models of jihad, and required Mawdudi to reconstruct the early Muslim armies as liberators and freedom fighters, rather than imperialists or colonisers. He does this, perhaps unconvincingly, by drawing a distinction between the motivations of the Muslim fighters, and the perceptions of their foes – that is, the invaded would have seen them as colonisers, but the early Muslims, he argues, had the motivation of liberators. Similarly, Riḍā and 'Abduh felt a need to accommodate early Muslim conquest into their defensive jihad doctrine somehow. Needless to say, it required some significant historical revisionism to turn conquest into defensive wars.

It is blindingly obvious that these theories of jihad stand in stark contrast to the doctrine of holy war in medieval Christendom. On either view, no jihad could be launched against non-Muslims merely over a matter of religious difference. Disbelief was not a legitimate pretext for war. Nor, even, was imperial conquest. The most cited Qur'anic verse in this connection is 2:256: 'Let there be no compulsion in religion. Truth stands clear from error.'

However, it must be frankly admitted that some verses within the Qur'an appear to adopt a markedly more aggressive posture. Perhaps the verse most commonly cited in this regard is 9:5, often called the 'Verse of the Sword', which reads:

> And so, when the sacred months are over, slay the idolators wherever you may come upon them, and take them captive, and besiege them, and lie in wait for them at every conceivable place . . .

More belligerent commentators invoke this and similar verses to argue that Islam requires Muslims to slaughter non-Muslims indiscriminately in any location, at any time, and in any context.

This reading relies on nothing more than the text (or worse, a translation of the text), in complete isolation from its textual and historical context. Accordingly, this was not the view of the earliest Qur'anic commentators, who held that the verse was restricted in a number of important ways. First, the verse addressed 'idolators' (in Arabic, the *'mushrikīn'*), and not the 'people of the book' (*'ahl al-kitāb'*), which was usually understood to mean Jews and Christians. Accordingly, for masters such as al-Qurṭubī and al-Nawawī, whatever the verse meant, it had no application to Christians and Jews. Second, as master jurists Abū Ḥanīfa and Aḥmad ibn Ḥanbal noted, the historical context of the verse indicated that the particular 'idolators' in question were those specifically located in the Arabian peninsula at the time of the prophet Muhammad, relegating the verse to dead-letter law subsequently. This is supported by the preceding verse, which clarifies that the war is not waged on

> ... those with whom you have made a covenant and who thereafter have in no way failed to fulfil their obligations towards you, and neither have aided anyone against you: observe, then, your covenant with them until the end of the term agreed with them. Verily, God loves those who are conscious of Him.

It becomes clear, then, that the polytheists to be fought are those who had broken their covenant with the Muslims. The violation of a covenant, of course, is tantamount to a declaration of war, and it is against that background that 9:5 commands the Muslims to fight. Accordingly, for the great Qur'anic commentator of Moorish Spain, Abū Bakr ibn al-'Arabī, 'it is clear that the intended meaning of the verse is to kill those polytheists who are waging war against you'. Proponents of defensive theories of jihad could therefore maintain their position, while accounting for the 'Verse of the Sword'. It was apparent to them that 9:5 referred to a war already in progress. The command to kill the enemy wherever they are found is therefore restricted clearly to circumstances of warfare, and would no doubt be a constant and universal imperative in the context of military engagement.

Nevertheless, some classical exegetes concluded that the 'Verse of the Sword' implied a more universal, perpetual approach to war. Accordingly, in the mid-seventh century, Muslim armies expanded quickly into modern-day Egypt, Syria and Iraq. Upon the establishment of the Umayyad dynasty in 661, Muslim conquests occurred rapidly in all directions. To the east, the Umayyads entered Afghanistan, the Indian subcontinent and Central Asia; to the north they conquered Armenia and the Caucasus; and to the west they took control of much of North Africa and even southern Europe: taking the Iberian peninsula in 701 and entering France before being defeated by Charles Martel at Poitiers in 732. This sudden imperial surge is perhaps one of the most remarkable in human history, particularly given the Arabs had not previously demonstrated any capacity to conquer even nearby lands.

This imperial expansion did have the doctrinal support of one strand of classical Islamic thought, where the purpose of jihad was held to be to expand the territories ruled by the Muslims. This was often conceived as a means to facilitate preaching at a time where preaching the non-state religion could be risky. From this emerged a view of the world that divided it into two notional regions: the abode of Islam (*dār al-Islām*) and the abode of war (*dār al-ḥarb*). The borders of each region were theoretically fluid, meaning one must ultimately prevail over the other. The two could cease hostilities for a period, but this was only temporary. According to this theory, military jihad was a perpetual obligation. Non-Muslim empires were to be given the choice of accepting Muslim rule, or fighting. War, then, could theoretically be a perpetual endeavour.

We should perhaps not be surprised that the Umayyads adopted such a thoroughly imperialist stance. Theirs was an entirely imperial age and it is difficult to resist the conclusion that they were the products of their time. In the absence of a peace treaty, a state of perpetual war was the international relations norm. Even treaties were easily dissolved when politically convenient for the stronger party. Military expansion was a matter of common custom and, to some extent, it was another form of survival. Imperial conflict was unavoidable. Those who did not attack would, in all likelihood, eventually be attacked.

Nevertheless, this bifurcated worldview was entirely constructed. The prophet Muhammad never spoke of *dār al-Islām* or *dār al-ḥarb*; they were extrapolated from a particular reading of the Islamic primary texts. Still, this was the doctrinal driving force of the Umayyad dynasty, which is why it has legitimately been called a 'Jihad State'. But inevitably, this perpetual war theory was entirely unsustainable. The empire could only expand so far, and as the Umayyads suffered losses, the entire economy, which was built on war booty, collapsed. The empire's vast lands became impossible to administer, and a power vacuum emerged in its heartland resulting in its overthrow. It was a classic example of imperial overstretch. The empire simply got too big for itself, and being sustained by war, was doomed to implode. Unsurprisingly, then, the Umayyad dynasty did not last long, coming to its demise in 749.

The Umayyads' theory of perpetual war is the most aggressive jihad doctrine known to pre-modern Islam. It was also contrary to the position taken by many eminent early scholars, including people who were companions of the prophet Muhammad himself, such as 'Abd Allāh ibn 'Umar. Giants of the next generations, such as Ibn Shibrama, Sufyān al-Thawrī and 'Amr bin Dinār, also shunned a theory of perpetual, universal war. But even this Umayyad aggression cannot be equated with the Christian doctrine of holy war. The Umayyads were imperialists; their aim was to gain political control over as much land as they could. They were concerned primarily with political supremacy. The Umayyad case for war ceased once Muslims had political dominance. This perpetual war theory, unlike holy war, was therefore prepared to tolerate religious difference. The shallow, polemical reading that the Qur'an permitted Muslims to slaughter 'infidels' indiscriminately was thoroughly rejected in Islamic thought – even by the Umayyads. Occupants of conquered lands were not forced to convert to Islam. Non-Muslims remained free to practise their respective faiths. Again: 'Let there be no compulsion in religion,' demanded the Qur'an.

This contrasts clearly with the doctrine of holy war, which embraced forced conversion and the massacre of entire 'pagan' populations. In holy war, the mere existence of disbelievers was an affront that could forcibly be rectified. In even the most aggressive jihad theory, this was not the case. This is why the cliché that Islam spread by the sword is folly. Certainly, Islamic rule, like any other of the period, spread through conquest. It is also true that conversions to Islam often followed. But these conversions were voluntary, which is why Muslims ruled as a minority for centuries. Moreover, the spread of Islam into East Africa, Southeast Asia and parts of Central Asia was not accompanied by any conquest at all.

With the Umayyads' demise, the theory of the Jihad State came quickly to be rejected by most classical scholars as unsound and unsustainable. Khalid Blankinship, in *The End of the Jihâd State*, asserts that the Umayyads remain the only polity in Islamic history to have based their foreign policy on perpetual warfare against non-Muslims. There is an argument to say it was revived in southeastern Europe with the Ottoman conquests of Kosovo in the fourteenth century, Constantinople in the fifteenth, and Hungary in the sixteenth. There is an Umayyad echo here, and the Ottomans suffered the same difficulties of imperial overstretch and, ultimately, the same fate. Still, there was something more to the Ottomans: they discovered the art of diplomacy in a way the Umayyads could not.

The Abbasids succeeded the Umayyads and ushered in a new era of Islamic foreign policy, which opted for extended periods of truce and diplomatic relations. Perhaps accordingly, the Abbasids survived for five centuries, until 1258 – substantially longer than their Umayyad predecessors. Concepts such as *dār al-Islām* and *dār al-ḥarb* were still used, but in a more nuanced way. Master jurist Muḥammad ibn Idrīs al-Shāfiʿī argued that a land, even if populated and ruled by non-Muslims, could not be called *dār al-ḥarb* if its polity was not at war with Muslims. Such was al-Shāfiʿī's influence that his legal methodology became the basis of one of the four main schools of Sunni Islamic jurisprudence. Subsequent scholars of the Shāfiʿī school came to define *dār al-Islām* as anywhere Muslims were free to practise their religion, even if under non-Muslim rule. Interestingly, this definition would include much of the modern West as *dār al-Islām* and exclude much of the Muslim world.

The subtleties of these definitions inevitably accompanied a proliferation of other conceptual regions or 'abodes': *dār al-ṣulḥ* or *dār al-hudna* ('the abode of neutrality or truce'); *dār al-ʿamn* ('the abode of security'); *dār al-ʿadl* ('the abode of justice'). All of these were categories that encompassed non-Muslim regions with which the Muslim world would have peaceful relations. No legitimate pretext to attack such regions existed, indicating a theory of armed jihad that, in contrast to that of the Umayyads, was neither perpetual nor universal.

Thus did Islamic politics, as early as 750, take on a collaborative posture. More restrained scholarly theories of jihad had always existed in tension with Umayyad imperialism. To be sure, divergent theories continued to compete. But now, more negotiable approaches assumed greater political purchase.

This did not mean that Muslims shunned conquest altogether. The ninth and tenth centuries saw some minor Muslim incursions into Sicily and southern Italy, for example. But it is certainly true that this slowed considerably as Muslims focused more on building great civilisations than on military expansion. The golden age of Islamic civilisation, particularly in Iraq and Spain, is located largely within the Abbasid period.

Additionally, it was around this time that Western Christian militancy was approaching its zenith. Holy war was on the way, meaning the majority of wars Muslims fought in this period were defensive. Muslim attempts to repel the regrouping armies of Christendom were not always successful. The Muslims in southern France were quickly vanquished, followed over the next century by their co-religionists in Italy. By the mid-tenth century, Western Christian armies began descending upon Moorish Spain and, with the exception of the city of Granada, succeeded in expelling the Muslims by the thirteenth century. Granada itself fell in 1492.

And, of course, there were the Crusades, which spanned several centuries and comprised a series of attacks into the very heartlands of Islam. Even here, many Muslim rulers had little concern for these wars, some even allying themselves with the Crusaders at various points in time. The Fatimid rulers in Egypt struggled to rally popular support for a jihad to defeat the invaders. By now, any notion that armed jihad was a perpetual, binding, religious obligation on Muslims had well and truly lost its political grip.

But the imperative for armed action intensified dramatically in the thirteenth century when the Mongols, led initially by Genghis Khan, launched their brutal invasion upon Muslim lands from Central Asia to eastern Persia and Iraq. The Abbasid caliphate fell in the process, and Baghdad was destroyed in a manner not seen again until the US invasion of 2003. Only the Mamluks in Egypt were able to prevent the Mongols from travelling further west. About 50 years later, the Mongols themselves became Muslims, but continued attacking Muslim polities in Egypt and Syria.

The Crusades loom large in the Western historical memory. The Muslim world, however, was typically more concerned with the Mongol invasions. No threat since the Byzantines had preoccupied Muslim thinkers so wholly, and none was so brutal. It is in this climate that we find a resurgence in the scholarly discussion of jihad.

However, most of this discussion focused on questions of legitimate conduct in jihad and what weaponry could be used, and added little to earlier thought concerning the fundamental, conceptual basis of armed jihad.

What we have, then, is a complicated, diverse, dynamic doctrinal landscape concerning armed jihad. This is a term that encompasses imperialist, defensive, revivalist, and even resistance ideas. Clearly, the practice of rendering jihad invariably as holy war is impossibly crude – and particularly since none of the above could accurately be described as holy war in the first place.

These differences only multiply when one considers Islamic rules of military engagement. Volumes of classical Islamic jurisprudence delve into the restrictions on Islamic warriors to define the limits of acceptable conduct in war. For this, Muslim scholars looked particularly to the instructions of the prophet Muhammad during war. There, classical jurists found clear, uncompromising prohibitions on targeting any non-combatants, which is why their sanctity became a point of consensus in Islamic laws of war. Only Ibn Ḥazm, a fiery theologian from Moorish Spain who wrote with the impending threat of the Christian reconquest, held that it was permissible to target male non-combatants (but, oddly, not merchants and travellers). However, so overwhelming was the scriptural evidence to the contrary, and such was his failure to deal with the clear mandates of the prophet Muhammad, that his position was resoundingly rejected. Still, even Ibn Ḥazm emphasised the sanctity of women and children, which has always been a point of absolute unanimity.

War, in Islamic thought, was only to be directed towards a confirmed military foe. This prohibition on harming the civilian population even extended to causing indirect harm by poisoning water supplies or destroying fruit-bearing trees. Al-Ḥakim al-Tirmidhī prohibited hamstringing horses. As the Christian armies, fresh from expelling the Moors from Spain, bore down upon Morocco, fifteenth-century jurist Aḥmad al-Wansharīsī emphasised the sanctity of women and children, and prohibited killing even wounded enemy combatants once the battle had finished.

Even the most imperial jihad theorists accepted such strictures, particularly concerning non-combatants. As a result, there was significant disagreement among the jurists as to whether it was permissible to use mangonels, or catapults, in warfare. The principal objection to them was that they had the potential to kill non-combatants, or, as the Moroccan jurist Ibn Abī Zaminayn argued, they were indiscriminate killing machines. Accordingly, they were traditionally rejected as illegitimate weapons. It is only during the Crusades that alternative views came to the fore. This clear concern to avoid what is now termed 'collateral damage' also led to a related debate about the permissibility of attacking an enemy that uses human shields. Many medieval jurists held that attacking was acceptable in this situation, provided only combatants were targeted. This position was largely reversed during the Mongol invasions, owing mainly to the fact that the Mongols used human shields on a scale not previously encountered.

Such restrictions were not features of medieval Christian theories of holy war. By and large, holy war permitted soldiers to wipe out entire populations of infidels indiscriminately.

But perhaps most instructively, the prophet Muhammad forbade the killing of religious leaders: priests, rabbis and monks. American Islamic scholar Hamza Yusuf has commented that this reflects Islam's recognition of the inviolable right of people to worship freely, irrespective of their religious persuasion. Religious communities are reliant on their leaders and theologians for guidance, and so to strike at those leaders would grossly undermine this freedom of religion.

This further underscored the fact that war could not be used for the purposes of converting people. To force conversion on people with the sword only creates hypocrites who are compelled to profess Islam but inwardly have no faith in it. This point, in particular, is an essential feature distinguishing jihad from holy war. The holy war doctrine had no quibble with forced conversion.

It is clear from this doctrinal history that the dominant conceptions of jihad have little in common with the medieval

Christian doctrine of holy war. By far the closest approximation to be found in the Christian, and subsequently, Western tradition is the theory of just war. It is instructive that Ibn Rushd's theory of jihad written in the twelfth century is reproduced a century later, almost as if by translation, in the just war discourse of St Thomas Aquinas. Of course, even this generalisation is fraught with danger, because jihad is not a static, singular concept. Still, to translate jihad as 'just war' would be a vast improvement in accuracy on the current popular practice of equating the concept of jihad with one of the ugliest doctrines in Christendom's often proud history. Even the most aggressive, imperialist theories of jihad exhibit significant differences to holy war.

To be clear, it is not my contention that Muslims have never, unlike Christians, perpetrated unjust wars on illegitimate pretexts. As any honest Muslim would acknowledge, imperial oppression is shared and we have our own measure of it. Nor is the above an assertion that the Crusades represent the spirit of mainstream Christian thought. My intention here is simply to demonstrate that, at a doctrinal level, the mainstream Islamic concept of jihad cannot, in all good conscience, be rendered synonymous with the now defunct doctrine of holy war.

It may seem like a small point, but this has profound consequences for our public conversation. It has become almost impossible for a Muslim in the public space even to utter the dreaded j-word without generating some degree of public hysteria. The confusion surrounding jihad has taken root so stubbornly in our discourse that jihad has become, of itself, something to be condemned and resisted in much the same way holy war has been. We are witnessing a kind of jihad against jihad.

Muslims might be familiar with jihad's military tradition, but most have little understanding of holy war. It is not uncommon for Muslims, then, to concede that part of the meaning of 'jihad' is holy war. Of course, they are blissfully unaware how this sounds to the Western ear, which is familiar with the meaning of 'holy war' but is either unfamiliar with, or polemically ignorant of, 'jihad'. This continuing, and seemingly unending, popular confusion surrounding the Islamic concept of jihad makes it almost impossible for doctrinally minded Muslims and broader Western societies to communicate on this issue. None can talk sense in the eyes of the other because the parameters are so radically different, which is only made worse by the fact that the same words are being used. Add the emotive senselessness generated by terrorism, and you are left only with mutually invincible ignorance masquerading as a conversation.

It is, admittedly, further complicated by the fact that terrorists are co-opting the language of jihad for their crimes, while journalists faithfully, and uncritically, reproduce their narrative. The senseless indiscrimination of terrorism done in the name of Islam does conjure up images of holy war. But it is certainly not jihad.

As terrorism has become the highest-profile (although illegitimate) expression of jihad, the phoney connection between jihad and holy war has only become entrenched in the public consciousness. While a steady stream of talking heads has spent considerable time reiterating Islam's absolute and unequivocal condemnation of terrorism, few have had the opportunity, or the desire, to reclaim jihad from terrorism in a similar way.

It is tragic, really, because, far from being synonymous with it, terrorism is jihad's exact opposite. Since September 11, several Muslim orators have quipped that terrorism is to jihad what adultery is to marriage. That is true in a sense, but at a deeper level, the relationship is even more distant. In the classical Islamic vocabulary, the conduct of those who attacked innocents, irrespective of their motives or the justness of their cause, was not called jihad at all; it belonged to an entirely different species called *ḥirāba*: banditry and brigandage, or in modern vocabulary, terrorism. To call this jihad is to give it an echo of legitimacy the classical Islamic tradition always denied it. Yet, thanks to the lazy sloppiness of many public commentators, and, it must be acknowledged, the deranged rhetoric of terrorist leaders themselves, we have long lost sight of this, if indeed we ever saw it.

We have seen that jihad has been based variously on notions of political expansion, defence and the establishment of justice. By contrast, al-Qaʻida's discourse is almost entirely one of revenge. Its communiqué of 24 April 2002, in which it attempts to provide an Islamic justification for the attacks of September 11, is little more than a propaganda tract alleging a series of crimes perpetrated by the United States against Muslim populations, followed by a pledge to repay the Americans in kind. Al-Qaʻida speaks of killing innocent Americans 'to teach others a lesson'. In *Under the Shadow of the Spears*, al-Qaʻida spokesman Sulayman Abu Ghaith is even more explicit:

> We are attracted to the Americans and they to us. We will not be saved if they are; there is no good in us if our firing ceases, and no power or nobility if we do not take vengeance for our brothers in Palestine, Iraq, Afghanistan, and every place.

This warped perversion of jihad rests consistently on 2:194 of the Qur'an:

> A sacred month for a sacred month: for sacred things, too, there is a law of retribution. Thus, if anyone commits aggression against you, attack him just as he has attacked you – but remain conscious of God, and know that God is with those who are conscious of Him.

The historical and textual context of this verse makes it clear that it was addressing the question of whether or not it was permissible to fight the pagan Arabs if they attacked the Muslims during the months of the year in which, according to custom, war was prohibited. The verse merely gives permission to fight back if attacked during those months, but even then implies restraint by reminding the Muslims to remain conscious of God. The text simply does not bear the unprincipled and unrestrained interpretation al-Qaʻida wishes to give it – one which would undo 1400 years of Islamic scholarship in an instant. I am unaware of any classical scholar invoking this or similar verses to permit the suspension of the Islamic rules of war. Yet, for al-Qaʿida, this hopelessly out-of-place verse is sufficient to justify every immorality. If the Americans have killed millions of innocent Muslims, al-Qaʿida claims the right to kill the same number of Americans. The United States has used depleted uranium, so al-Qaʿida claims the right to use chemical and biological weapons. Thus does bin Laden pledge to continue his attacks 'until we obtain a balance in terror'. Compare the Prophet's famous command: 'Let there be neither harm, nor reciprocating harm.'

Al-Qaʿida's is a view of warfare that is entrenched deeply in anger and revenge: two motivations that are completely unacceptable from the perspective of jihad. The limitations on the conduct of armed jihad mean it is done with a great deal of restraint. The true *mujāhid* is in control of his own emotions and motivations. This is why many of the early scholars emphasised the importance of the inner, spiritual jihad even while engaging in armed, physical jihad. They understood that the instant one fights in anger, one has left the realm of jihad and entered into the realm of ego and oppression.

ʿAlī ibn Abī Ṭālib was the prophet Muhammad's cousin, and an accomplished warrior. In a famous incident during what Muslim historians call the Battle of the Trench, ʿAlī had successfully subdued an enemy to the point where he was in a position to deliver the killer blow. As ʿAlī raised his sword, his enemy spat in ʿAlī's face. At that point, ʿAlī paused and withdrew his sword, enabling his enemy to escape after striking ʿAlī twice. Asked later why he had spared his enemy, ʿAlī responded: 'I was afraid that I would strike him in vengeance for myself, so I lifted my sword.' ʿAlī was a man who understood the difference between war (*ḥarb*) and jihad.

Jihad is a struggle. The very defining characteristic of jihad is that it is difficult. Anger and revenge are easy. They are jihad's negative image. With every al-Qa'ida statement of anger and revenge, they make themselves even more distant from jihad. That they attempt to claim their thoughts and actions for jihad is a profound insult to the tradition of Islam.

But it does at least expose the rank hypocrisy terrorism so violently embodies. Its rhetoric complains of injustice but itself inflicts the most manifest injustice on the innocent. It uses a discourse of resistance to hegemony, but is itself deeply hegemonic. Sometimes it is easier to die for something than to live by it.

Terrorism, then, far from being an act of fervent religiosity, is an act of rampant disbelief. By straying beyond the legitimate bounds of armed jihad, both in pretext and in conduct, the terrorist is confessing that God's ability to restore justice and reward the oppressed – common themes in traditional Islamic theology – cannot be considered reliable. It impersonates strength, yet it is hopelessly weak. It feigns victory, but is nothing more than a frank admission of moral defeat. This is in stark contrast to the actions of the prophet Muhammad's companions, who faced far greater persecution than most terrorists ever would have, yet spent over a dozen years bearing it and relying on the arrival of divine help. Persecution did not provide them with an excuse to violate Islamic restrictions on warfare. These people knew who they were. Terrorism is exactly everything it pretends it is not.

This false thread connecting terrorism, jihad and holy war sets stubborn, confining parameters on our thoughts, with profound implications. The consequent syllogism runs thus: if terrorism is jihad; and jihad is holy war in Islamic form; and holy war is a relic of medieval Christian theology; then terrorism is an expression of medieval Islamic theology. As we have seen, there is no medieval Islamic precedent for the idea of killing civilians and non-combatants indiscriminately. Still, it is one of the most common mantras of the war on terror that terrorism, or more generally, Muslim radicalism, is a medieval affront to modernity. As we will see, this misguided diagnosis reveals a persistent ignorance of the natures of both radical thought and modernity.

7

What is so medieval about al-Qa'ida?

At some point, we must come to terms with the fact that the world is bigger than us. Failure to do so leads to small-minded conclusions, and threatens to weaken almost any diagnosis of our present condition – at least to the extent it involves something we perceive to be somehow foreign. The war on terror is, sadly and urgently, not an exception to this. 'Islam,' writes Francis Fukuyama in *The Wall Street Journal*, 'is the only cultural system that seems regularly to produce people like Osama bin Laden or the Taliban who reject modernity lock, stock and barrel'. Here Fukuyama articulates one of the war on terror's great political shibboleths: that al-Qa'ida and the Taliban are medieval.

It may be that the religious authoritarianism of the Taliban, and the absolutist fanaticism of al-Qa'ida, revive in the Western consciousness the dark spectres of its own medieval past. The voracious doctrinal intolerance and the diminished value of human life possibly rekindle the flames of the medieval Church. Here, again, emerges the persistent tendency towards projection. To the extent the parallels are meaningful at all, these medieval characteristics are particularly Western. They have comparatively little to do with the Muslim world, whose medieval memory is of a very different spirit. For those of the Western commentariat for whom the West is modern, and its enemies must be its diametric opposite, this is difficult to grasp. Once more, though, the central reference point is the Western self-image. Once more, the analysis reveals more about the analyst than the subject.

To be fair, the Taliban and al-Qaʻida do appropriate medieval language. They attempt to invoke the authority of the Islamic tradition, and adopt some of the more unsavoury precedents medieval Islam has to offer. But, in truth, any similarities with the medieval world are superficial, perhaps illusory. Though the clichés of Western politicians will encourage a different conclusion, these groups are not, in their essence, medieval. They are, in fact, radically modern.

If they have any pre-modern Islamic reflection, it is perhaps in the Kharijites: precisely the word Saudis often use to describe terrorists. These were a sect of violent puritans from the very earliest period of Islam, who rebelled against the Muslim leadership for departing from their particular interpretation of Islamic law. The Kharijite catch-cry of 'no sovereignty but God's' might be familiar to modern Muslim radicals, but the Kharijites were immediately and overwhelmingly rejected by mainstream Islam to the extent that it is understood unequivocally to be an insult to be called by that name. Hence, when the Jordanian scholar Nāṣir al-Dīn al-Albānī wrote a critique of terrorism called *From the Methodology of the Kharijites*, those he described took deep offence and wailed in protest. Bin Laden himself makes a point of objecting to any such description. If the Kharijites are a premodern echo of al-Qaʻida, this only emphasises that al-Qaʻida is not medieval. Medieval Muslims emphatically rejected the Kharijites, which demonstrates how unlike their medieval counterparts are today's radical Muslim ideologues.

This is why they are best described as *radical*. Literally. Their ideology is a regressive, but thoroughly new, invention with little true connection to classical thought. It is difficult to speak singularly about medieval or classical Islam with any coherence because it is so dizzyingly diverse, but it is possible to identify some of its general features – enough, certainly, to recognise that the radical Muslim ideologues of today represent a revolutionary departure from the tradition with which they are ostensibly associated.

It should not come as a surprise that radical Muslim thought is profoundly modern. It is fashionable, but thoughtless, to believe that to be modern is, by definition, to be liberal, tolerant and secular. There have been many greatly illiberal and intolerant manifestations of modernity, Western ones such as Nazism among them. Moreover, there are plenty of medieval examples of diverse, relatively tolerant societies: the Moors, medieval Buddhist India, ancient China. Tolerance is not exclusively liberal, Western, modern and secular, and repression is not exclusively medieval, religious and Eastern.

There are, of course, some immediately obvious ways in which al-Qa'ida's modernity is readily observable. Among them is its famed exploitation of modern technology, or more instructively, its understanding of the pivotal, global role mass media plays in modern warfare. Structurally, it is a loose, privatised, multinational network. It resembles more the international drug cartels of modernity than traditional central command models. It is sustained by the globalisation that permits terrorist organisations to move money around the world silently and with ease. Al-Qa'ida's financial survival would not be possible in a pre-globalisation age. Indeed, as an operational matter, al-Qai'da simply could not exist as it does in a pre-modern era.

The imperial terrain of medieval times was not fertile ground for al-Qa'ida's non-state variety of militancy. The modern world, consisting not of empires, but nation states, is far more accommodating. This is particularly true in the post-colonial societies of the Muslim world, where ill-conceived borders surround divided populations crippled by the colonial experience. When, as is inevitable, these dynamics leave behind a string of failed states, a vacuum is created, to be filled by non-state actors with the militant will to step into the breach. Organisations such as al-Qa'ida can exist in a variety of environments, but thrive most notably in such a context of weak or failed states. Again, modern times suit them.

It is true that non-state militancy existed in pre-modern times, but al-Qa'ida's particular brand of irregular warfare is distinctly a phenomenon of modernity, and has clearly modern ideological roots. It proceeds from the idea, resoundingly alien to classical Islamic thought, of effecting change through the violence of a revolutionary vanguard. This is a clear philosophical bequest, not from the prophet Muhammad or Saladin, but from Lenin. Its first Muslim expression is found in *Milestones on the Road* by Sayyid Qutb, which prescribed that a vanguard seize power and establish an Islamic state in order to Islamicise society from the top down. Many of Qutb's peers in the Muslim Brotherhood movement, and the more traditionalist Al-Azhar University in Cairo, denounced the book as heretical. Other twentieth-century thinkers, like India's Abul A'la Mawdudi embraced this idea, casting Islam's purpose as 'universal, all-embracing revolution'. Similarly, Ayatollah Khomeini called on Muslims to 'transform themselves into a powerful force so that they may overthrow the tyrannical regime imperialism has imposed on us and set up an Islamic government', which is precisely what he did.

Muslims are divided on whether Qutb himself advocated violent revolution, or this was the product of subsequent misinterpretation. Certainly, he never partook in violence himself. Whatever the case, the ideological genealogy to al-Qai'da, even if indirect, is clear enough. Abdullah Azzam, the leader of the Afghan jihad against the Soviets, who adopted the idea of suicide bombing from the Tamil Tigers in Sri Lanka, drew inspiration in turn from Qutb's Leninist borrowing. Azzam was Osama bin Laden's intellectual mentor during those years, and despite their disagreements (which ultimately led to bin Laden's implication in Azzam's death), Azzam's ideological imprint on bin Laden is indelible. Indeed, bin Laden took an Islamic studies course taught by Azzam, and Sayyid Qutb's younger brother, Muhammad, whose work bin Laden recommends. Bin Laden's other profound ideological influence was his current deputy Ayman al-Zawahiri, who was previously imprisoned and tortured in Egypt as a member of the Muslim Brotherhood movement, of which Sayyid Qutb is a landmark ideologue.

The worldview of classical Islamic theologians was more inclined towards introspection. 'Verily, God does not change the condition of a people until they change what is within themselves,' advises the Qur'an, buttressing the classical view that when Muslims suffer a calamity, they should look within for the cause. But in sharp contradistinction, after the attacks of September 11, 2001, Sulayman Abu Ghaith, spokesman for al-Qa'ida, thundered that 'America is the reason for every injustice, wrong, and oppression to befall the Muslims. It is behind all of the disasters that have happened and continue to happen to the Muslims.'

To the extent that Muslims bear any responsibility in the radical view, it is for the sole reason that they have abandoned jihad – or, more accurately, the radical's particular version of it. As Abdullah Azzam opined in his will:

> ... every Muslim on earth bears the responsibility of abandoning jihad and the sin of abandoning the gun. Every Muslim who passes away without a gun in his hand faces God with the sin of abandoning fighting ... I believe that the Muslim *umma* [global community] is responsible for the honour of every Muslim woman that is being violated in Afghanistan and is responsible for every drop of Muslim blood that is being shed unjustly – therefore they are an accessory to these crimes.

This charge of abandoning jihad aside, radical Muslim ideology proceeds from a conviction that there is a worldwide conspiracy designed to destroy the Muslims and eliminate Islam. They find considerable support for this idea from the fact that Muslims in disparate parts of the world have in recent decades found themselves the weaker party in apparently unconnected conflicts in the Middle East, Chechnya, the Balkans, Somalia, Kashmir and the Philippines. They find further support from the statement attributed to the prophet Muhammad that 'the nations are about to flock against [the Muslims] from every horizon, just as hungry people flock to a kettle'. The report is popular in an age where Muslims are politically humiliated, but it is telling that it was rarely cited in classical Islamic literature. Perhaps this is because it would have found little resonance among medieval Muslims to whom Islam was ascendant. Whatever the reason, the ultimate fact is that the classical mind was far from conspiratorial. That mindset is modern.

With this untraditional outlook in place, it is easy to see how radical Muslims, like Leninist radicals, would lead a revolutionary vanguard; positioning themselves rhetorically as forces of purity against evil. Accordingly, in al-Qa'ida we see military jihad ripped from the exclusive realm of government. This may be a replication of the Bolshevik model, but it is certainly a radical departure from the classical Islamic one. Here is the first clue that the modernity of radical Muslim activists is not merely operational, but more profoundly philosophical as well.

Conservative British philosopher John Gray argues that the philosophy of modernity begins with a group of thinkers known to history as the Positivists. The Positivists were devoutly rationalist, and argued that objective, universal criteria could and should become the singular reference point for all the enquiries of society. It begins with Count Henri de Saint-Simon's view that human progress is a product of scientific knowledge. As the world acquires such knowledge, every sphere of life could be governed by it. Accordingly, ethics and morality could become an exact science.

The Positivist view was clearly misguided, but this has not prevented it from being highly influential. Karl Marx, and subsequent Marxist thinkers, embraced the doctrine that increased knowledge would lead humanity to the best condition it had known. Like Saint-Simon, Marx argued that conflict would cease and government could be abolished. More recently, neoconservative thinkers such as Francis Fukuyama built the idea of the universal free market on the assumptions of the Positivists. Indeed, perhaps Positivism's most profound contemporary impact has been on economic discourse, which treats what is essentially the imprecise study of human behaviour as though it were Newtonian physics.

If, as the Positivists believed, the conundrums of the world are reducible to, and objectively soluble in the manner of, an equation, it becomes possible to eliminate evil. Hunger, poverty, war and conflict can be eradicated by an objective, unarguable pathway. Disagreement becomes a thing of the past. Progress – material, existential and moral – becomes our objectively determinable fate.

The Positivists were convinced of the all-conquering power of the human intellect. This is perhaps their most marked philosophical difference from radical Muslim ideologues, who tend to be staunch enemies of rationalism. This, however, does not render them any more medieval. This radical rejection of reason echoes more loudly the counter-Enlightenment than classical Islam, which was more inclined to regard reason as an integral aspect of attaining faith. The Qur'an's tendency is to speak of disbelief almost as though it were a failure of reason. Qutb, by contrast, saw disbelief, and for that matter, faith, as a matter of subjective experience. It was almost an act of will rather than reason. Qutb sounds more like Kierkegaarde, or even Nietzsche, than any medieval Muslim theologian. Abdal Hakim Murad has quipped that '[f]undamentalism is the belief that revelation forces us to be stupid'. Via Qutb, radical thinkers adopt that position wholesale. As Gray argues, it is this resolute rejection of reason that, in part, exposes radical Muslim thought for the modernism it is.

Still, radical Muslim thought treats theology in rather a Positivist manner: as a matter of science, and not humanities. Like

Saint-Simon, radicals approach ethics and morality as though they are the outcome of an objective equation. The only reference points are to the primary sacred texts, almost always devoid of context, and interpreted singularly in accordance with the reader's most radical prejudices.

When religion becomes science, culture becomes merely a corruptive deviation from the objective truth – an impurity that is best eliminated. 'The more radical the terrorists, the more they do not embody a traditional culture or a culture at all,' wrote Olivier Roy in the Spring 2005 edition of the *ISIM Review*. For Roy, Islamic radicalisation 'is an endeavour to reconstruct a "pure" religion outside traditional or Western cultures, outside the very concept of culture itself'. For the radical ideologue, then, pure religion does not find a broad range of diverse, yet authentic cultural expressions. '[W]hat we consider to be Islamic culture, Islamic sources, Islamic philosophy and Islamic thought are also constructs of *jāhiliyya* [un-Islamic ignorance],' wrote Qutb, imploring Muslims to return to the 'pure source ... free from any mixing or pollution'. Clearly, such pollution is not uniquely Western for Qutb. Rather, Islam provides a mode of living 'such that you will look upon all other modes, whether Eastern or Western, with contempt'. Radicalism is profoundly anti-cultural. In this way, it is also profoundly untraditional. The conceptual relationship between Islam and culture has, traditionally, been highly convivial.

Medieval Islam incorporated cultural differences throughout the Muslim world into a plurality of Islamic thought. At one level, this was an inevitable outcome of diverse environments impacting upon Muslim thinkers. But more deeply, it was a pluralism embedded in classical Islamic legal theory itself. 'Cultural usage shall have the weight of law', goes the long established Islamic legal maxim. Expanding on this in the nineteenth century, Al-Tusūlī held that 'allowing the people to follow their customs, usages, and general aspirations in life is obligatory. To hand down rulings in opposition to this is gross deviation and tyranny.' And here, in the fourteenth century and in typically emphatic fashion, is Syrian jurist Ibn al-Qayyim al-Jawziyya:

> Whoever issues legal rulings to the people merely on the basis of what is transmitted in the compendia despite differences in their customs, usages, times, places, conditions, and the special circumstances of their situations has gone astray and leads others astray. His crime against the religion is greater than the crime of a physician who gives people medical prescriptions without regard to the differences of their climes, norms, the times they live in, and their physical natures but merely in accord with what he finds written down in some medical book about people with similar anatomies. He is an ignorant physician, but the other is an ignorant jurisconsult but much more detrimental.

In this spirit, traditional Islamic jurists often gave legal force to local customs, so that local culture would not simply be tolerated, but play a formative role in the development of Islamic law in the region. Hence the classical Islamic principle that legal rulings are valid only for the time and place in which they are given. Hence, also, the (oft-forgotten) requirement of a qualified Islamic jurist that she or he must have an in-depth knowledge of the local culture.

It is therefore unsurprising that traditional Islamic thought and practice always bears the marks of the culture in which it is manifest. Subcontinental Islam retains many patriarchal pre-Islamic practices, while in Southeast Asia, one can find matriarchal social structures in particular Muslim villages. Similarly, the differences between the Islam of Africa and its counterparts in the Middle East or the Caucasus are profoundly marked.

This cultural openness imbued classical Islamic thought with the powerful flexibility to respond to its environment. It would develop organically in its social context and become entwined with local culture. It is precisely for this reason that the cultural colouring of Islam in a given society is rarely perceived by locals. At least until the recent influx of Islamic literature from Saudi Arabia made an impact, Indonesian or Somali Muslims were unlikely to apprehend the Indonesian or Somali flavour of their Islam; as far as they were concerned, this was the only Islam they need have known. Accordingly, in spite of their very real religious differences, Muslims from the subcontinent, for example, often have far more in common with local Sikhs or Hindus than they do with their co-religionists from, say, the Balkans. Each had a pre-Islamic culture that the arrival of Islam may have regulated in some way, but that unquestionably remains.

Mosques in China resemble local temples in their architecture, and in their interior design often feature a marriage of Chinese and Arabic calligraphy. Medieval Muslims were quite prepared to learn even from cultures of peoples they had conquered: the domes now so iconic of mosque architecture entered the Muslim world via the Ottomans, who borrowed from the design of the Byzantine churches of Constantinople. One of the great secrets of early Islamic expansion was the ability of Muslims to adopt the mainstream culture of the civilisation's frontiers without compromising religious integrity.

There is something of Burkeian conservatism in this. It implies an acknowledgment that societies and their cultures are complex organisms, the product of centuries of social evolution, and that change, if necessary at all, is most likely to be accepted where it causes minimal social and cultural upheaval.

Now compare Qutb's condemnation of the suggestion that Muslims could embrace even the tiniest aspect of a non-Muslim's culture except 'in relation to science and technology'. Any suggestion to the contrary was, for Qutb, 'one of the tricks played by world Jewry ... so that the Jews may penetrate into the body politic of the whole world and then be free to perpetuate their evil designs'. The bigotry of radical Muslim ideology is profoundly ahistorical. Unlike its medieval predecessor, it fails to account for the complexities of human societies and human history, instead appealing to its own 'objective' universal set of laws; its own, singular interpretation of Islam. Anything short of complete and radical upheaval, wrote Qutb, is merely 'rationalisation ... to appease people's desires'.

It is easy to see how this philosophical outlook lends itself to utopian delusions. At the turn of the twentieth century, the Bolsheviks emerged with a Marxist belief in the power of objective knowledge to bring about inexorable human progress. Theirs was a utopian mission to abolish social classes and, ultimately, the State. The result was the precise opposite: the establishment of a totalitarian Soviet state, and the state-sanctioned murder of millions of people. The Nazis, too, embraced a similarly modern project. Their utopia was built on a firm belief in the ability of science to generate a better species of human. Again, their utopian zeal led them to torture and murder millions.

Today, radical Muslim ideologues seek their own religious version of utopia. It is true that their rhetoric draws heavily on the plight of Muslim populations around the world that have suffered at the hands of Western (and other) foreign policies. But they also draw heavily, and perhaps more ardently, on popular Muslim resentment of leaders in the Muslim world. Some of bin Laden's most spiteful venom is directed at the Saudi regime, which he regards as one of the Muslim world's 'oppressive, debauched, infidel governments', who are 'part of the organisation of global unbelief'. Perhaps inconceivably to Western observers, the Taliban spoke of Iranian religious leaders, not as devout or pious, but as 'wicked' and 'corrupt'; as promoters of adultery. These ideologues make little secret of the fact that they desire to see Islamic rule return, at the very least, to the Muslim lands.

That, in itself, is not utopian. But it is clear that their particular version of Islamic rule, perhaps exemplified best by the Taliban (the 'divine blessing' with whom bin Laden said he shared a 'doctrinal relationship' and to whom he pledged his allegiance), is. It is a political vision that seeks to eliminate everything it considers vice, leaving only a residual kind of virtue. The aspiration is for a society built according to a divine plan; a society that is perfect. This, naturally, presupposes that the radical ideologue has complete, unmitigated knowledge and access to this divine plan – or perhaps that Islam is so simple and singular that the divine plan is unambiguously obvious.

That might recall the medieval Church, but in an Islamic context, it immediately exposes this radical ideology as deeply untraditional. As discussed in Chapter 3, classical thought resolutely recognised the crucial distinction between the absolute Truth of the divine message, and the fallibility of any human's interpretation of it. This gave rise to the development of diverse juridical and theological schools, some of which became entrenched in the Islamic tradition, while others faded into history. To some degree, it should be said, this was a pragmatic measure. In the absence of a Church-like structure to determine official doctrine, the alternative to amicable pluralism was violent sectarianism, which, frankly, was not much of an option. Of course, this did not prevent sectarian rivalry completely. At various points of Islamic history such rivalry was perfectly scalding. A vivid example is the controversy between al-Ṭabarī and the followers of Aḥmad ibn Ḥanbal, which, according to one report, led ibn Ḥanbal's students to bury al-Ṭabarī's corpse in a non-Muslim graveyard. Other schools of thought essentially perished, natural selection style, as a result of sectarian debate. Still, nearly all classicists will agree, with varying degrees of width, that other schools of thought are to be given deep respect.

For the radical, nothing could be further from the truth. When the Gama'at al-Islamiyya in Egypt published a justification of its terrorist methodology, it called it *Al-qawl al-qaṭi'* ('The Definitive Word'). Following the group's massacre of 58 tourists at the Temple of Queen Hatshepsut in Luxor in November 1997, it suffered an enormous backlash from the Egyptian public. The group retreated by saying it would never again attack tourists, but revealed itself as incapable of admitting its action had been a mistake. Classical scholars habitually concluded their written and oral statements with the phrase 'and God knows best'. It is an expression entrenched in Islamic discourse to this day. Yet, it is conspicuously absent from the statements of radical groups such as al-Qa'ida.

Indeed, radical ideologues are fixated with distinguishing 'true' Muslims from 'false' Muslims, whom they usually label hypocrites or apostates. In this way, radicals claim the authority to define who is, and who is not, a Muslim. As Qutb did, they liberally condemn large numbers of Muslims, perhaps entire societies, to the realm of apostasy. Such apostates include almost anyone who does not share their vision of society, and does not devote him- or herself to the radical's brand of militancy. Indeed, a month after the September 11 attacks, bin Laden unhesitatingly declared Muslims who condemned them, and lamented the loss of American life, 'immoral, dissolute, apostates'. This concept of quasi-excommunication, known as *takfīr*, was known to classical Muslims, but was usually confined to the judiciary and was very rarely used. Unlike in Christendom, heresy trials were very rare. The charge of calling a Muslim an apostate was spiritually a grave one: as a tradition of the Prophet warns, if the accuser is mistaken, the accusation returns to the one who uttered it.

Clearly, in an Islamic context, utopian, exclusionary fundamentalism is radically untraditional. But it is akin to the dogmatism of the Bolsheviks who hijacked Marxism with their particular reading of it, and insisted on the total exclusion of alternative interpretations of the foundational text. This, too, was a feature of the Taliban in the most authoritarian way. Hence the prescription of punishment for acts, such as shaving one's beard, which various Muslim jurists did not even consider sinful, let alone worthy of state punishment.

It is the nature of utopian dreams that, in practice, they end inevitably in authoritarianism. That is the inescapable result of a movement that seeks to create an ideal society. Often, this carries with it the elimination of any diversity. Such attempts are destined for frustration, leaving only the option of forced compliance. Traditional Islamic political theory did not generally seek to eradicate social difference. It sought only to moderate any resultant tension. It manages and negotiates – but does not hastily abolish. Even where an injustice or other human imperfection was concerned, change would best be gradual, and only in a manner that did not cause greater evil than it sought to remove. As Hamza Yusuf, a contemporary American Muslim scholar of traditional schooling, observed: 'I have a problem with people who say their objective is "getting rid of the evildoers." First, nobody has done it in the past and second, those ridding the world of evildoers also do evil.'

We have seen that classical Islamic thought, proceeding from an acknowledgment of the fallibility of human understanding, adopted a pluralist ethos. This idea did not exist merely at the realm of abstract theology. It found intelligible expression in Islamic political science. As Nizām al-Mulk, a master political theorist of Sunni Islam, argued, Islamic polity seeks not to enforce a singular norm; it requires the acceptance of many norms. That is to say, it is, of its nature, anti-authoritarian. It is entirely understandable, then, that medieval Islamic civilisation demonstrated a far greater tendency to create pluralist societies than its Christian counterparts.

Here, the obvious, almost cliché reference is to al-Andalus: the medieval Islamic caliphate of the Moors in southern Spain. The Moors were famed for the *convivencia* of their empire: the spirit of conviviality that existed between Muslims, Christians and Jews and was unparalleled anywhere else in Europe. Jewish historians, in particular, have written extensively of the quality of Jewish life under Moorish rule, and of the fact that this nurtured a Jewish golden age as much as an Islamic one. In some ways, this ethic of interfaith toleration was the lifeblood of the Moors. When the Almoravids took control of al-Andalus, and the culture of pluralism consequently began to decline, so did the empire. Today, in the former Moorish capital of Cordoba, a museum is dedicated to the celebration of this unique historical example of interfaith harmony. This is an expression of the fame of this Moorish legacy, and of the pride it creates in modern-day Cordobans.

Later, when the Indian subcontinent came under Muslim rule, early Moghul rulers, and most famously Akbar the Great, were relatively tolerant towards the Hindu majority. Awrangzeb's violence against Hindus in the late seventeenth century, towards the end of the Moghul period, was unlike what came before it. Similarly, the Ottoman Empire, though worthy of more criticism than the Moors, particularly as it entered decline, sustained a level of pluralism that would be unknown in the West for centuries to come. They preferred their *millet* system to occupation. The result gave non-Muslim populations, and even diverse Muslim populations, substantial autonomy over their public affairs and governance.

This did not mean the Ottomans could not be ruthless. Indeed, any community that indicated separatist intentions, or demonstrated subversive political aspirations, could count on the Ottomans to crush them swiftly and mercilessly. But where communities posed no challenge to Ottoman political rule, the Ottomans were generally content to let communities across their vast empire, Muslim and non-Muslim, regulate themselves. Once more, this only changed substantially as the empire decayed.

It is true that the glory of this famed pluralism is often overstated. Ostensibly, Islamic governments were perfectly capable of instituting discriminatory laws against non-Muslims (though they did so inconsistently and most typically in areas surrounding military conflict with Christians, rather than across the whole empire). Life, even under the Moors, was not the interfaith utopia of much historical romanticism, particularly from the late tenth century under the caliphate of al-Manṣūr. But, there can be no doubt, particularly when judged by the standards of their contemporaries, that medieval Islamic governments were remarkable for their capacity to preserve and rule over vast, pluralist empires without descending into authoritarianism. Only the most dedicated, ideologically motivated historical revisionist could (and does) argue otherwise.

Which brings us, by way of stark contrast, back to the Taliban. The key distinction between it and its medieval counterparts was that it almost entirely failed to recognise any difference between sin and crime. Accordingly, its own particular view of Islamic morality, itself highly questionable, automatically became a matter of governmental law. In this way, the Taliban's governmental design accommodated little, if any, pluralism. The prevailing conception of government was total: the minutiae of women's (and men's) clothing became the domain of strict, harsh governmental enforcement. Where every classical Islamic society, from the Umayyads to the Ottomans, had its own music and arts, the Taliban quashed much artistic expression, including a total ban on music.

The Taliban's approach to Afghan diversity was not one of classical self-regulation and accommodation. In classical Islamic political theory, Islamic law applied only to Muslims. Other communities were permitted to establish their own governance. This is an inherently medieval model. The Taliban's particularly perverse brand of Islamic law, however, was applied territorially. It was a modern nation state. It certainly did succeed in restoring order to parts of the country that had been ravaged by decades of constant war, but those with tribal or religious differences with the polity often suffered terribly.

The Taliban's actions were those of people attempting to remake the human condition by force. Mawdudi and Qutb similarly promote a concept of jihad that aims to cure the world of its ills, or in Qutb's formulation, 'to wipe out tyranny and introduce true freedom to mankind'. Al-Qa'ida falls into the same trap, and believes this can be achieved by executing spectacular, preferably symbolic acts of destruction. The attacks of

September 11, 2001, demonstrate nothing if not this. It was not enough to destroy people: the World Trade Center had to be destroyed with them. What mattered was not merely slaughter, but symbolism. Bin Laden was explicit on this point in an interview published in Pakistani daily newspaper *Ausaf*: 'The targets of September 11 were not women and children. The main targets were the symbol of the United States: their economic and military power.' As Gray observes, this theme was familiar to Bolshevik revolutionaries, a fact reflected in Joseph Conrad's novel *The Secret Agent*, where we see the first secretary to the Russian Embassy in London order the destruction of the Observatory at Greenwich – a symbol of science. Decades later, al-Qa'ida would target symbols of economics and high finance. Revolutionary violence destroys the symbolic, what Conrad's first secretary called the 'sacrosanct fetish' of the world at the time. Such symbolism is designed to play a major role in remaking the world. When the World Trade Center towers collapsed on September 11, a symbolic embodiment of economic might collapsed with them.

Such an idea would be completely alien to the medieval mind. It is, however, entirely resonant with the Positivist view that it is possible to remake the human condition. To the extent that radical Muslim ideologues promote this, they share it in common with Lenin, Bakunin, Marx, Mao and Fukuyama. This view is a modern, Western philosophical position before it is a medieval Islamic one. Medieval armies fought for political, often imperial reasons, but not for human happiness. Perhaps for the glory and happiness of the king, but not of humanity generally. They sought to remake (or preserve) the political landscape, but not the human condition. The latter is a modern invention. It is also a necessary philosophical precursor to revolutionary violence.

By comparison, the conservatism of classical Muslim thought led scholars to respond to new challenges in a slow, self-scrutinising, cautious way. Indeed, arguably, too much so. The quintessential example here is the refusal of Muslim scholars to accept the introduction of the printing press, particularly to print Arabic, in the early to mid-Ottoman period. This has naturally led scholars from the colonial and post-colonial age to argue that, in many ways, the Muslim world was ripe for colonisation once classical scholars lost their dynamism; when the established schools of thought became akin to institutions and the doors of *ijtihād* (reasoned developments in legal thought) were closed to preserve doctrinal integrity. There is merit to this argument, but for present purposes, it is enough to note the caution with which classical Islamic thought proceeded, antithetically to radicalism. The model ruler of al-Fārābī's Virtuous City was not a utopian revolutionary. Rather, his governance maintained the integrity of his predecessor's, and developed it. Even the imperialist Umayyads declined for 70 years to impose a single, Arabic-speaking administrative system across the Empire. Greek remained the official language in Syria's revenue department, and local Christians ran the administration. Except in fiscal matters, the conquered provinces were allowed to continue the traditions of the previous regime.

Accordingly, in circumstances of conflict and political tension, the classical jurist was more inclined to pragmatism than revolution. According to Cambridge theologian Abdal Hakim Murad, since the great medieval political theorists of the Seljuk period, the traditional approach had been to negotiate with the sultan rather than overthrow him. This has led many observers to the exaggerated conclusion that classical Islamic scholarship was quietist.

Even in response to non-Muslim challenge, classical Muslim scholars, though cautious, were often conciliatory and pragmatic in their approach. Among the Palestinians, initial violence against Israel was predominantly perpetrated by secular groups, to the point that Hamas felt the need in 1987 to refute suggestions that Muslims had never played a part in the resistance. Thinkers in traditional Islamic movements, even those with stricter approaches to Islamic law, came largely to oppose Partition in India. Other inheritors of the classical paradigm in Tsarist Russia, such as Shihāb al-Dīn Marjānī, argued that the Tsar's domains could be embraced as part of *dār al-Islām* (the abode of Islam) rather than *dār al-ḥarb* (the abode of war) – an important medieval classification which implied the loyalty to the ruler. The traditional Ḥanafī school of Islamic law reached the same consensus regarding the Raj in British India. This, perhaps, was a reflection of the position long held by several jurists of the Shāfi'ī school that anywhere it is possible to practise Islam safely is considered *dār al-Islām*, even if the ruler is a non-Muslim. And today, here is the emphatic discourse of Hamza Yusuf, speaking in London a few months after the 2005 London bombings, on Muslims living in the West:

> ... in non-Muslim lands, you are obliged to follow the law. If you don't like the law then you need to move. The most common response is to say there is no place to make *hijrah* [migrate]. Allah says the world is vast. If people don't want to live here they should go and live in certain Muslim lands and see how long they last before this country starts looking more like *dār al-Islām*.

Yusuf is far from alone in his assessment, but for Qutb or bin Laden, this would be pure anathema. It constitutes a spirit of unacceptable acquiescence. They are more likely to draw inspiration from the writings of Aḥmad ibn Taymiyya, who was violently opposed to the brutal Mongol Empire. But, the radical ideologue goes abominably further than ibn Taymiyya. He or she sees nobility in eliminating the enemies of Islam as he or she deems them, whether combatant or not, just as Lenin rationalised mass killing on the basis that it was necessary to eliminate the enemies of progress. This radically modern ideology quickly descends into a moral abyss, where the utopian ends justify all imaginable means. That was precisely the message of Gama'at al-Islamiyya when it responded to criticism for its tactics of massacring tourists in Egypt. The group frankly admitted that its methods, which included the killing of Muslims, could only be accepted when one saw that its goal of establishing an Islamic state in Egypt justified these means in order to attain it.

Thus, it becomes permissible for the al-Qaʻida operative to drink alcohol for the purposes of social camouflage, or to abandon ritual prayers which the prophet Muhammad once described as the dividing line between a believer and a disbeliever. The Qur'an is one of the few religious texts of the world to condemn suicide unequivocally, and the Prophet's rejection of it is ardently forthright, yet the radical ideologue embraces suicide bombing, which prior to the 1990s was almost unknown among Muslim movements. If, as bin Laden concluded, Islam's enemies include all Americans without distinction such that it was some warped duty of his devotees to kill all Americans everywhere, then the inherent immorality of this proposal could be easily accommodated within this (un)ethical framework.

So it was for Lenin and Trotsky. Lenin's dream was the creation of a communist utopia in which the State could be abolished. If it was necessary to embark on a phase of revolutionary terror, killing millions of people to achieve this, then it became legitimate. Trotsky, too, rationalised the taking and killing of hostages as a necessary stage in the realisation of his utopia.

For utopian and revolutionary groups, this remains true even, and perhaps especially, if the victims are those from within their own communities. In this vision, nothing is more vile than the enemy within. Sendero Luminoso terrorists in Peru routinely killed mayors and village leaders in poor areas who, in their view, had collaborated with the enemy. When Lenin seized power in Russia, he immediately established the Cheka, a secret police network that, within a few years of its creation, was executing around a thousand people per month. Stalin's Communist Party went on to kill substantially more. Pol Pot's Maoist regime in Cambodia, the Red Brigades in Italy, and the Irish Republican Army have all seen fit to kill their own.

Similarly, a group of young British Muslims were arrested in

February 2007 for plotting to abduct and behead a fellow Muslim who had served in the British army in Afghanistan. Likewise, in a communiqué attempting to justify the September 11 attacks, al-Qa'ida stated flatly: 'It is permitted to treat a Muslim who helps the disbelievers and strengthens them so that he is numbered among them.' For them, that was sufficient response to the charge that they had killed Muslims on September 11, too. Muslims living in the West are simply fair game. They are the enemy.

So, too, are secularist and irreligious Muslims living in the Muslim world. Take, for example, Palestinian radical Abu Qatada, who specifically advocated the 'killing of the children of the apostates'; or bin Laden's condemnation of 'secular, apostate opportunists' from whom 'it is therefore permitted to take their money and their blood'. Similarly, when Pakistani authorities arrested Ramzi bin al-Shibh, one of the masterminds of the September 11 attacks, one radical Muslim website, www.azzam.com, condemned the entire nation of Pakistan, including ordinary civilians, in the following terms:

> The whole nation of Pakistan is guilty before the Lord of the Worlds for betraying those *mujahidin*. It is incorrect to blame only the leaders and the government, for the armed forces, police, intelligence, and media all comprise ordinary Pakistanis from ordinary walks of life. Those who tipped off the Pakistani authorities were... ordinary Pakistanis. When a nation allows its leaders to fight Islam, it is only a matter of time before Allah's punishment comes to that nation, either in the form of natural disasters, or worse, by Allah taking Islam away from that country as He did with Turkey after the people of Turkey supported Kemal Ataturk in destroying Islam in Turkey.

Radical ideologues have no qualms engaging in utopian warfare upon their own community. This kind of war does not enter Islamic thought or practice until well into the post-medieval period. The originator and archetype is Muhammad ibn Abdul Wahhab, who generated a brand of reformist Islam that was fanatically intolerant of religious difference. Ibn Abdul Wahhab's venom was reserved primarily for Sufis and Shiites, but extended to all Muslims he considered to be deviant, which was in line with his utopian aim to purify Islamic practice.

From the mid-eighteenth century, ibn Abdul Wahhab's followers declared war on other Muslims. In 1802 they destroyed the holy Shiite city of Karbala, and over the next decade occupied Mecca and Medina where they destroyed countless Sufi shrines. This militancy was made possible by the readiness of this school to dismiss other Muslims as unbelievers. Around the same time, Usaman Dan Fodio, though decidedly more pluralist than the Wahhabis, prosecuted his own wars of purification upon Muslims in Nigeria. Dan Fodio's activism also has a utopian ring to it: he claimed to bring the Sword of Truth; to differentiate between good and evil. A century later, Muḥammad Aḥmad named himself the *mahdī* – a title reserved in Islamic literature for an eschatological saviour – and launched similar wars into the Sudan.

Such was rarely, if ever, the method of pre-modernity. Russia's Tsarist regime was responsible for unforgivable oppression, but never mass killings on the scale of the subsequent Bolsheviks, and certainly not with the Positivist-style aim of improving the human condition. Indeed, such a scale of slaughter had never been known to history. Al-Qaʿida, not having controlled the apparatus of a functioning state, has not yet wrought anywhere near as much human destruction. Still, the spirit is the same. Both are simultaneously ideological and nihilistic. Their revolutionary zeal permits the suspension of moral strictures. Yet, the idea that morality and ethics can be rendered subordinate to the higher cause is found nowhere in classical Islam.

It is crucial here to note the seriousness with which classical

Islam took the divine command. This, in part, was the reason for its cautiousness in development. Whatever the circumstance, however grave the oppression, however hot the politics and lawless the terrain, for the classical jurist the divine command, and all the ethical strictures it entails, remained. It would evolve, admit flexibility and even the creation of exceptions in cases of necessity, but not at the expense of another's rights.

Aḥmad al-Wansharīsī, a Moroccan Islamic jurist of the early sixteenth century, provides a good example of this, noted briefly in the previous chapter. Catholic armies had just vanquished the Moors from Spain and were threatening to descend mercilessly upon Morocco as he wrote. Al-Wansharīsī, then, was under the intense pressure of a deadly threat. He was known to find flexibility in Islamic law or to reinterpret it creatively for the benefit of the Muslims. Still, he insisted upon the ethics of classical Islamic warfare: he prohibited the killing of innocent women and children, held that Muslim governments were bound to contracts made with non-Muslims, and forbade killing enemy wounded who were helpless after a battle.

God, according to the Islamic tradition, had forbidden oppression for Himself, and would not accept it from humans. This remained true in the context of conflict. For the classicist, God is the master of history and the human condition. There can therefore be no advantage in attempting to improve one's condition by violating the moral boundaries He prescribed. Indeed, the divine command is most necessary under conditions of stress; where anger and ethics lead to different, often opposite, destinations. 'Let the judge not judge when he is angry,' proclaimed the Muslim jurists. 'Do not let the injustice of others lead you into injustice,' insists the Qur'an. For the classicist, ethics could never be suspended. This ethos was not sufficiently nihilist to accept that the ends could justify the means.

Modern Muslim radicals, like the various revolutionaries from whom they seem to have inherited so much, gleefully embrace this nihilist mantra. The disciplined strictures of medieval Muslim jurists are more than alien to them: they are contemptible; complicit in oppressive circumstances; bowed to a world order in which Muslims have little political muscle. The truth is nearer the opposite. It is the radical ideologue that has most profoundly bowed to the contemporary political order by inheriting its moral logic. This is precisely the step the classical mind is unwilling to take.

It should, then, come as no surprise that the idea of targeting civilians, that hallmark of terrorist methodology, is itself quintessentially modern. Certainly it was, and is, unimaginable to classical Muslim jurists and thinkers. Pre-modern warfare may have wrought havoc upon civilian populations (often via recreational ventures), but it was principally confined to the battlefield where soldiers met face to face. This changed significantly in the twentieth century when a string of militant groups, from the Baader-Meinhof Gang in Germany to the Sendoro Luminoso in Peru, began murdering unarmed civilians, including children. World War II demonstrated that Western states, too, in the context of war, possess a clear willingness to target innocent civilians. In the early 1940s, Winston Churchill conceived of a campaign of 'terror bombing' German cities, including their civilians, convinced that it was the most effective way of striking back at Germany. His strategy was not purely military. Its target was not the German army, but quite explicitly the 'morale of the enemy civil population'. New weapons, such as incendiary bombs, were designed to destroy private homes. Half a million German civilians were slaughtered as a result. Eventually, Churchill came to review this tactic 'of bombing German cities simply for the sake of increasing the terror, though under other pretexts', not because it was immoral, but because otherwise, Britain 'shall come into control of an utterly ruined land'. As a matter of morality, Churchill would defend the terror campaign until his death. Indeed, he owed his popularity to it.

No medieval theorist of war could have inspired Churchill's tactics. It was the stuff of twentieth-century military theorists such as General Giulio Douhet or Basil Liddell Hart, for whom the object of war was the subjugation of the enemy's will, and any 'attack on the centres of government and population' are merely appropriate 'means to that end'. The legitimisation of civilian targets is largely a bequest of this modern legacy.

Intentional civilian murder is only possible, either when strategic imperatives demand it, or as Melbourne-based columnist Paul Gray suggests, when one commits the intellectual folly of believing it is possible to attack an abstract evil by killing physical people. The former may be true for the radical ideologue, but the latter almost certainly is. It is as if he or she assumes that ideas are literally embodied in flesh. This was part of the madness expressed when the Taliban destroyed the gigantic, historic statues of Buddha at Bamiyan, much to bin Laden's delight; an entirely modern act betraying a deeply untraditional approach to the nature of ideas. Testament to this is the fact that no medieval or classical Islamic civilisation undertook such destruction over the centuries during which those statues stood. Quite simply, it was not a medieval Islamic way of thinking to conceive of destroying them, particularly as some kind of attack on idolatry. Classical Islamic thinkers understood that idolatry was a function of the heart. An idolater without idols will simply make them, even out of food as the pre-Islamic pagan Arabs used to do. Alternatively, they would worship a more abstract idol such as themselves. Indeed, by the time of the conquest of Mecca when the prophet Muhammad destroyed the idols housed inside the Ka'bah, idolatry was almost abandoned as a belief system. There was scarcely anyone left to worship them, in any event. The Prophet's action was designed to restore the Ka'bah itself to its original function as a house of monotheism, rather than pursuant to some vain hope that idolatry would be smashed with the idols.

Even in the context of war, classical Islamic thought did not conceive of killing an idea through the slaughter of people. That is much closer (though not equivalent) to the medieval Christian doctrine of holy war, which, as discussed in the previous chapter, is doctrinally alien to Islamic theories of war. Certainly, some Muslim politicians were imperial, but their imperialism was about political control, not the vanquishing of ideas. This is why, upon assuming political control, other ideas and religions were still allowed to survive under Islamic government to the extent that Muslim polities ruled as a religious minority for centuries, until around 850.

All this implies that the war on terror is not a war on a renewed medievalism. It is more accurately a war on the most grotesque manifestations of modernity. That being so, there is little hope of success in attempting to oppose it through the assertion of the modernity that spawned it. In this context, it becomes clear that the approach of the United States and its allies in combating terrorism is little short of the obstinate courting of disaster.

Under the guise of being tough on terrorism, the Bush administration in the United States has resorted to the abandonment of principle and the refuge of repression. The CIA has confirmed that terror suspects have been escorted by the United States to countries such as Syria, Morocco, Egypt, Jordan, Afghanistan and Uzbekistan, where the authorities have no qualms with attempting to extract intelligence through the use of torture – a practice euphemistically called 'rendition'. Not that the US authorities were entirely resistant to the use of torture themselves: in a memorandum written in 2002, the assistant attorney-general, Jay Bybee, argued that CIA interrogators who tortured detainees could be exonerated, provided their intention was to extract information rather than inflict pain. Moreover, Bybee argued that it was legal to inflict pain up to a point equivalent with 'organ failure', because this would fall short of 'severe physical pain and suffering', which he held to be the legal definition of torture. Meanwhile, the United States detained terror suspects, mostly picked up during the war with Afghanistan, in Guantanamo Bay, Cuba, with the apparent intention of keeping them beyond the reach of the US courts. This naturally raised questions about the manner of their treatment.

Perhaps unsurprisingly, allegations of torture at Guantanamo were plentiful. The Red Cross and several UN Special Rapporteurs were among those to make them. The detailed allegations make for sobering reading: extended periods of solitary confinement, sensory deprivation and regular beatings. Military psychologists were instructed to determine each detainee's specific phobias and, according to *The New York Times*, subsequently advised interrogators on how to exploit 'a detainee's fears and longings to increase distress'. Letters from family were passed on with all messages of love and support blacked out. An FBI agent sent a memorandum to headquarters in November 2002 reporting that one detainee was 'evidencing behavior consistent with extreme psychological trauma', including talking to non-existent people. Another FBI agent reported that a detainee 'was almost unconscious on the floor, with a pile of hair next to him. He had apparently been literally pulling his own hair out throughout the night.' Dozens of detainees have attempted suicide. In June 2006, three succeeded. In May 2007, so did another.

The Bush administration, expectedly, rationalised whatever was happening at Guantanamo Bay on the basis that the detainees were 'cold-blooded killers'; the 'worst of the worst'. And perhaps that is true of some of them. But this is almost certainly not true of at least ten detainees who were arrested because they were wearing internationally available Casio watches that, according to the US Defense Department, resemble a model used by al-Qa'ida for making bombs. It also may not be true of a Saudi man held in Guantanamo because he spent a couple of weeks at a Taliban bean farm. According to him, the Taliban had imprisoned him there because they suspected he was a Saudi spy. There is no public evidence it is true of Sami al-Hajj, whose only crime appears to have been that he was a cameraman for the often anti-American Al-Jazeera television network. A study of US government documentation against all detainees undertaken by the Seton Hall Law School found that

WHAT IS SO MEDIEVAL ABOUT AL-QA'IDA?

US forces were not responsible for the arrest of 86 per cent of Guantanamo detainees. These people were arrested by Afghan and Pakistani mercenaries, who were paid US$5000 for every captive they presented. Fliers dropped over Afghanistan at the time promised informants 'wealth and power beyond your dreams', and 'enough money to take care of your family, your tribe, your village, for the rest of your life. Pay for livestock and doctors and school books'. Moreover, many detainees were actually arrested in Pakistan, not Afghanistan. Some 55 per cent were not accused of committing any hostile act against the United States. Only about 8 per cent were classified as al-Qa'ida fighters. There are probably many more random Casio-watch-wearers in Guantanamo. Peasants in the wrong place at the wrong time.

We will probably never know what percentage of detainees was guilty of any crime. A tiny minority have been charged. And even that minority were to be tried in unique military tribunals, established to prosecute detainees at Guantanamo Bay. Here was a system that admitted evidence obtained by coercion, despite the fact that this is plainly immoral and has long been considered unreliable by lawyers, in any case. Worse, the accused could be denied the right even to hear the evidence against him. It all raises the question of why this should be necessary: as Richard Ackland, radio presenter, journalist and lawyer, argued in *The Sydney Morning Herald*, '[y]ou'd think it wouldn't be all that difficult giving fair trials and securing convictions for the worst of the worst.'

This represents an aggressive erosion of the moral foundations on which the best of Western civilisation is built. It sends a message that, like the monsters of modernity they are fighting, Western governments accept the doing of evil for the sake of a greater good. It embodies a disturbing symmetry.

It is also a doomed failure. This has not subdued al-Qa'ida. If anything, it is likely to embolden it because it proclaims to all a humiliating desperation and the intensity of Western fears. Those who reach for torture and repression disclose that they have exhausted their ideas. There is no further deterrent available. There is no further philosophical triumph to be sought. They have spent their last resort and abandoned themselves. These are not the responses of an assured people, upright and certain of victory.

They are, however, precisely the sorts of responses on which revolutionary movements thrive. As French revolutionary theorist Regis Debray has argued, revolutionary war is possible only in a revolutionary environment. It can grow only in certain conditions. Radical Muslim groups, too, although recently developing a globalist outlook, first emerged as resistance movements in local, radicalised environments: Palestine, occupied Lebanon, Chechnya, Kashmir and, originally, Egypt, where the government's brutal repression of the Muslim Brotherhood served only to radicalise its members further, especially Ayman al-Zawahiri – now bin Laden's deputy at al-Qa'ida. Revolutionary movements, perhaps paradoxically, depend for survival on the repressive actions of those they seek to overthrow. They cannot be fought on terrain bereft of ethics. This merely lends authority to revolutionary rhetoric, and serves as potent recruitment propaganda, as evidenced by bin Laden's repeated invocation of America's human rights violations. It also provides a steady stream of martyrs to inspire continued revolution. In purely strategic terms, it is a colossal own goal.

In November 2005, US marines are alleged to have rampaged through a small Iraqi town, screaming abuse, forcibly entering houses of civilians and intentionally slaughtering whoever they encountered: women, children, university students, taxi drivers, an elderly man in a wheelchair. The victims begged helplessly for their lives, and were shot in the coldest imaginable blood. Allegedly, 24 civilians were massacred. When reports surfaced in June 2006, military inquiries began, and senior military officers immediately warned President Bush to 'expect the worst'. In December 2006, eight marines were charged. Samir al-Sumaidaie, the Iraqi ambassador to the United States, believes this is not an isolated incident, claiming marines intentionally killed his cousin months earlier. Perhaps the deliberate killing of civilians is a more pervasive feature of modernity than we willingly acknowledge.

By now, most of the world has probably long forgotten this incident. It is just another event buried in the quagmire of war. But like the victims of modernity in New York, Bali, Madrid or London, these Iraqis had names and lives. Their families have emotions.

And their little town has a name we should not forget: Haditha – the Arabic word for 'modern'.

8

Reformists, Reformation and Renaissance

Despite the insistence of US president George W. Bush, radical Muslim groups engaged in terrorist activity are not 'Islamic fascists'. Certainly, they have some fascist-like features; they are authoritarian, intolerant of dissent, and trade on a militant kind of nostalgia, but otherwise they have little in common with Italian dictator Benito Mussolini from whose rule in the 1920s to the 1940s the term 'fascism' arose.

Fascism is inherently nationalistic. As with the Nazis, inclusion in Mussolini's Italy was based on race. Al-Qa'ida is globalist, spanning all the races of the world. In political science terms, the difference is crucial. Anyone could conceivably convert to al-Qa'ida's ideology. But fascism's barriers are insurmountable. It is impossible, for example, to convert to the Aryan race. One movement is ideological; the other, partly biological.

Likewise, for all the similarities between Muslim radicalism and modern revolutionary ideologies, it would be a mistake to argue that groups such as the Taliban or al-Qa'ida are simply the Bolsheviks or the Nazis *redux*. The commonalities are several and important, but to describe radical Muslims completely is substantially more complex than to render them mere duplications of a known, recent past. Unlike the Bolsheviks, Muslim radicals claim to draw inspiration from history. The Bolsheviks were entirely progressive; Muslim radicals are, at least in their language, regressive. Bolshevism was manifest in totalitarian government; the Taliban was authoritarian, but certainly not totalitarian, because it did not patrol its population with the surveillance of a mass party.

Moreover, radical Muslim ideology is resoundingly apocalyptic. The Bolsheviks and the Nazis were concerned with creating a perfect nation or world, but aside from the occasional comment from Adolf Hitler that he was doing God's work, neither seems to have had any spiritual aspirations. Muslim radicals, by contrast, add an otherworldly chapter to their utopian sequence. They remain committed to remaking the world in this life, but their ultimate reward lies in the next. It is a worldly plan seeking a heavenly reward.

Allusions to martyrdom and paradise are frequent. A suicide operation does not mark the termination of one's existence, but merely a new phase in it. Radical discourse places a heavy reliance on eschatological texts: the global conspiracy against Muslims, and the thorough lack of militancy in Muslim populations that radicals so regularly lament all point the radical ideologue to the end of the Earth and the impending arrival of Judgment Day. It is safe to say these were not motivational features of either Bolshevism or Nazism.

The fact is that Muslim radicalism is a new beast. Such ideologues are inauthentic, untraditional and modern; they draw little more than language from medieval Islamic thought, but this is not to absolve Muslims of the problem they pose. Indeed, it implies the precise opposite.

Modern Islamic thought has a crisis to confront. It is, of course, dangerously naïve to presume that terrorist activity is purely an ideological product. Humans are not wandering balls of ideology, and terrorism, like all crimes and acts of war, is still a human act. It inevitably proceeds from a mix of ideological, sociological and psychological factors.

Radicalism appeals to those with a revolutionary zeal; to those whose religiosity owes more to the identity politics of modernity than the motivations of traditional piety. As much can be observed by a brief survey of those who perpetrate it.

This was certainly true of Hasib Hussain, one of the London bombers, who suddenly, ardently found Islam only eighteen months prior to the attack, having previously been a wild drinker. The same may be said for Abu Musab al-Zarqawi, who, according to Jordanian intelligence reports, was imprisoned in the 1980s for drug possession and sexual assault before stumbling upon a religiosity that gave expression to his criminality, and who was killed while leading the insurgency in Iraq. Modern terror groups, it seems, latch most devastatingly on to those seeking to atone for a guilty past.

It happens that such a profile is instructively common. Convicted 'shoe bomber' Richard Reid, the London-born son of an English mother and Jamaican father, was involved in street crime as a youth, and ended up several times in the Feltham Young Offenders' Institution. It was there that he converted to Islam. Mohamed Atta, the operational leader of the September 11 attacks, had no particularly religious leanings until he entered his radical phase in the mid-1990s in Germany. Jamaican-born Germaine Lindsay, according to a report in British local paper *The Huddersfield Daily Examiner*, had violent tendencies as a teenager and was dealing in heroin and crack cocaine at age fourteen. Suddenly, at fifteen, he converted to Islam and rejected his old friends and habits. In July 2005, he executed the most deadly attack of the London bombings, killing 26 people on the Piccadilly Line.

The once popular image of a terrorist raised on doctrinal hatred from childhood before maturing into an indiscriminate killer is largely imaginary. More commonly, terrorists have a relatively short history of religiosity, preceded by an irreligious, or even deeply unholy past. The archetype has undergone some kind of conversion; whether from another faith (such as Reid or Lindsay) or as 'internal converts' from non-observance to devotion (Atta, Hussain or al-Zarqawi). Lifelong devotees such as Osama bin Laden are exceptions.

This should not be terribly surprising. People of longstanding piety are usually too familiar with mainstream religion to buy the radical message. They recognise radical ideology as immediately foreign. Life for the newly devout, however, is considerably more difficult. Their religious knowledge and experience is typically dwarfed by their zeal and, in those circumstances, navigating a spiritual path can become a hazardous exercise. When such people also feel the need to atone for a guilty past, the result can be overcompensation. American Muslim convert and writer Siraji Umm Zaid calls it 'convertitis': the common affliction of converts moving to instant absolutism, rebelling against their past as they seek to forge a new identity. This is a relatively common sociological phenomenon across all faith and ideological groups.

It is the newly devout who are most dangerously susceptible to the insemination of radical thought. Thus does the intersection of sociology and ideology become, sometimes literally, explosive. Radicalism's simple certainty and purity appeals at what is often a time of confusion and emotional upheaval. For most, this is a short passing phase before they settle in a more centred position. Tragically, a few fall into more dangerous company, even if briefly.

Radical ideology's success with converts and newly observant Muslims points to a disastrous failure of mainstream religious leadership. Radicals can only thrive where the complacent mainstream has failed to provide a compelling intellectual and spiritual alternative. Particularly in the West, there is a worrying dearth of quality Muslim scholars who can communicate effectively with increasingly perplexed and alienated Muslim youth. Militant radicals take advantage of this vacuum. Muslim radicalism is, therefore, ultimately a Muslim problem. It simply cannot be spirited away without an Islamic contribution.

There is no doubt that the war on terror, with its mass Muslim civilian casualties, amplifies Muslim grievances of injustice, and assists the radical cause. Certainly, Western responses have the potential to nurture and exacerbate the problem, or to deny it oxygen. But Muslims must ultimately take ownership of it. This should be an empowering fact for Muslims. This realisation gives Muslims a degree of control over their condition. The alternative, in addition to being intellectually untenable, can only leave Muslims at the whim of those who would seek to solve the problem on Muslims' behalf. This is the very dynamic that produces nonsensical prescriptions of 'moderate' Islam.

Certainly, many observers intuit that any intellectual and spiritual response to radicalism must be Islamic. This undoubtedly lies beneath endless calls from Western governments and commentators for Muslims to condemn terrorism. It never seems to occur to such people that many Muslim spokespeople have already done this. Nor does it seem to be recognised that this will ultimately achieve nothing to dismantle radical ideology. A summit of some 800 Muslim scholars in Putrajaya, Malaysia, in 2003 specifically denounced al-Qa'ida, but this has not saved any lives. Radical groups construct themselves as warriors for purity against a corrupt world. Their very identity is based on their marginality. They are *meant* to be repudiated by the mainstream. It only entrenches their position, reiterates the corruption of the world, and confirms for them their role as true purifiers. They are akin to cults. They recognise scant authority outside of themselves.

If radicalism cannot be fought by condemnation, it remains only to defeat it in the realm of ideas. This, it seems, is what sits behind the wildly popular prescription that Islam is in desperate need of its own Reformation. 'What is needed is a move beyond tradition,' wrote Salman Rushdie in *The Washington Post* a month after the 2005 London bombings. '[N]othing less than a reform movement to bring the core concepts of Islam into the modern age, a Muslim Reformation to combat not only the jihadist ideologues but also the dusty, stifling seminaries of the traditionalists, throwing open the windows to let in much-needed fresh air . . . This is how to take up the "profound challenge" of the bombers.'

That is a reasonable account of what the Protestant Reformation of the sixteenth century achieved in Christendom. For Martin Luther, perhaps the Reformation's most recognised and seminal figure, the Church had fallen into heresy. Luther argued that the Bible was the sole measure of theology, and that, examined against it, the Church's doctrinal corruption was plain. The Reformation therefore held Church doctrine to biblical account; it emphasised the biblical text over the canonical law, and insisted on direct biblical interpretation. The defining purpose of a Reformation, then, is that it alleges and seeks to eradicate identified corruptions and deviances of orthodoxy. In accusing the orthodoxy, or at least parts of it, of heresy, it stands apart from tradition, seeking to return religious thought to a purer form.

In truth, this made perfect sense in Western Christianity. Having emerged from the Dark Ages with its attendant Church-led persecution, it experienced the Renaissance and acquired a new thirst for knowledge. As Western Christendom faced increasing political unrest through the fourteenth and fifteenth centuries, the environment was such that a challenge to orthodoxy was inevitable.

Still, Rushdie's critique has considerably more surface appeal than substance. Precisely why we should assume the products, even of the Protestant Reformation, are necessarily positive is a mystery. Fundamentalist Christians who parade with placards asserting that 'God hates fags' (and establishing websites to the same effect), or who bomb abortion clinics, are also modern products of the Reformation. So are the Ku Klux Klan.

The deeper question is what Reformation might mean in an

Islamic context. Here, we must surely conclude that Islam has already had its Martin Luther. The blindingly obvious parallel is Muhammad ibn Abdul Wahhab, who, in the eighteenth century, raged against what he perceived to be the doctrinal deviations of the Islamic tradition, and advocated a return to Islamic purity. Luther fought the Church's practice of selling indulgences; ibn Abdul Wahhab accused vast Muslim populations of engaging in idolatry through practices he deemed to be grave worship. In true Reformation style, the Wahhabis asserted the primacy of the Islamic sacred texts over the voluminous body of traditional Islamic thought, and advocated their direct interpretation. Wahhabism is a clear intellectual rebellion against orthodoxy.

Some of ibn Abdul Wahhab's doctrinal criticisms were perfectly valid, but his thinking was almost unprecedented in Islamic history in its preparedness to declare other Muslims to be outside the pale of Islam. Various Sufi and Shiite groups were particularly maligned. Islamic theologians of his day emphatically denounced ibn Abdul Wahhab. His own brother, Sulaymān, himself a respected scholar, was particularly scathing, dismissing him as ill-educated and intolerant. None of this did anything to dampen ibn Abdul Wahhab's zeal.

What followed were several wars of purification launched by ibn Abdul Wahhab's more militant successors against other Muslims that led the Wahhabis ultimately to take control of the sacred mosques of Mecca and Medina. The traditionalist Ottoman Empire reclaimed the mosques briefly, but following the Ottoman fall of 1924, and having forged an alliance with the Saud family, the Wahhabis rose to political prominence and founded the modern nation of Saudi Arabia. Those wishing to see the fruits of an Islamic Reformation need look no further than that country. This should not be entirely surprising. The Protestant Reformation yielded puritan religious movements of its own.

Wahhabism, it should be noted, today encompasses a broad range of Muslim thought, much of which is not remotely as extreme as the militant puritanism of ibn Abdul Wahhab's early followers. Nevertheless, the radicalism of al-Qaʿida is recognisably one of its more extreme offshoots. Accordingly, Rushdie's analysis, though fashionable, is the exact opposite of correct. It is disastrously wrongheaded to expect the Taliban, al-Qaʿida and their ideological brethren to be cured by Reformation. They *are* the Reformation.

Nevertheless, we can expect the Islamic Reformation catchcry to persist. Few embody this Reformation, its Western popularity, and its inevitable failure as quintessentially as Canadian journalist Irshad Manji, of whom Rushdie is an unabashed fan. Manji burst into the public conversation in 2003 with her book *The Trouble with Islam*, and certainly, there can be no denying Manji's short-term impact with Western readers. She quickly became a keynote speaker at countless influential forums. Her media folio is impressively prolific, having been interviewed on an extraordinary range of news and current affairs programs, from BBC Television's *Newsnight* and BBC Radio 4's *Today*, to *The O'Reilly Factor* on Fox News. She has been profiled and her work reviewed in mainstream publications from North America to Scandinavia, Britain, Continental Europe, the Middle East, Australia and Israel. From nowhere, she became a purported expert commentator on issues to which she had little connection: a prime example being her interview on Australia's highest-powered current affairs program, *Lateline*, to offer her views on how the prime minister should engage the Australian Muslim community. Within a few short years, she became a Fellow at Yale University. The World Economic Forum named her a 'Young Global Leader'.

Manji's rise is a product of her image as Islam's uber-reformist archetype: a Muslim woman who does not wear a headscarf, is open about her homosexuality, and is a self-declared warrior for truth and clarity with the courage to tell it like it is. The Muslim with the preparedness to blow the whistle on the Muslim world and expose everything that is wrong with it, and to do it with punchy turns of phrase and the skills of a television presenter.

With these populist credentials, it is wholly unsurprising that she has found a captive audience among non-Muslims in the West. The problem is that her book purports to be an open letter to her fellow Muslims. And for that audience it has been overwhelmingly irrelevant. If the goal is to find an intellectual response to modern Muslim radicalism, those who put their faith in Manji are destined to be hopelessly disappointed.

This book is not a response to Manji's. Nevertheless, some discussion of Manji's work is necessary here in order to demonstrate the weakness of the Islamic Reformation she is seen to represent. In part this is because the bulk of her book is not a discussion of Islam at all, but is rather spent detailing the failings of the Muslim world and coming eagerly to the defence of the United States, and particularly Israel. To that extent, Manji's discourse is largely political; one that acknowledges only briefly the very real, legitimate grievances of the Muslim world and, where Israel is concerned, the Palestinians. Principally, Manji's work is a spirited blaming of Muslims for the woes of the world.

A detailed discussion of Manji's political commentary is beside the point of this chapter. Suffice to say that it has met with heavy attack for its historical revisionism, and, while some Muslims find it offensive, few, in my experience, even take it seriously. Symbolic of this reception is that Tarek Fatah, a man Manji thanks in her acknowledgments, was moved to request that any mention of him be removed from subsequent editions of the book in an article for *The Globe and Mail*, published elsewhere online under the instructive title, 'Thanks, but no thanks: Irshad Manji's book is for Muslim haters, not Muslims'. For Fatah, Manji's work is 'aimed at making Muslim haters feel secure in their thinking' by validating their every prejudice.

At the crux of Fatah's objection is a conviction that Manji's work is not written in good faith. And if my own experience is any guide, this appears to be largely how Manji's work has been received among even the most self-critical, liberal, reform-minded Muslims.

This does not augur well for Manji's credentials as a meaningful force for change. But to assess her potential for such a role, it is what she has to contribute to Islamic thought that is most relevant. Here, however, Manji's considerable irrelevance to Muslim audiences is only compounded. Invariably, what she does have to say is absurdly ignorant and simplistic, or contributes nothing new. Often both.

Manji's primary target is the Qur'an, which she asserts is 'contradictory and ambiguous', has 'wild mood swings' and is 'profoundly at war with itself'. It embodies an 'incitement of hate against Jews', despite the fact that no classical theologian of any note seems to have discovered this. Muslim anti-Semitism, which is indeed a serious sickness today, is very much a phenomenon of the last 60 years. If classical Islam has a despised Other, it is probably Zoroastrianism.

Manji makes these statements, ostensibly as some sort of intellectual challenge. In her own view, she is asking 'questions from which we can no longer hide'. But in truth, they are simple and tired. The Qur'an itself admits its ambiguity at 3:7, declaring 'in it [the Qur'an] are verses of clear meaning; they are the foundation of the Book; others are allegorical'. As we have seen, Qur'anic ambiguity was universally acknowledged in, and became a central assumption of, classical Islamic thought.

But no classical Islamic thinker would have been swayed by Manji's claim that the Qur'an is replete with contradiction. Partly, this is because Manji does not clearly, and explicitly, identify the contradictions she tells us are so ubiquitous. Partly, also, it is because the Qur'an itself denies this claim. Most relevantly, however, it is because apparent tensions in the text can often easily be resolved with reference to the historical contexts of the verses in question. Manji seems lamentably ignorant of this basic method, writing that 'it's not clear which verses came to Muhammad when', despite the libraries of classical literature that prove otherwise. But even without this elementary knowledge, the few contradictions Manji does purport to identify are quite clearly a function, not of the Qur'anic text, but of her own ineptitude.

Generally, these relate to the Qur'an's attitude towards war and international relations, which were discussed more fully in Chapter 6. But Manji's most coherent challenge concerns the Qur'an's stance towards non-Muslims. On the one hand, she identifies that the Qur'an positions its message as a continuation of the Judeo–Christian tradition. It claims to emanate from the God of Abraham, Moses and Jesus, and affirms the truth of the revelations brought by those prophets. However, Manji argues, the Qur'an 'also discourages Muslims from taking Jews and Christians as friends, lest we become "one of them"'. This is an apparent reference to 5:51, which reads:

> Oh you who believe: do not take the Jews and Christians as *awliyā*; they are *awliyā* (only) of each other. And whoever among you turns to them is certainly one of them.

The key word, which is often translated as 'friends', is '*awliyā*'. But *awliyā* connotes far more than mere friendship. It conveys a sense of guardianship, akin to the relationship of a parent to a child. It implies not simply love or conviviality, but dependency. This verse therefore implies that communities tend to guard themselves, and cannot always be relied upon for protection. Understood this way, it is advising Muslims to strive for independence. This was especially so in the context of the prophet Muhammad's community, which was regularly entangled in the treacherous tribal politics of Arabia.

Yet, because the Prophet did forge alliances with non-Muslim tribes, exegetes usually understand this verse to be speaking of people who were politically hostile to the fledgling Muslims. As for those non-Muslims who are not in this hostile category, there is no prohibition on friendship, or in some circumstances, marriage. This fact is clear when the above verse is read in conjunction with 60:8–9, which says:

> God does not forbid you, with regard to those who do not fight you on account of your religion nor drive you out of your homes, to treat them with goodness and to be just to them; truly, God loves those who are just. Indeed, God forbids you (only) with regard to those who fight you on account of religion and drive you out of your homes, and assist (others) in driving you out, that you turn to them; and whoever turns to them, they are wrongdoers.

It is not my intention to embark upon a lengthy dissertation on the Qur'an's vision of relations between Muslims and non-Muslims. It is merely to demonstrate the shallowness of Manji's glib analysis. In this instance, the alleged contradiction stems from a misleading translation of the Qur'anic text, and a refusal to consider the range of verses relevant to the issue at hand. There is nothing sufficiently probing in Manji's challenge to trigger even the poorest imitation of a ripple in Islamic thought. Perhaps more instructively, Manji's challenges are little more than the reproduction of the kinds of charges Christian evangelists, and occasionally Western Orientalist writers, have been making against Islam for decades, even centuries. That does not necessarily mean they are unworthy of response. But it does indicate that there is no new intellectual contribution here. If this is the Islamic Reformation that we are supposed to hope will defuse the bombs of radicalism, radical ideologues will be grinning vastly.

Where Manji does make a novel theological charge, its novelty invariably derives either from deliberate distortion or jaw-dropping ignorance. In an attempt to demonstrate the torpor of Islamic thought, Manji asserts that an Islamic orthodoxy has prevailed which holds that Muslims must obey the Qur'an 'without asking how'. The phrase is a translation of *'bi lā kayf'*, and does indeed refer to a widely held scholarly view within classical Islam. But Manji's rendering of the doctrine is absurd. For her, it means that the Qur'an 'stands for itself. It is our job to comply.' The implication Manji articulates more explicitly elsewhere is that, under this doctrine, the Qur'an is not interpreted, but merely imitated. This doctrine is therefore said to preclude an inquisitive approach to theology completely; to prevent Muslims from looking for deeper meaning within the Qur'an.

This is a perverse fabrication of Islamic thought. The *bi lā kayf* doctrine emerged from an esoteric theological controversy about the meaning of Qur'anic references to God's 'Hand' or other apparently human-like features. The Qur'an is adamant that God is completely unique, and does not resemble the creation in any way. Islamic theologians were therefore united in their rejection of anthropomorphism. But this caused Islamic exegetes to wonder how God could be said to have human body parts, such as hands, while maintaining total uniqueness.

Ultimately, two responses developed. One school held these terms to be positively metaphorical. References to God's 'Hand', for example, connoted God's power, control or assistance. A second school held there was no way to be certain these terms are metaphorical, but that it was nevertheless unquestionable that God did not resemble the creation. This school therefore said that God has a Hand, but that it was totally unlike anything humans can understand. The precise meaning of 'Hand' is a mystery. Accordingly, these exegetes asserted that the correct interpretation was to accept the existence of God's Hand '*bi lā kayf*': without asking how this is the case. It had nothing to do with adopting a brainless approach to the Qur'an. In fact, this position stems from, and relies upon, the mystery of the divine word.

Manji's confused, perhaps desperate, attempt to prove the inherent thoughtlessness of Islam leads her to assert that the centres of Muslim creativity 'existed on the periphery' and 'didn't steer the direction of Islam'. This is an incredible claim, given the high Islamic civilisation that developed in the Muslim heartlands, such as Iraq, and other major centres such as Spain, which contributed acknowledged fathers of Western civilisation's Renaissance such as Ibn Rushd. Moorish Spain may have been geographically peripheral in the medieval Muslim world, but it is purely imaginary to suggest it 'didn't steer the direction of Islam'. The *Mezquita*, the grand mosque of Cordoba, was one of the most significant in the Muslim world during its prime. Some of the greatest and most influential Islamic jurists, theologians and philosophers were products of Moorish Spain. The Spanish contribution to the Islamic tradition is immense.

But Manji insists that Islam has always been driven from the desert and, as such, that it is dominated by Arab tribalism. This, we are told, is the reason Islam is incompatible with equality. Equality must always perish for the survival of the tribe. It is this 'desert personality of Islam' that Manji would have us believe allows dishonoured clans in Pakistan to rape women of rival clans in retribution, even if the woman was not responsible for any transgression. Similarly in the case of honour killings in Jordan. And certainly, Manji is right to identify that tribal honour, in which women are treated as communal property, plays a major role in these atrocities. Indeed, these honour crimes, particularly in Pakistan and Afghanistan, are often produced by ancient tribal legal systems. But these predate the arrival of Islam. Manji anticipates this response, and asserts that Islam is difficult to extricate from these tribal norms, which demonstrates that 'there is something profoundly tribal about the religion to begin with'.

This is perhaps Manji's most revealing howler. Of all the criticisms that might be levelled at Islam, inherent tribalism is the least plausible. Even the most cursory glance at the prophet Muhammad's life is enough to demonstrate that the precise reason Islam's arrival in Arabia was so ardently resisted by the pagan Arabs was that it was radically *anti*-tribal. The early Muslim community was entirely novel in its context because it was abnormally multicultural. Its mix of Persians, Africans and, of course, Arabs of wildly varying classes and tribes registered the monumental achievement of shattering tribal barriers and establishing new human bonds of faith. 'O Humankind! We created you from a male and a female, and made you into nations and tribes that you may know one another,' informs the Qur'an. 'All people are equal, like the teeth of a comb,' the prophet Muhammad is reported to have said. 'There is no virtue in an Arab over a non-Arab nor a non-Arab over an Arab; white has no superiority over black nor black over white except by one's consciousness of God and good action,' he added elsewhere. To us these appear obvious motherhood statements. To the Prophet's contemporaries, they were revolutionary ideas. Manji's assertion that Islam is captive to Arab tribalism is the precise opposite of the truth.

The evidence Manji invokes in support of her claim only confirms this. Muslims have an attachment to the Arabic language and even pray in Arabic. Worse, they pray facing Mecca. This is sufficient for Manji to enquire whether or not Muslims are 'desert-whipped'. She invites us to see evidence here of Arab imperialism. It is a claim Muslims, with very few exceptions, will find startlingly alien. Muslim attachment to the Arabic language stems from a desire to be able to access the Qur'an directly, without the filter of someone else's translation. Given the difficulties discussed above that Manji has found in interpreting the Qur'an via a poor translation, one would have thought this entirely understandable. This does not render all other languages irrelevant. Indeed, so vast is the body of Islamic literature in Farsi, Turkish and even Swahili, that knowledge of these languages would be of tremendous value to the student of Islam.

Indeed, Muslims do face Mecca for their daily ritual prayers. More accurately, they face the Ka'bah: a small granite building that, in the Islamic tradition, is recognised as the first building dedicated to monotheism. Initially they faced Jerusalem. The Qur'an makes it clear that the direction of prayer is not singularly important: 'Righteousness is not constituted in whether you face the East or the West,' it declares. But it remains an awesome, spiritually uplifting thought for many Muslims that all over the world, their co-religionists are facing the same direction; that they are unified by a single focal point. It has nothing whatsoever to do with Arab imperialism or Muslims being 'desert-whipped'.

It is true that aspects of these ritual prayers, especially the Qur'anic recitation, are said in Arabic. This is what allows Muslims from every country on Earth to pray in one congregation as they do at least annually during the pilgrimage to Mecca. But Manji ignores that there is room within this ritual for Muslims to incorporate their own prayers in their own languages. Moreover, there is unlimited scope for Muslims to engage in their own informal prayers in any language they wish.

But undeterred, Manji presses on with her Arab tribalism thesis. The Arabs assumed that everything pre-Islamic all over the word was ignorant, she argues in a profound perversion of history. The truth is nearer the opposite. The early Muslims had tremendous respect for the wisdoms of advanced, ancient civilisations. The eleventh-century Islamic philosopher Aḥmad ibn Muḥammad Miskawayh argued that Greek ethics were more reflective of Islamic ideals than pre-Islamic Arab morality. I have earlier noted the influence of Socrates, Plato and Aristotle on the work of Islamic philosophers and political theorists. Even Manji is compelled to admit the cultural openness of early Islam, quoting Muslim scientist and philosopher al-Kindī thanking 'former generations and foreign peoples' because 'if they had not lived, it would have been impossible for us, despite our zeal, during the whole of our lifetime, to assemble these principles of truth'. As we have seen, one of the great secrets of early Muslim expansion was the ability of the Muslims to preserve the (usually non-Arab) cultures they conquered, and to absorb them within the breadth of Islamic practice. But for Manji, this was a brief interlude, reversed irrevocably once the Mongols invaded the Muslim lands, leaving Islam's arrival in Arabia as its only source of 'undisputed glory'. The fact that Islam has remained entwined in diverse local cultures around the Muslim world since that time refutes this. As does the fact that the last of Islam's great empires, which flourished after the Mongol invasions, was that of the Ottoman Turks.

Manji would have been correct to identify a worrying trend in modern Islam to conflate Arab dress and culture with religion. But this is entirely a modern phenomenon: largely a function of the wild global proliferation of Islamic materials from Saudi Arabia in the last few decades. Manji's analysis falls apart so comprehensively because she seeks to paint this as something that has been inherent in the Islamic mind since its inception, when this is unequivocally not the case.

It is little wonder that Manji sees a 'serious problem with the guts of this religion'. This, she asserts, is partly attributable to Islamic thought's reliance on the words and conduct of the prophet Muhammad, which necessarily results in unthinking imitation and total closure to any intellectual development. To this end, she quotes the Prophet's warning to 'beware of newly invented matters' because 'every innovation is a going astray' as evidence that Islamic thought shunned all manner of progress. It is a staggering misrepresentation. Manji either does not know, or fails to disclose, that, for over a millennium, Islamic scholars have understood this prophetic statement to be directed only to matters of religion, particularly core rituals and theological ideas. It is intended to prevent Muslims from worshipping five gods, not from inventing computers. This kind of basic blunder is all too common in Manji's analysis. Given this, it is hardly surprising that she believes Muslim reliance on sacred texts leads them to 'a destination called Brain-Dead'. This is an easy conclusion to reach, but it does not occur to Manji that the same people who emphasised the prophetic message managed to build some of history's most knowledge-centred societies and a tradition of intellectual dynamism.

Such obvious unfamiliarity with Islamic thought is manifest in Manji's declaration that '[i]nstigating change means not taking the Koran literally'. She fails to realise that no one does, or at least no one has since the literalist Ẓāhirī school, which flourished briefly in Moorish Spain, died out centuries ago. Today's radicals, like most fundamentalists, are only selectively literal with the Qur'anic text. They do not fight wars on horseback as the Qur'an describes; nor are they averse to killing people with fire (through the use of bombs), which the prophet Muhammad specifically prohibited. Militant ideologues are forced to rely, often explicitly, on declaring large swathes of the Qur'an to be abrogated precisely because a complete reading of the Qur'an would dismantle their ideology. Their disease is not literalism, but modernism and an associated preparedness to depart from Qur'anic and prophetic disciplines. Perhaps what Manji really means to advocate is not that Muslims stop taking the Qur'an literally, but that they abandon taking it seriously.

There is enough highly questionable material in Manji's work to invite volumes of analysis. Only the simplest shortcomings have been noted here, while some of the most serious are not. This is not intended to be a comprehensive refutation of her work, for that was done centuries ago. But it is intended to demonstrate why her work is likely to be of so little value in instigating badly needed change in Muslim communities and modern Islamic thought. The trouble with Manji is that while she might be wildly popular among non-Muslims, the people she purports to be addressing in her 'letter', with few exceptions, will find it terrifically difficult to take her seriously.

In some ways, this is a shame. Amid her populist confusions, Manji raises issues of genuine, burning urgency for contemporary Muslim communities. It is true that as glorious as Islam's intellectual history is, its intellectual present is not. In Muslim-majority societies, mistreatment of, and discrimination against, non-Muslim minorities is disturbingly common. The atrocious abuses faced by many Muslim women must surely sicken anyone with the most mildly functioning moral compass. Manji's diagnoses are often disastrously amiss, but she is right to be outraged.

And she does propose some meaningful solutions. Generally,

these are socioeconomic and sociopolitical in nature, rather than theological. Manji is not the first to advocate the provision of micro-finance to Muslim women in repressive societies to encourage entrepreneurship and give them independence. Indeed, Bangladeshi economist Muhammad Yunus won the 2006 Nobel Peace Prize for inventing the concept, and implementing it through his own Grameen Bank. Clearly, it is a suggestion with exciting potential that must surely be explored further.

But the great tragedy is that Manji risks doing profound damage to the cause of change in Muslim thought and society. So obviously unlearned is her discourse, so obviously alien to her co-religionists, that she is easily dismissed as a lightweight and derided as a Trojan horse. Worse, she is fast becoming symbolic. It is now despairingly easy for the more regressive and resistant to change to label anyone calling for self-criticism an 'Irshad Manji', thus ending, and avoiding, the most important conversations. It is an instant, convenient put-down, and in my experience, it is devastatingly effective. Manji's ineptitude has become everyone else's problem. Agitation for change is important. But done poorly, it only sets back the clock considerably.

This is the reality of the Islamic Reformation. It might make Salman Rushdie smile, but it will achieve little else, except perhaps harm. A profile in *The New York Times* dubbed Manji 'Osama bin Laden's worst nightmare', but the truth is nearer the opposite. Both quintessentially represent the Islamic Reformation. Both sideline the Islamic tradition (though Manji does so more explicitly), and approach the Qur'anic text superficially and without any coherent methodology. Both are happy to discard whatever Islamic strictures they find inconvenient without developing any rigorous methodological justification for this departure. As a result, both concoct religions of convenience. Far from opposites, they are theological twins. One can never be the antidote for the other. Indeed, each depends on the other for its rhetorical survival. Relying on Manji to fight bin Laden is naïve and dangerously confused.

And Salman Rushdie's oft-echoed call for Islam to be modernised simply buys into this confusion. Rushdie decries as hopelessly weak any reliance on 'traditional, essentially orthodox Muslims to help eradicate Islamist radicalism' precisely because he fails to grasp that this radicalism *is* modern.

Thus is Rushdie's ignorance of traditional Islam revealed. For him, the central problem is that traditional Muslims are incapable of interpreting the Qur'an in the context of history. This prevents Muslims from understanding that it is 'legitimate to reinterpret it to suit the new conditions of successive new ages'. An Islamic Reformation, he muddles, would drive a realisation that 'all ideas, even sacred ones, must adapt to altered realities'. Here, we come to a central point of difference between the Islamic and Christian contexts. The Christian orthodoxy against which the Reformation protested had a very different legacy to that of classical Islam, one which was markedly less accommodating of political dissent. Partly this was because the absence of a church in Islam made the historical dynamics more open to theological diversity.

Classical Islamic thought has always been a living organism. As noted earlier, it has thrived on the very idea that changes in social conditions necessitate developments in legal thinking. Its ideas very much 'adapt to altered realities'. But classical Islamic thought has always done so within ethical limits. The single most catastrophic failure of modern radicalism is that it is quite prepared to breach these limits for its utopian ends. How does Rushdie account for the fact that it is precisely radicalism's preparedness to alter sacred ideas to altered realities that has permitted it to justify killing civilians where none before them did?

The central flaw in Rushdie's thinking is his assumption that traditional Islam's view of the Qur'anic text as the infallible word of God 'renders analytical, scholarly discourse all but impossible'. With one sentence, Rushdie airbrushes entire libraries of classical Islamic scholarship from the face of intellectual history. In truth, classical Islamic scholars were far more prolific and subtle in their debates and analyses than their modern counterparts. If the bottom has fallen out of much Islamic scholarly discourse (and it has), then this is a recent malaise. Rushdie is more correct when he says there is a need for 'scholarship to replace the literalist diktats and narrow dogmatisms that plague present-day Muslim thinking'. But people like Manji simply do not have the tools to provide it.

No, we do not need any further attempts at an Islamic Reformation. As is so often the case with proposed solutions for Islam's perceived woes, this is a thoroughly Western prescription that fails to take account of the Islamic context. The narrative of Western history proceeds from Dark Ages, to Renaissance, Reformation and Enlightenment. Western commentators often forget that the Muslim world has already had its enlightenment. It has travelled subsequently via Reformation to its Dark Ages, in which it is presently plunged.

There is no doubt that, at least since the colonial period, and probably since the mid-Ottoman period, Islamic scholarship has been in deep crisis. The truly active intellects of the past have receded, and practitioners of rote-learned regurgitation now stand largely in their place. Knowledge now subsists in how well one can quote the dead, rather than in bringing the sacred texts meaningfully to life. Islamic scholarship was once immersed in the perpetual tensions of the world in which we live. Today, it almost always sits irrelevantly outside them.

The solution to Islamic thought's current malaise lies in recapturing the dynamism of Islam's traditional past. This does not mean the excision and unthinking application of swathes of medieval text in a modern context. Indeed, in some ways, that would be a modern approach. It does, however, mean the reinvigoration of classical thought and the emergence of the best traditions of Islamic history. What is needed so desperately is renewal. Not merely slogans to the effect that 'Islam is the solution'. Not a nostalgic movement that exaggerates and reminisces about Islam's former greatness as though that is sufficient, without a preparedness to embark upon the unglamorous task of self-rectification in the present. Neither a movement to expunge the entire Islamic tradition, nor one simply to imitate the past. Rather, a new appreciation of the classics and their vibrancy. Literally, a Renaissance: a rebirth. And while, undoubtedly, a figure like Manji is a publicist's dream, she is a Renaissance's nightmare.

Classical thought understood it was in a constant, if slow and steady, state of flux. It is more a process than, as is commonly misconceived, a repository of immutable conclusions. As Shihāb al-Dīn al-Qarāfī said in the thirteenth century of those who would render Islamic legal thought static: 'Their blind adherence to what is written down in the legal compendia is misguidance in the religion of Islam and utter ignorance of the ultimate objectives behind the rulings of the earlier scholars and great personages of the past whom they claim to be imitating'. In the next century Ibn al-Qayyim al-Jawziyya remarked that such stagnancy would cause 'grave errors [to be] committed in reference to the Islamic sacred law. As a result, hardship and severity [would be] brought forth [upon people].' Classical theory has, built within it, its own mechanisms for responding to modernity.

The challenge, then, is not to develop a modern Islam, for we have already seen how grotesque this can be. Rather, it is to identify, encourage and pursue a classical Islamic response to the challenges of modernity. Irshad Manji advocates the revival of *ijtihād*, the Islamic tradition of human reasoning and textual interpretation, and she is right to do so. But classically minded scholars have long been calling for and engaging in it. The problem is that there are not enough of them.

Yet, here we must frankly acknowledge that classical Islam was, and is, a diverse feast. Moreover, it was not uniformly enlightened. Like all empires, each Islamic dynasty entered a period of decline, which was regularly accompanied by oppressive conduct towards Muslims and non-Muslims alike. Islamic rulers were still politicians, and were perfectly capable of succumbing to the sinister forces of politics. Governments often sought to align themselves with one theological school over another, occasionally persecuting the theologians of alternative schools, only to reverse their policies when the political winds changed.

But invariably such persecutors are pathetically forgotten. No one quotes them because they left nothing worthy of quotation. Theirs is the domain of the incompetent and inconsequential. Instructively, this was not the domain of the masters who, more often, were the ones persecuted. We can be thankful that it is the masters who leave behind the legacy of classical Islamic thought. The more limited persecutors need not detain us.

How, then, might an Islamic Renaissance be manifest in conditions of modernity? One needs only to survey the breadth of classical discourse on, for example, jihad to appreciate the varied expressions this could take. And indeed, in our world, this is perhaps the most pertinent example to contemplate.

Here, one must consider that, since medieval times, the political landscape of the world has changed in at least two important ways. First, the imperial terrain of history has been replaced, at least nominally, by horizontal relationships between nation states in an international political system. Where once the default relationship between polities was one of war, now the starting point, recognised internationally and reciprocally, is peace. This is not to say there are not wars. Clearly, there are. But under contemporary international relations, military hostility requires at least some kind of attempt at objective justification. That is markedly different from the medieval imperial prerogative to wage war.

Second, the nature of modern war is far deadlier, and less discriminate, than its medieval predecessor. Only the modern world has seen the use of chemical, biological and nuclear weaponry, with their potential for widespread devastation, often disproportionately upon civilian populations and the natural environment. Ours is an era of daisy cutters and cluster bombs that desolate towns and massacre the innocent. All this lends itself to the obvious, perhaps inescapable conclusion that the decision to go to war now is far weightier than it once was. The damage wrought, at least in wars involving powerful states, is longer-lasting and deadlier.

As we have seen, classical formulations of jihad were varied, but none finds its logical extension in terrorism. For present purposes, the instructive point is that classical Islamic foreign policies were deeply rooted in their environments. The prophet Muhammad himself acted within the conventions of the inter-tribal politics of Arabia. Indeed his conduct can only be understood fully when viewed through that prism. The most aggressive jihad theory was decidedly imperialist, but it was also the product of an imperial age. The significantly altered political and technological landscape identified above is alone sufficient reason to doubt that a classical consensus would form around continued imperialism in the modern world. The world has changed; so, too, will the appropriate conclusions. That is the classical way.

This is well demonstrated by the analysis of Zaid Shakir, a classically educated Muslim theologian and political scientist from the United States. Shakir has argued persuasively and often that the natural expression of classical Islamic approaches to war and international relations in the modern world would be fruitful participation in the international community, and not the imperialism of yesteryear. This draws heavily on the influential theories of Islamic foreign policy from the Abbasid period, which placed a strong emphasis on diplomacy and the forging of treaties. For Shakir, the 'evolution of an international political regime, which has made peace the norm governing international relations' has created a political landscape 'in opposition to pre-modern times when war prevailed'. True to classical form, Shakir formulates his position on jihad accordingly.

The touchstones of Shakir's analysis are the objectives of Islamic law, on which Muslim jurists have overwhelmingly agreed since at least the time of al-Ghazālī in the twelfth century. The consensus holds that Islam aims to achieve the preservation of religion, of life, of property, of the intellect and of lineage. Scholarly discussions on these themes are too nuanced and voluminous to repeat here, except to say that a significant body of scholarship explains how well established Islamic norms serve these overarching objectives. The prohibition on consuming intoxicants, for example, aims to preserve the intellect. Prescribed forms of worship, such as fasting during the month of Ramadan or the five, daily, ritual prayers, inculcate the preservation of religion. Condemnation of murder and the strictures of warfare that protect non-combatants give expression to the imperative to preserve life. Prohibitions on theft, the rendering sacred of private property, and the denunciation of inequitable trade practices speak to the preservation of property. And so it goes.

The inherent classicism of Shakir's approach is that it seeks to develop Islamic theories on war and international relations in the modern environment in ways that are consistent with these overarching objectives. Contemporary warfare, he argues, has a savage tendency to violate these objectives. Its deadly and indiscriminate nature clearly poses massive threats to life – particularly non-combatant life. Its demonstrated tendency to leave towns and even nations in utter ruin, such that they may never fully recover, clearly compromises the preservation of property. Thus does the analysis continue.

This does not necessarily mean that modern warfare could not be justified under any circumstances. But given the astronomical human and environmental costs, Shakir considers that those circumstances are becoming fewer and fewer. The classical response to modernity would therefore be one devoted to avoidance of war unless it was absolutely necessary.

Shakir's analysis would quite obviously seem alien, even heretical, to al-Qa'ida. This is not merely because its orientation towards peace stands in diametric opposition to al-Qa'ida's ideology. It is also because Shakir's methodology is far too conciliatory, pragmatic and sober for al-Qa'ida's taste. For bin Laden, Muslims such as Shakir, who advocate involvement in the international political system, do 'not understand their religion', and are 'hypocrites who are trying to deceive God and His Prophet and those who believe'. Shakir remains a strident critic of Western foreign policy, but the reactionary, nihilistic approach of al-Qaʿida is conspicuously absent from his thought. His classical *ijtihād* is the true antidote to the disease of al-Qaʿida, and radical ideologues would instantly know it.

Those who call for 'moderate' Islam are not calling for anything coherent. They are, in truth, calling for Muslims to articulate a set of (usually political) conclusions with which they feel comfortable. How those conclusions are reached is simply irrelevant detail. Moderate Islam, then, like radicalism, becomes simply a religion of political convenience.

Such an approach is doomed to inexorable failure, and those who advocate a classical Renaissance understand this. Radicalism succeeds because it provides a coherent, if simplistic, narrative of the world and the radical ideologue's place within it. This will not be cured by an Islam that proceeds from no consistent philosophical base; that simply reaches for whatever conclusions are politically benign.

Here, it becomes apparent that a resurgence of classical Islamic thought has far more to contribute than merely a peaceable approach to questions of war and international relations in the modern world. Such approaches in isolation can easily be abandoned under stress. More profoundly, it can contribute a comprehensive theological disposition in the presence of which radicalism must inevitably become dismantled. Foundational classical concepts such as introspection, self-criticism and conciliatory pragmatism could come to the fore. Most crucially, it would reiterate ethical strictures, and command principled restraint. The radical reliance on vengeance must then be unequivocally rejected: traditional Muslims do not derive their morality from the transgressions of others.

In short, it can recapture Islam as a traditional faith. It can halt its reduction to an ideology where every Qur'anic imperative is given unprecedented, adversarial political meanings. Where Qutb writes that the 'foremost duty of Islam in this world is ... to take leadership in its own hands and enforce the particular way of life which is its permanent feature', classicism can restore the primacy of personal salvation to Islamic thought, and confirm that any worldly or political prominence is distantly secondary. This is a reorientation towards the soul, away from the world, for the benefit of both. It immediately erodes the ideological propensity to prefer expediency over morality.

It is now the non-derogable duty of classically educated Islamic theologians to communicate such classical norms to Muslim populations persuasively enough to expose the nihilistic, reactionary egotism of radical ideology for the heresy it is. Ed Husain, author of *The Islamist*, which tells of his deliverance from radicalism, is a valuable illustration of this: it was his introduction to the richness and diversity of traditional Islamic thought through dynamic, traditionalist scholars like Hamza Yusuf that, he believes, saved him because it gave him an authentic (and superior) alternative. 'Without that, I probably would have been a suicide bomber,' he told altmuslim.com. 'Seriously, I'm not joking'.

The good news is that this is beginning to happen in the Muslim heartlands. A report published by London international affairs think tank Chatham House, and released in 2006 to coincide with the fifth anniversary of the September 11 terrorist attacks, found that al-Qaʿida had suffered dwindling support in the Muslim world. This is largely because, while al-Qaʿida promotes itself as a defender of Muslim honour, it is killing innocent Muslims in numbers that far outweigh those of its non-Muslim victims, particularly in Saudi Arabia, Jordan and Iraq. In this way, it mirrors the experience of the Gamaʿat al-Islamiyya, which brought about its own downfall by targeting foreign tourists in Egypt, bringing the Egyptian economy to its knees, and turning the Egyptian public furiously against it. This, it seems, is the inescapable logic of terrorist groups. The depravity of their actions confesses immediately to profound moral defeat. Thus does their true grotesqueness expose itself, causing them to collapse under the weight of their own hypocrisy.

This creates a vacuum and, according to Chatham House, traditional Islamic scholars are asserting themselves in this space, with an emphatic message that Muslims must reject terrorism as heresy. Against the backdrop of al-Qaʻida's crumbling credibility, this message is making significant inroads.

The process has started. It is unhappily embryonic, but the signs are there that the rhetorical dismantling of al-Qaʻida will, in the presence of a strong traditional alternative, complete itself. As a classicist might argue, this is its inexorable course: falsehood will inevitably perish.

But it will take time. The phases of history are measured in decades, even centuries, not months. So stagnant has Islamic scholarship been for so long, and so emasculated were many of the traditional centres of Islamic scholarship during the colonial period, that Renaissance will be no simple task. The Western journey from Renaissance to Enlightenment took centuries, and brought much ugly scenery. Under conditions of modernity, an Islamic version might be more rapid, but possibly more ugly.

In the meantime, we will still share the same planet. The intellectual process is important, but it is not everything, and it is certainly not immediate. The world will not suspend its motion while Muslim communities struggle through the intellectual processes of Renaissance. International political crises are unlikely to vacate our landscape. Action will bring reaction. Politicians all over the world can be relied upon to act as belligerently and divisively as is inevitably popular, for there is much political capital to be made from exploiting fear and antipathy.

It will be left to private people to navigate these predictable but poisonous dynamics. And this will only be possible by recognising the most obvious, and incontestable truth of all.

9

Seeking the human

> You don't understand the humiliation of it – to be tricked out of the single assumption which makes our existence viable – that somebody is *watching* . . .
>
> Don't you see?! We're *actors* – we're the opposite of people!
>
> *Rosencrantz and Guildenstern are Dead*, by Tom Stoppard; Act Two

Yasmine Ahmed is a young, firecracker of a woman – the kind you don't forget upon meeting even fleetingly. There are few conversations she does not naturally dominate. Her energy is exhausting, her voice, like her laugh, piercing and engaging. She wears a seemingly permanent smile that flashes broadly and brightly across her face. In almost any context, she is an endless stream of wit and story. But Yasmine is not simply a source of entertainment. She is also intelligent, brave and irrepressibly active.

Yasmine studied law and journalism at Macquarie University in Sydney, before transferring to the University of Adelaide to complete her law degree. In her penultimate year, she backpacked alone around Europe, and completed an intensive course in international law as an exchange student at the University of Uppsala in Sweden. During her final year, she worked for six months as an intern at the United Nations International Criminal Tribunal for the Former Yugoslavia in The Hague. There, she did legal work on the prosecution of Pavle Strugar, a commander in the then Yugoslav People's Army, for war crimes in the bombing of Dubrovnik, Croatia, in late 1991.

Yasmine wears the hijab. During her time in The Hague, she was refused entry to a restaurant because of this. At first, the manager insisted this was due to restaurant policy that patrons remove their hats. Later, he confessed to one of Yasmine's friends that he 'didn't want those kinds of people in the restaurant'. It was an intensely isolating experience. Yasmine had spent time in early post-apartheid South Africa, where the remnants of that policy could still be seen, but says she has never felt as excluded as that restaurateur made her feel. She swiftly lodged a complaint with an equal opportunity tribunal, and obtained a judgment against the restaurant ordering it to change its policy. Yasmine is a woman of action.

She returned to Australia at the end of her internship, but left again only a week later. While working at The Hague, she applied for another legal internship in Timor Leste, formerly East Timor. Her application was successful, and she spent five months working in the United Nations Serious Crimes Unit there as part of the team prosecuting POLRI, the Indonesian Police Force. It never crossed Yasmine's mind that she was in an unusual position for a Muslim. For her, it was a simple matter of justice. Crimes had been committed, and needed to be prosecuted. The religious identity of the accused was wholly irrelevant. Her only concern was for how the Timorese would receive her. She found they did so with an astonishing warmth.

Since then, Yasmine has worked as a legal associate for John Sulan, a Supreme Court judge in South Australia, where she did complex legal research, drafted judgments, and ran the court when Sulan was presiding. Presently she is an international lawyer in the Federal Attorney-General's department. From her time with Sulan, Yasmine recalls a ceremony on the fifth anniversary of the September 11 terrorist attacks in which about a hundred young lawyers were admitted to the legal profession. It was an enormous moment for them; the culmination of nearly twenty years of study. On that symbolically loaded day, Yasmine was the legal associate chosen to preside over the proceedings. As she described to me the contentment she felt that day, I could not help but feel that this moment captured the best of Australia's potential. So, too, does the fact that Justice Sulan, whom Yasmine habitually describes as an invaluable personal and professional mentor, is a devout and active member of the South Australian Jewish community.

But if there is one story that, for me, defines Yasmine, it occurred in December 2005 in Mecca, Saudi Arabia, in the weeks leading up to the annual Muslim pilgrimage. This was Yasmine's fourth time on the pilgrimage. She keeps coming back because, for her, it is 'the most unique, beautiful experience' she can find. For Yasmine, this is particularly true as a woman: 'A lot of other places as a woman you feel excluded and not part of the congregation,' she explains. 'At the pilgrimage you feel like you're really there as a human being, not a man or a woman . . . just a soul.' Partly, this is because it is an intense spiritual experience. It is moving for Muslims to visit Islam's holiest site, the Ka'bah: the black, cube-shaped, granite building that Muslims believe was built by the prophet Abraham as the first house dedicated to monotheism, and which Muslims all over the world face five times daily in prayer. But for Yasmine it is also because the Ka'bah 'is one of the only mosques where men and women pray side by side'. The arrangement is inevitable and necessary. Crowds of over two million descend upon Mecca for the pilgrimage every year. Women unaccompanied by men can be physically unsafe in the crushing density of the crowds, and if men and women in a group are separated from one another during prayer, they may never find each other again. In a strange city awash with foreigners, it is easy to get lost, unable to find either your companions or your accommodation.

These days, the Ka'bah stands dwarfed by the huge stadium-like marble complex that surrounds it. It rests in the centre of a marble courtyard, which resembles a sporting arena encircled by multi-level grandstands. It is understandable that Muslims visiting the Ka'bah will covet the chance to pray as near it as possible, and will therefore often seek to make their way to the courtyard area. Yasmine is no different, and on her previous trips to Mecca had never found any difficulty in doing this. Praying in the courtyard within throwing distance of the Ka'bah was an eagerly anticipated highlight for her.

But this time would be different. Yasmine went to the sacred mosque with a group of three other women and two men. As the time approached for the afternoon prayers, they took their positions in the courtyard, the women sitting together amid a large section of women, the men about ten metres away among other men. About twenty minutes before the time for congregational prayer, Yasmine noticed guards approaching. They demanded that the women leave the courtyard, and did so in a tone that conveyed an expectation of silent, immediate compliance. Apparently, for some unknown reason, the courtyard was henceforth an exclusively men's space. Naturally, some women, confronted by the aggressive demands of a Saudi male guard, obeyed instantly. Yasmine did not. When the guard demanded specifically that she move, her reply was swift and emphatic.

'No. Absolutely not!'

The guard kept looking at her, incredulous, and repeated his demand. 'Move! Move!' His insistence caused most of the women around Yasmine's group to get up and leave. Yasmine implored them to stay, to stand their ground, not to be cowed, but it was to no avail. As the women cleared out, men moved in to fill the vacuum, leaving Yasmine and her friends isolated.

Still, Yasmine was not deterred. The guard's brusque, unexpected demand had hurt her deeply. 'This is my right to have a spiritual experience,' she explained to me later. 'It has been this way since the time of the Prophet,' she thought at the time. 'How dare you take this away from me?' She steadfastly kept refusing the guard's order. If she gave in, she thought, there would be no stopping this bizarre campaign to exclude women.

The guard left. Yasmine thought momentarily that it was over, but the guard returned, this time with three other men. One was dressed in finer clothing, which denoted that he was of a higher rank, perhaps of the religious establishment. The guards in their newly emboldened numbers kept repeating the demand.

Yasmine's group resolved to ignore them. The one thing in their favour was that they were women and the guards would not dare to remove them physically. Still, there was no point attempting to reason with them. For their part, the guards simply continued barking their aggressive orders.

It was at this time that Yasmine decided to stand up and pray a voluntary prayer. It was a brilliantly resourceful response, because it left the guards in a quandary. A person praying is entitled to an area of inviolable space on which they prostrate. They have receded temporarily from the world, meaning they are immediately disengaged from the conversations around them. The guards only grew more and more frustrated, realising their commands must now fall on deaf ears. But they, too, were resourceful. One grabbed a nearby Afghan man, and shoved him directly in front of Yasmine, pushed up against her so that she couldn't move, violating her prayer space. Yasmine had no choice but to push him out of the way, and he scurried off, perhaps a little scared, but definitely uncomfortable at his involuntary inclusion in this quarrel. Yasmine kept praying. Eventually, though, she finished, and sat down on her prayer mat, which one of the guards tried to yank out from underneath her. Yasmine snatched it back and managed to hold on to it.

By now, almost everyone in the vicinity was looking at

Yasmine and her group. She was angry, but more overwhelmingly, upset. Some of the men nearby were providing moral support, encouraging the women to keep standing up for themselves. Others were scowling at them for causing a scene and acting in a manner unbecoming of women. Meanwhile, the guards had managed to identify the men who had come with Yasmine. Now they had her defeated. They physically removed the men. Yasmine yielded, fearing the men might be in physical danger or sent to prison. As she left, Yasmine had a parting message: 'How dare you do this?' she yelled. 'This is my right as a Muslim and you're taking that right away from us.' Then she turned to the men around her: 'You're part of this. You're contributing to this oppression.' Half of them probably couldn't understand; others didn't care.

As the guards beamed with satisfaction, Yasmine and her group moved towards the back of the mosque, as far from the Ka'bah as possible where, apparently, for the first time in 1400 years, Muslim women now belonged. 'Good on you for trying,' came a voice from among a group of nearby men as they left. Some women who had watched the incident also offered their encouragement.

'It was one of the most disempowering moments of my life,' Yasmine recalls now. As an Australian Muslim woman who wears the hijab, she faces discrimination in life regularly. This, she explains, she can handle. But her faith was her last sanctuary. At that moment, in the most sacred space in her religious tradition, she felt her faith being ripped away from her. 'Being told I couldn't be there at that place because I was a woman was just awful, really disempowering.' But there is nothing powerless about Yasmine. Her definitive stand in Mecca was one of immense conviction and courage.

It is little wonder, then, that a year after the Bali bombings of October 2002, when a major daily newspaper was writing a feature about the discrimination faced by Australian Muslims since the attacks, they contacted Yasmine for an interview. She duly obliged. A few days later they sent to her house a photographer who had been briefed about the story.

'Would you mind putting on one of those things that covers your face, and leaves only your eyes exposed?' he asked Yasmine.

'What?!' she said.

'I was just wondering if you could put it on for the photo,' he said with a straight face.

'No way!' Yasmine replied. 'I'm not going to put something on my face. I don't wear it usually, so why would I wear it for a photograph?'

The photographer sought to explain himself. 'Well, if I don't ask, I'll be in trouble with my picture editor, because he'll ask me why I didn't get a photo like that.'

Yasmine proceeded to lambast him: 'All you're doing is perpetuating the stereotype of who Muslim women are. Only a minority of Muslim women dress like that and you're just creating a false image. It defies the very point of the article.' Apologetic, the photographer searched for an alternative.

'Can you just go near the bars on the window and we'll take a photo near there?' he asked. Yasmine immediately sensed that the photo would make her look caged, imprisoned. 'I think it would be a nicer picture outside,' she countered, and led the photographer out of the house.

Yasmine's smile is permanent. The photographer wanted something else. 'Can we do one with a sullen face?' He explained that this might suit the story better, since it was about discrimination. Yasmine acquiesced, suspicious of his argument. Was this not a contrived image of the Muslim woman? Here was every stereotype imaginable compressed into one photograph. The only consolation was that she had not satisfied the paper's fetish by wearing a face veil. The next day, Yasmine opened the newspaper to look at the article. There was no accompanying picture.

Three years later, the same newspaper interviewed Yasmine again for a similar story. Again, a photographer came to her house. After an exchange of pleasantries, it was time to set up the photo shoot.

'Is there any possibility that you could put something over your face for the photograph?'

Clearly, Yasmine was of no independent, inherent value to the photographic editor. She was there to play a role. She was not a bold, intelligent, dynamic woman. She was an image designed for the consumption of an audience expecting to be fed a stereotype. Her reality was not relevant. The shabby imperatives of mass media were. Here, Yasmine was an actor. As Stoppard would have it, the opposite of a person.

This is precisely where the issues discussed in this book lead us. Caged by labels such as 'moderate' and 'fundamentalist', engagement with Muslims becomes little more than an exercise in crude taxonomy. Upon entering public contemplation, every Muslim must immediately be reduced to a one-dimensional fiction. The moderate is good (or at least benign), the fundamentalist is nasty, and there is little, if anything, in between. There are tolerable Muslims and intolerable Muslims. But no Muslim can be complex, which is to say, human.

In this public environment, the Muslim naturally has one of a defined set of roles to play. The fundamentalist repulses, frightens and inflames, and the moderate condemns, but neither is permitted to connect to mainstream society. All individuality is lost as a civilisation, and its people, like Yasmine, are reduced to roles, their humanity consumed.

The Muslim world, too, plays its role: ally, trade partner, oil supplier, military base, military threat and, perhaps, invaded nation. Ultimately, then, Muslims as a whole exist for their Western audience. They are the opposite of people.

Our nomenclature is political, not human. This fact merely gives structure to the inherently political prism through which Western commentators often gaze upon, and ultimately construct, an essentialised Muslim world. Consider *The Age*'s editorial from 8 December 2005, which opened: 'Saudi Arabia was recently likened by a long-time observer to "a sort of oily heart of darkness" that has come to envelop all that is anti-American.' Here, an entire nation is reduced to a one-dimensional 'heart of darkness'. It belongs quite simply in the 'evil' box. These are not a people with histories, identities, social struggles, or human complexities.

But most revealingly, this summary of Saudi Arabia is built on two quintessential images. It is a heart of darkness, but it is – to be sure – an oily one. Similarly, the reader is invited to infer that the Saudi darkness subsists in the fact that it envelops 'all that is anti-American'.

Such descriptions of Saudi Arabia that gather around oil and anti-Americanism demonstrate an apprehension of the Muslim world defined exclusively by Western political interests. Saudi Arabia's relevant features are its resources and its attitudes towards the West. That is all the reader is told because, it seems, that is all the reader need know. We aspire to no greater understanding of this nation and its people.

Thus are popular conceptions of the Muslim world, and indeed Islamic thought, reduced to the personification of a handful of clichés. Both apologists and polemicists seem destined to frame the discourse on Islam only in terms of terrorism, misogyny and authoritarianism. The superimposition of this analytical model on to Islam and the Muslim world means many Western commentators have little to say about either that does not fit within this narrative.

In the West, we study our own societies and traditions with pedantic precision and attention to subtle and nuanced detail, but we do not afford the same to Muslim communities, locally or globally. There is limited space in the public discourse to reflect upon the spiritual, material, and human aspirations and struggles of Muslims. These are publicly stripped away by political solvent. The public eye is unable to see, the public mind unable to comprehend, the human.

There are exceptions. In a rarely nuanced article for *The Independent* in July 2004, British author and television presenter

Simon Reeve provided a useful account of Saudi Arabia as a kingdom in flux, subject to incredible social tensions. Yet even such noble attempts, it seems, must ultimately resort to caricatures. Making the case that 'Saudi Arabia is a land of staggering contradictions', Reeve's exhibit A is that 'Saudis profess loathing for the American government' yet 'McDonald's is hugely popular'. Surely there are more meaningful social contradictions to be found than this; ones that might tell us more about the internal dynamics of Saudi society?

In a sense, Reeve's hand is forced. Had he produced more telling contradictions, it is doubtful that readers would have had the necessary familiarity with Saudi society to understand them. We relate easily and immediately to the competing images of anti-Americanism and McDonald's, not because they are meaningful, but because they are about *us*. This, ultimately, is how we have come to engage with Muslim communities. Our apprehension of them is far more about us than it is about them. And more specifically, it is more about our own political horizons than it is about their social histories and evolution. It is *egocentric*.

Accordingly, Islam and Muslims only enter our serious contemplation when something we deem to be newsworthy has occurred. This most often means the detonation of a bomb in some place where we have an economic, political or cultural interest (and nowhere else), but it can also mean a harrowing tale of misogyny or the gross violation of human rights. Suddenly we find an eruption of material presented to us, seeking to explain Muslims at home and abroad. People who confess to having known nothing about Islam before September 11 become sudden, self-proclaimed, auto-didactic experts. No sustained, in-depth discussion of Muslim communities or contemporary Islamic thought precedes these attention-grabbing triggers because, in the absence of a newsworthy event, the Muslim world is not deemed worthy of comment.

Little room exists in our public conversation for the dispassionate study of Islamic societies away from an environment of political turmoil. As long as this approach persists, we will never come to have a thorough, or even balanced grasp of Muslim societies. The context in which Islam and Muslims enter our thoughts is simply too compromised. That we have only ever come to study Islam in an environment of conflict necessarily colours our reading of it.

Thus, we find books in the 'Islam' section of our bookstores with titles such as *Islam Exposed*, *Islam Revealed* or *The Myth of Islamic Tolerance*. Certainly, scriptural and religious criticism is welcome, but we cannot pretend these are works produced in a motivational vacuum. Like much of the Orientalist material they regurgitate, these texts ride shotgun to a political agenda. You will find no equivalent titles in the Christianity or Judaism sections, despite the fact that there is plenty of scriptural grist available for the polemical mill. You might, however, find similar material about Jews and Judaism in some Muslim bookshops that pursue an anti-Israeli political agenda and service aggressively anti-Israeli clientele. The bandwagon of politically motivated polemic, it seems, rolls on.

It is clear that the politicisation of a discourse naturally leads to the grotesque simplification of the subject matter. Most familiarly, we do this with our meaningless categorisation of political debate in terms of Left and Right; a binary so brilliantly dismantled by British journalist Andrew Kenny in an essay for *The Spectator* in 2005. As Kenny notes, this often 'replaced rational argument with a playground division into two gangs who understood nothing clearly except how much they hated each other'. Thus can the Muslim world, and Islam itself, become reduced in a way that would be incomprehensible and unacceptable if done to our own societies and philosophies. The countless diverse nations, histories, traditions, languages, cultures and identities that inform the realities of Muslims all over the world are collapsed into one mental construct we call 'the world of Islam'.

This is, of course, hopelessly false. As we have earlier explored, a Muslim from sub-Saharan Africa usually has far more in common with a Christian or animist from the same region than he or she might with a fellow Muslim from Uzbekistan. No doubt the religious identities of these people play an important part in shaping their respective worldviews, but it is intellectually reckless to make Islam the dominant reference point for analysing their behaviour. Human behaviour is far too complex to be understood so one-dimensionally.

In this light, and given that the Muslim world only enters our consciousness when something shockingly newsworthy draws our attention to it, we are naturally invited to consider such oppressive, criminal and antisocial behaviour and practices an inherent function of Muslim existence. When a Muslim does something evil, it is therefore because that is what Muslims are.

Thus, the practice of female genital mutilation becomes linked inextricably with Islam because of its existence in some Muslim communities. Any Muslim woman who frequently gives presentations about Islam will be asked to condemn the practice. The same is never asked of Christians, despite the fact that Christian tribes in places such as sub-Saharan Africa engage in the same practice. We are too familiar with Christianity to essentialise it in the same way.

Similarly, suicide bombing becomes an 'Islamic' phenomenon, despite the fact that Palestinian Christian priests have also praised it, and that it finds its genesis, and still much of its expression, in non-Muslim or secular resistance groups such as the Tamil Tigers. So, too, does honour killing, which occurs, as noted in Chapter 5, among Hindu and Sikh families in the subcontinent, Christian families in the Middle East, and Italian and Greek migrant communities in Britain. The common thread has more to do with low socioeconomic class, feudalism and poor education than religion, but honour killings nevertheless feed into an essentialised discourse on Islamic misogyny far more often than they do a socioeconomic one.

None of this excuses the barbarism that exists in some Muslim societies. But it does indicate that too often we have not been serious in attempting to explain it, preferring instead to use news selectively to perpetuate and bolster our clichéd narrative. All evil actions of Muslims proceed simply from who they are. We find little beyond our discourse of good and evil; of fundamentalist and moderate; of Islam and the West. We do not perceive our world as a human creation, so we have no human discourse to describe it. It might be tempting to believe that the inhumanity of terrorism means terrorists are not human. Perhaps one day we will realise that, for all the depravity of their actions, they are only too human and seek solutions accordingly. Until then, the clash of civilisations, in reality a clash of ignorance, must surely continue.

The dehumanising nature of much Western discourse about Muslims works mainly because it operates in an environment of unfamiliarity and laziness when it comes to such matters. The public conversation, at least to the extent it is conducted via mass media, is always worryingly crude. Very few experts on any issue would express contentment with media treatment of matters in their specific field. This is true of lawyers, doctors, even athletes. Most relevantly, it is definitely true of religious communities, including Christian ones. If the approximations of mass media are misleading in the context of a familiar religious tradition such as Christianity, the dehumanising distortions can only multiply rapidly for Islam, with which Western societies remain profoundly unfamiliar.

By contrast, Muslim conversations operate in a very different environment, where the other world, that of the West, is far more familiar. The Muslim heartlands, with the exception of Turkey, went through nearly a century of colonisation by the British and the French. This had the inevitable result that the colonising cultures wove their way into the local language and culture, particularly among the elite. In some Muslim countries, such as Senegal, the language of the colonisers (in that case, French) is now predominant. In places such as Morocco, or Lebanon, dialects of Arabic are primary, but French is widely spoken. Most of the professional classes in Egypt have functional English. Even among the masses in the Arab world, it is common to hear sentences punctuated with the odd French or English word, possibly even without the speaker realising its very recent, Western etymology. The mark of the colonisers is readily observable in the clothing and even sociology of many Muslim societies, which is hardly surprising, given that the colonial project was to 'civilise' the colonies through Westernisation.

But the presence of Western culture in Muslim societies has not waned in the post-colonial period. Today, the Western world, and particularly the United States, is remarkably successful in exporting its popular culture all over the world, and the Muslim world is no exception. Television shows such as *Dallas* and *Baywatch* have been widely popular in the Middle East, a fact which *Baywatch* actor David Hasselhoff claimed would liberate women in Iran who are 'sitting there oppressed', but 'pull back their burqas and they've got blonde hair'. Large portions of the Muslim world are regularly exposed to the American entertainment industry. Pop singers and Hollywood actors are widely known and loved throughout the Middle East.

Moreover, it remains inescapable that the United States is the only contemporary world superpower. This renders domestic American politics a matter of international concern. US elections are watched closely by nearly every nation, and especially Muslim-majority nations.

The prevailing world order means simply that the Muslim world has no choice but to learn about, and take an interest in, the United States in particular, and the West more generally. Until very recently, that interest was simply not required. That is the nature of power imbalances. It is exactly why Australians are far more familiar with American culture and society than the reverse. It is also why the politically ascendant Islamic civilisations of history paid far less attention to Christendom than Christendom paid to them – even during the time of the Crusades. This seems a universal law of human behaviour.

And finally, significant Muslim populations now call the Western world home, millions having been born and raised there. Their familiarity with Western societies is first-hand. Comparatively few Westerners can say the same of Muslim societies. Net migration flows into the Western world, not out of it.

We might expect this substantially higher level of Muslim familiarity with the Western world to lead to a more nuanced public conversation than exists in the West about Muslims. Yet, not all Muslim discourses on the West have avoided similar pitfalls, and often for similar reasons. Where the Western tendency is to apprehend Muslims with reference to Western interests, and to view them through narrow political prisms, more reactionary Muslim polemics apprehend the West in similarly reductionist terms of cultural and military hegemony. The Western world makes Muslim news principally as a political force, particularly a belligerent one, or when it demonstrates some other form of hostility towards Muslims or Islam. A politician speaking out against the practice of women wearing veils, or better yet, a law that bans it domestically, will always make mainstream news in the Muslim world. The nuances of a debate about the importance of pluralism in Western societies will not. Thus is the story familiar: the only news from the West deemed relevant is that which has to do with Muslims; and it is most often conveying a form of hostility. That is usually the context in which the West, as a political entity, enters Muslim contemplation.

The result is a strand of public Muslim discourse on the West with the capacity to be every bit as essentialised and egocentric as prevails in the West about Muslims. Usually, this has the political West assuming a fixed role of hegemonic hubris, and fanatical anti-Muslim murderousness. This is an effortless enterprise for Muslim commentators in the context of the Middle East conflict, or the invasions of Afghanistan and Iraq. Certainly, there is a strong argument that US foreign policy has often had a devastating impact on the Muslim world. But the most extreme discourses place the West, and specifically the United States, on the enemy side in every conflict, even if this requires an exact reversal of the facts. So, al-Qa'ida spokesman Sulayman Abu Ghaith complains of 'America's support of world Christians against the Muslims... in the Sudan, the Philippines, Indonesia, Kashmir, Macedonia, Bosnia, and other places'. The list is instructive for its incoherence.

The protracted conflict over Kashmir involves neither Americans nor Christians. For decades the US was highly critical of India's role in the conflict, and only in recent years has it cooled towards Pakistan, but at no stage has its role in the conflict been significant. And while it is true that the world's most powerful nations were, at best, woefully lethargic and, at worst, criminally negligent in watching on as Serbs perpetrated their 'ethnic cleansing' of Bosnian Muslims, it is also true that a belated US-led military intervention in the Balkans ultimately saved the lives of thousands of Kosovar Muslims by striking at Christian Serbia. Still, this regularly forms a plank of Muslim grievance with the United States, usually on the grounds that the intervention was disastrously late, only occurring once the US no longer had any choice, and that the US had earlier upheld an arms embargo that prevented Bosnians from defending themselves. The oft-stated assumption is that action would have been immediate were the victims Christian. This overlooks the fact that the greatest failure of the United States to act in this period was not in the Balkans, but in Rwanda – an overwhelmingly Christian country that plunged itself into a genocide the US had the power to prevent. Bill Clinton would later nominate this as his greatest regret as US president.

Such inversions of political history demonstrate the unthinking ease with which the West must be constructed as the oppressive enemy in this discourse. Quite simply, wherever Muslims have suffered, it is assumed to be the fault of the United States. That, after all, is its designated role. This is how conspiratorial narratives take root in the Muslim world, with surveys finding that majorities in Egypt, Indonesia, Jordan and Turkey do not believe

Arabs carried out the terrorist attacks of September 11, 2001. The irony is that, in the process, the Muslim world dehumanises itself by assuming a corresponding, fixed role as victim.

There is little room for a human apprehension of the West in such a confined political narrative. And certainly in the case of al-Qaʻida's rhetoric, that is exactly how it becomes possible to kill Western civilians indiscriminately. Dehumanisation does not always lead to oppression, but it must always precede it.

Where, then, can the Muslim world turn for a human view of Westerners? Current migration patterns mean there are few sizeable communities from Western countries living in the Muslim world. Such Westerners as there are tend not to be migrants, but professionals stopping by temporarily. This contrasts with the significant and growing Muslim populations living in the West, which, for all the stigma that attaches to them, at least provide a point of human contact, and in media terms, provide opportunities for human interest stories. Such opportunities are considerably rarer in the Muslim world.

Muslim apprehensions of the West as a cultural entity can suffer accordingly. Muslims might be well acquainted with Hollywood, but the problem is that for many, this is the most authoritative view of Western culture they get. A 2005 Gallup poll of 8000 Muslim women from Egypt, Iran, Jordan, Lebanon, Morocco, Pakistan, Saudi Arabia and Turkey found that most of the women did not believe that 'adopting Western values will help Muslims progress'. This itself is unremarkable, but more telling was Gallup Muslim Studies executive director Dalia Mogahed's observation that the Muslim respondents were put off by 'a certain cultural degradation of women' they perceived in the West, which stemmed largely 'from Hollywood films, which are, of course, consumed readily in the Muslim world'.

To simplify, the constructed world of Hollywood is often a world of violent action, crime, drugs, big money, and impossibly heightened sexuality. It implies pervasive immorality, and even where Hollywood does attempt some articulation of moral principle, it appears in an entirely secular environment. If taken as a window on the West, it is easy to see how some Muslims conclude that Western society is built on three pillars: sexual immorality, capitalist greed, and godlessness. One radical cyber-commentator, Ali al-Aliyani, manages to compress an impressive list of stereotypes into one sentence in asserting that Westerners are 'raised in addiction to drugs, wallowing in the mire of sex and freedom from the higher qualities'. It is no surprise that similar themes are regularly repeated in more highbrow Muslim criticisms of the West.

Consider, for example, Maryam Jameelah's lengthy denunciation of 'westernism' in *Islam and Western Society*. Jameelah portrays American society as one of 'absolute cultural and moral freedom' that has become reduced to 'a hectic search in quest of superficial, fickle and irresponsible pleasures'. Accordingly, it is lawless and flighty, such that '[c]rime and violence are general for who can be expected to abide by laws destined to be obsolete tomorrow?'. American society's '[i]ndividualism becomes mere selfishness and egotism knows no limits'. It is defined by 'atheism and materialism'.

Jameelah was writing in the 1970s 'for the English-speaking, modern-educated Muslim in Muslim lands specifically and for the intelligentsia in Asia and Africa generally'. She is a New Yorker, formerly a Jew, who at the time of writing lived in Lahore, Pakistan. Many of her critiques sound remarkably similar to those of socially conservative Western commentators. The difference is that those critiques come from within, and convey an innate understanding of the dynamics of the internal cultural debate. Jameelah must have known of those critiques, but the nuance seems largely absent from her discourse. Accordingly, her characterisation of American society is appallingly one-dimensional and selective. She must have realised that she had reduced the Western world to an '-ism', hence 'westernism'. But her stated aim was to convince her readers, many of whom would have been unfamiliar with the West, of the mortal danger posed by the 'adoption of Western culture and values by increasing multitudes of Muslims'.

Yet, these caricatures are not restricted to material fed to Muslim audiences in Asia and Africa. It can also appear from the pens of Western Muslims addressing Western Muslim audiences, sometimes in even cruder form.

'Walking through the centre of any major city on a Friday night makes one realise that Western society has become similar to a herd of wild animals that can't control their desires,' writes Briton Abdul Hamid Jassat in the August 2002 edition of *Khalifah Magazine* – a publication of the isolationist Muslim movement, Hizb ut-Tahrir. 'The West promotes notions of "finding true love" or "following your heart"; in reality what people in Western society follow is their lust.' The unashamed use of phrases such as 'people in Western society' is immediately revealing. Western society is a singular, decadent phenomenon in this vision. Maryam Jameelah at least had the sense to talk about the 'trend' in Western society, and she was writing soon after the sexual revolution. For Jassat, there is no trend. The West is an animalistic monolith. It is, quite explicitly, not a matter of diverse, human complexity. Indeed, it is expressly dehumanised; reduced to 'a herd of wild animals'. Here, we find an echo in Sayyid Qutb's description in *Milestones on the Road* of America's 'animal-like' mixing of the sexes.

Precisely what it is that makes Jassat's hysterical conclusion inevitable is, of course unstated. The oft-invoked stereotype of a morally decadent West simply fills this gap for us. To that extent, Jassat's comments are more than just a case of raving overstatement. Here, the entirety of Western civilisation is reduced to one highly dubious Friday-night snapshot. We can only infer that snapshot is one of sexual depravity, but if so, the honest will admit that this is neither of exclusively Western origin nor the subject of Western monopoly. Indeed, it would be possible to reach the same conclusion in any of the world's major cities upon exposure to its seedy underbelly. But, anyone who is prepared to come to a conclusion on such a limited basis must first confront the dishonesty of his or her approach. It proceeds from an extremely small sample of social behaviour from an extremely small portion of Western society.

Almost any society can be made to look the same on such a limited view. Perhaps red-light districts are more visible in the Western world (although Bangkok tourists would surely qualify this), but only the profoundly naïve could assert that the Muslim world itself is immune from such vices. Drugs, alcohol, prostitution – it is all readily available, even in Saudi Arabia; a fact not changed by the brutal presence of the religious police who attempt to provide a veneer of purity. This might facilitate pious propaganda about the contrast between Muslim moral propriety and Western sexual decadence, but the secret facts are more damning. A 2006 survey conducted by Google found that of the top ten countries for sex-related Google searches, only one – Poland – was European or Western. Six were Muslim-majority nations; the top two being Pakistan and Egypt in that order. Fourth was Iran and fifth, Morocco. Saudi Arabia came in at seventh, followed by Turkey. India, which ranked sixth, has a sizeable Muslim minority. The results are remarkable when one considers that personal internet connections are far more common in the Western world.

'A-ha', comes the reply. Such behaviour is obviously a violation of Islamic morality. It is true that Muslims fall into all sorts of transgressions, but this cannot be projected on to the religious tradition of Islam. True. But this only reveals the other flaw in this kind of rhetoric. In seeking to establish the cultural inferiority of the West, it regularly ends up contrasting Western reality with the Islamic ideal. Any social problems faced by Western societies are presented as an expression of their inherently flawed culture. Of course, that assumption does not apply when the failings of Muslim-majority societies are being considered, where it is suddenly not the philosophical foundations of society that are responsible, but human frailty. That, surely, is the more erudite explanation, which only raises the question: why should Western societies not be given benefit of it as well? It is an arrestingly arrogant and disingenuous double standard given the fact that some Muslim societies are among the most immoral and oppressive on Earth, even if they remain sexually conservative, which they sometimes do only selectively.

But it is clear that such essentialised anti-Western rhetoric depends exclusively on the superficial. Thus, continues Jassat, in the West 'it is abnormal for women to step out of their homes without layers of make-up, lipstick and wearing revealing clothes'. Once more we return to the familiar theme of determining a society's sexual promiscuity solely with reference to the amount of their bodies women (but seemingly never men) cover. But in any event, Jassat's statement is demonstrably false. Western women often leave their homes without layers of make-up and without wearing revealing clothes. There is nothing abnormal about this. It raises not an eyebrow.

Of course, it can scarcely be denied that Western nations tend to be more sexually liberal than their Muslim-majority counterparts, at least in the public sphere. Moreover, it is entirely reasonable to argue, as many Western commentators do, that the impact of the sexual revolution of the 1960s has not been entirely positive and that the public space in many Western societies has become more sexualised than is healthy. The problem is that rhetoric such as Jassat's moves well beyond a sober critique of sexual ethics in Western society. It merely appropriates this caricature to make broad, untenable generalisations about a diverse set of societies. Accordingly, it is possible for Jassat to draw upon any of the stereotypical pillars of Western society in the most irresponsibly pervasive way.

Hence, elsewhere, Jassat provides a critique of what he calls 'friendship in the West'. In this instance, he invokes the West as a capitalist entity to argue, outrageously, that '[f]riendship in the West is based on using each other'. It is 'normally false as the society is founded on greed, individualism and following lusts'.

This, apparently, is why friends in the West drift apart: a change in someone's personality and lifestyle renders them of no further use, so they are discarded like spent capital. After all, friends in the West 'even become status symbols'. A change in fashion means the termination of the relationship. This, of course, contrasts with friendship in Islam, which is 'true as it is based on sincerity, trust and *Taqwa* (piety)'.

It is almost too ridiculous an example to take seriously. And indeed, Jassat's voice must be said to be more extreme than that of his mainstream co-religionists. But it is not so far from Qutb, who raged against the 'rubbish heap of the West' and its 'materialistic attitude which deadens the spirit', and it is a particularly useful illustration of how some Muslim discourses essentialise Western people. Take the influential twentieth-century Indian reformist Abul A'la Mawdudi, who attempts to establish that Western individualism is perpetrating the 'genocide' of its own societies through 'anti-conceptionist propaganda' and high rates of abortion. In support of this claim, Mawdudi resorts to alarmist propaganda of his own, stating that '[d]estroying the young one in the womb has become as simple and common a thing for the people as getting a tooth extracted', as though women who have abortions do so with gleeful abandon, with no sense of the weight of their decision. But more tellingly, he cites the obscure story of a prostitute whose material selfishness was such that, at the death of her six-month-old child, 'she danced and sang out of sheer joy by its corpse'. 'My husband and I are greatly relieved by this one's death,' she says. 'Think what a little baby is; it cries all the time, it dirties its clothes, and one is never done with it.' The story is so bizarre, so obviously anomalous to anyone familiar with Western societies, that it carries no representative meaning; it simply does not provide a window of any breadth on Western societies. Yet, it is invoked here as an example of the depravity of the Other, much in the same way as the Australian government incorrectly told us Muslim refugees were throwing their children overboard for cynical gain. There is no better way to dehumanise a people than to claim they do not even love their own children.

Here, any richness in Western civilisation becomes completely lost in a series of dehumanising stereotypes: the West is godless, materialistic, morally bankrupt and sexually degenerate. This is so thoroughly its nature that it renders Westerners incapable of forming meaningful human relationships, even with their own children. Worse, they *are* children; what Sayyid Qutb considered to be emotional and moral infants, advanced in the technological sense, but otherwise 'abysmally primitive', below even 'the most primordial levels of existence'. It was in this context that Qutb, having spent several years of his youth in the United States, wrote of 'The Deformed Birth of the American Man' and 'The Secret of the Deformed American Character'.

Every aspect of Western life must be squeezed into this simple-minded template. In his hate propaganda tract *The America I Have Seen*, Qutb asserts that jazz is 'the music that the savage bushmen created to satisfy their primitive desires, and their desire for noise on the one hand, and the abundance of animal noises on the other'. Warming to his theme, he asserts that 'nothing existed within [the early American pilgrims] besides the crude power of the mind and the overwhelming lust for the sensual pleasure'. It is impossible, within the confines of such commentary, to see the West as encompassing an extraordinarily diverse range of nations and cultures, each with an astonishing internal breadth and diversity, each teeming with constantly changing social currents and counter-currents. Certainly, it becomes dangerous to make too many assumptions about France or Spain as though these nations were no different from the United States. It is dangerous enough to make blanket assumptions about New York and Los Angeles, or even Melbourne and Sydney. But this is precisely what much Muslim discourse on the West does. Jassat's rhetoric is extreme, but the difference in many cases is only one of degree.

But as we might expect by now, there is clear egocentricity at work here. We have seen earlier how some Western discussions of Muslims and Islam are in fact more revealing as a commentary on the West than on Muslims; how they do little more than construct a Muslim world that is the opposite of the relevant Western self-image. Similarly here, such descriptions of an essential, monolithic West bear little meaningful relationship to the myriad Western societies of the world. What we observe instead is the construction of the anti-Muslim; the precise opposite of whatever it is these Muslim commentators attribute to themselves. If the Muslim world is militarily weak, the West must be its ruthless oppressor with an incurable hatred of Islam that makes it bent on Islam's destruction. If Islam demands moral uprightness, the ability to resist the material world, and piety, then the West must always be morally bankrupt, materialistic and godless. Capitalism is its only compass, which means it is incurably greedy, cold and ruthless, and which, in turn, destines it to be militarily aggressive, prepared to dispense with any civilian life on which it does not place a monetary value. The fact that the United States is one of the world's most religious societies simply cannot be acknowledged in this narrative.

Thus, we return to those three familiar pillars: greed, sexual promiscuity and godlessness. These themes fit most effortlessly, and are therefore naturally most prominent, in religious rhetoric. This explains how, in an era of globalised information flow, they have managed to take root in certain Islamic movements even among Muslims living in the West. Muslims have every right to complain about the manner in which the Western public conversation dehumanises them. But they would do well to realise their discourse on the West can be no less caricatured, and no more human. Qutb's outrageous subheading, 'The Americans Are Free of Humanity', illustrates this explicitly.

Little wonder, then, that a 2006 Pew Global Attitudes Survey of more than 14,000 people in thirteen countries across Asia, Europe, Africa and America found that Muslims and Westerners tend to view each other in similarly bleak terms. Each is more inclined to blame the other for the world's woes than itself. Each tends to view the other as violent, intolerant, and disrespectful towards women. Muslims tended to add that Westerners are selfish, immoral and greedy, for good measure. The symmetry is compelling, and should cause us to pause for reflection. If Westerners immediately, and correctly, recognise that these Muslim perceptions of them are stereotyped nonsense, they may also be inclined to reconsider the accuracy of their own stereotyped view of Muslims. The reverse is equally true. Each, being the victim of caricature, seems strangely unable to recognise their role as perpetrator of the same. Instead, we tend to fall back on the clichés that support them.

But, perhaps, a note of hope. While it is true that stereotyped views of Western societies exist among them, the Pew Survey showed that, unlike their co-religionists abroad who have little or no contact with Western society, European Muslims' views of Westerners were generally positive: largely describing them as tolerant, generous, and respectful towards women. They reject, by large majorities, the suggestion that Westerners are violent. European Muslims occupied a precious middle ground in what was otherwise generally polarised terrain. Undoubtedly this is due to their inevitably more nuanced understanding of both Muslims and the West. If a gulf exists between the Muslim and Western worlds, it will be people whose knowledge and experience spans both who are capable of bridging it, for the simple, powerful reason that they are capable of seeing the humanity in both. Similarly, a study of Australian attitudes to Muslims, published in 2006 by Kevin Dunn at the University of New South Wales, found that younger people, who had more contact with Muslims than did older Australians, were less likely to view Islam as a threat. Familiarity, it seems, does not always breed contempt. It might be our best hope.

This truth is reflected at more scholarly levels. It is telling that Muslim thinkers with a more nuanced view of Western society tend also to be capable of seeing important areas of connection and compatibility with Islam. New York imam Feisal Abdul Rauf called his book *What's Right with Islam is What's Right with America*; a title that neatly encapsulates that approach. Rauf demonstrates a vision prepared to move beyond the amount of clothing women wear. He sees more meaningful connections in fundamental concepts such as the separation of powers, the independence of the courts and the accountability of government. In so doing, Rauf not only pays tribute to some of the United States' (and the West's) most admirable moral ideals, he presents them as Islamic ones as well. In Rauf's vision, the West is more than an arena for scantily clad women, rampant sexual impropriety and commercial exploitation. It is a civilisation built upon many universally shared values, diverse populations and robust, accountable systems of government.

My purpose here is not to endorse everything in Rauf's analysis. But it is to endorse the orientation of his thought. Only when we are prepared to take a subtle, complex – that is, human – view of one another, will our world begin to make sense. I say this, not as a feel-good motherhood statement; I say it because it is the only hope for any intellectual clarity. If we discard the most obvious assumption – that we are human – and all that flows from it, we simply cannot expect our thoughts to be anything but a fraudulent typecast of countless astonishingly diverse, complex societies.

Ultimately, when the chatter of the talking heads finally stops, when the nonsense of politically motivated and self-serving conversation is duly ignored, and when the clutter of endless analyses is cleared away, we are left with this one indisputable truth: that we are all human. This is a powerful realisation if we can truly come to it. It means that for all our variances, we share the same emotions, the same impulses, and at the very deepest level, the same motivations. We are, none of us, simple personifications of ideology. We are also complex products of our social and political histories, our socioeconomic conditions, our life experiences, our social environments, our educations. We are individually, and even collectively, capable of giving this noble or evil expression, but it is never true that entire societies are virtuous or vile. This much we understand of that which is familiar and dear to us. How much more sense we could make if we were prepared to concede to others what we expect for ourselves. How much we could achieve if we were capable of viewing each other in full, nuanced, human colour. Our humanity does not excuse our respective wrongdoings, but the fact that it is unquestionably in common gives us a frame of reference through which we can transport ourselves from a world of nonsense, to a world of coherence.

In the meantime, let us not assume that every vice of the other is a function of their difference. Let us resist the mutual temptation to assume that their world would be so much better if only they were like us. Such positions allow us to airbrush our own iniquities from our consciousness. They are easy, self-gratifying and all too common. Many Muslims once argued that the solution to Catholic–Protestant tensions could be solved if they all converted to Islam. What would they say now as Sunnis and Shiites slaughter each other in Iraq? As discussed, many Western voices assert that the Muslim world's salvation lies in a secular, modern, post-Reformation future. They ignore that Saddam Hussein was an arch secularist, while al-Qaʿida and the Taliban are both modern and, in an Islamic sense, post-Reformation. What we desperately need, and what is categorically missing in such discourses of conceit, is the humility to understand that our own self-declared wisdom is often more limited than we admit; that when we criticise and lecture those with a different history and sociology, we often expose little more than our ignorance.

It is possible, and desirable, to speak – and even to argue – across social, religious and cultural borders. The above is not remotely a call for moral relativism. But it requires a level of knowledge that a grotesque proportion of those engaged in the conversation are either too arrogant or lazy to obtain. It requires Western commentators looking at a veiled woman to see more than oppression, and Muslim critics looking at Michelangelo's *David* to see more than nudity. It requires the discovery of what is deeper, even if each ultimately chooses not to embrace it for themselves. Alas, listening is now a forgotten art among much of the commentariat, and genuine depth is considered dispensable. They prefer instead to pontificate from an impossible distance in furtherance of their respective causes. They decide what the symbols and practices of others mean on their behalf because it boosts their predetermined, and often prejudiced, narratives. So, Yasmine Ahmed is a veil and *David* is pornography. Yet, such ignorance does nothing to dent the confidence of those who espouse it. Sometimes, certainty is made possible only by stupidity.

This is truly a problem of ego: of the arrogance that makes a fruitful conversation impossible; the egocentricity that renders our analyses redundant. The resultant conversation is often as simplistic as it is frightening. In such a dichotomous world where each considers him– or herself the sole repository of virtue and enlightenment, the only outcome is perpetual and escalating conflict. It seems a disturbingly accurate description of our times. Ours is an age of arrogance. Ours is an age of ignorance. Whether this can be cured will depend on people like us.

Notes on sources

This book is intended to be more accessible than a formal academic work. Accordingly, for ease of use and flow, what follows is a chapter-by-chapter bibliography. Naturally, it does not reference every text consulted during the writing of this book, but seeks to identify the most important sources. Because each chapter is referenced separately, several sources are referenced numerous times.

In the interests of brevity, references to news reports and press articles have not been included here. Where practicable, such sources have been referenced in the text. Of course, with nearly all reputable newspapers in the world having active websites, most, if not all, of these references can easily be found online.

Introduction
Huntington, Samuel, 'The Clash of Civilizations?', *Foreign Affairs*, Summer 1993, 22–49.
Inglehart, Ronald and Norris, Pippa, 'Islam and the West: A "Clash of Civilizations"?', *Foreign Policy*, March/April 2003, 62–70.
Lewis, Bernard, 'The Roots of Muslim Rage', *The Atlantic Monthly*, September 1990, 47–60.

Chapter 1: A Danish snapshot
Bluitgen, Kåre, *Til gavn for de sorte: Om tilslørede øjne i den danske indvandrerdebat* (2002) Centrum.

Bluitgen's book, called *For the Benefit of the Blacks: Veiled Eyes in the Danish Immigration Debate*, is published only in Danish. I have not consulted the original work, however the passage to which I refer in Chapter 1 is quoted widely online. The relevant passage reads:

> Venstrefløjen skal gå i offensiven. Gå i optog ned ad Nørrebrogade i København klædt i burkha, chador, tørklæder og lange frakker slæbende på en vognpark af klap- og barnevogne for til sidst at kaste det hele i en container på Blågårds Plads og *stænke Koranen med menstruationsblod.* (My emphasis)

It may be translated as:

> The Left needs to go on the offensive. Hold a procession down Nørrebrogade in Copenhagen wearing burqas, chadors, and long, dragging jackets, with strollers and babycarriages, all the way to Blågårds Plads. Then they should throw everything into the rubbish and *splash the Koran with menstrual blood.* (My emphasis)

Phillips, Melanie, *Londonistan* (2006) New York: Encounter Books.

Chapter 2: How did we get here?
Abd-Allah, Dr Umar Faruq, 'Islam and the Cultural Imperative', A Nawawi Foundation Paper (2004) available at: http://www.nawawi.org/downloads/article3.pdf
Abou el Fadl, Khaled M, *Conference of the Books: The Search for Beauty in Islam* (2001) Lanham: University Press of America.

NOTES ON SOURCES

Ali, Daniel and Spencer, Robert, *Inside Islam: A Guide for Catholics* (2003) West Chester: Ascension Press.

Armstrong, Karen, *Muhammad: A Biography of the Prophet* (2004) London: Phoenix.

Butterworth, Charles E, 'Al-Fârâbî's Statecraft: War and the Well-Ordered Regime' in Johnson, James Turner and Kelsay, John (eds), *Cross, Crescent and Sword: The Justification and Limitation of War in Western and Islamic Tradition* (1990) Westport: Greenwood Press, 79–100.

Daniel, Norman, *Islam and the West: The Making of an Image* (2000) Oxford: Oneworld Publications.

Ibn Warraq (ed), *The Quest for the Historical Muhammad* (2000) Amherst: Prometheus Books.

Masud, Muhammad Khalid, 'The Scope of Pluralism in Islamic Moral Traditions' in Hashmi, Sohail H (ed), *Islamic Political Ethics: Civil Society, Pluralism, and Conflict* (2002) Princeton: Princeton University Press, 135–147.

Murad, Abdal Hakim, 'Bombing Without Moonlight: The Origins of Suicidal Terrorism', *Islamica Magazine*, Spring 2005, 59–76.

Ramadan, Tariq, *To Be A European Muslim: A Study of Islamic Sources in the European Context* (1999) Leicester: The Islamic Foundation.

Ramadan, Tariq, *The Messenger: The Meanings of the Life of Muhammad* (2007) London: Allen Lane.

Roded, Ruth, 'Alternate images of the Prophet Muhammad's virility' in Ouzgane, Lahoucine (ed), *Islamic Masculinities* (2006) London: Zed Books, 57–71.

Smith, Jane I, 'Islam and Christendom: Historical, Cultural, and Religious Interaction from the Seventh to the Fifteenth Centuries' in Esposito, John L (ed), *The Oxford History of Islam* (1999) New York: Oxford University Press, 305–345.

Steyn, Mark, *America Alone: The End of the World As We Know It* (2006) Washington DC: Regnery Publishing.

Ye'or, Bat, *Eurabia: The Euro-Arab Axis* (2005) Madison: Fairleigh Dickinson University Press.

Chapter 3: Don't call me a moderate!
Abou el Fadl, Khaled, *Speaking in God's Name: Islamic Law, Authority and Women*, (2001) Oxford: Oneworld Publications.
Abou el Fadl, Khaled M, *Conference of the Books: The Search for Beauty in Islam*, (2001) Lanham: University Press of America.
Abou el Fadl, Khaled, *Islam and the Challenge of Democracy* (2004) Princeton: Princeton University Press.
Kelsay, John, 'Islam and the Distinction between Combatants and Noncombatants' in Johnson, James Turner and Kelsay, John (eds), *Cross, Crescent and Sword: The Justification and Limitation of War in Western and Islamic Tradition* (1990) Westport: Greenwood Press, 197–220.
Leaman, Oliver, *An Introduction to Islamic Philosophy* (2002) Cambridge: Cambridge University Press.
Orwell, George, *Nineteen Eighty-Four* (1990) London: Penguin Books.
Trumpbour, John, 'The Clash of Civilizations: Samuel P. Huntington, Bernard Lewis, and the Remaking of the Post Cold-War World Order' in Qureshi, Emran and Sells, Michael A (eds), *The New Crusades: Constructing the Muslim Enemy* (2003) New York: Columbia University Press, 88–130.
Phillips, Melanie, *Londonistan* (2006) New York: Encounter Books.

Chapter 4: Save our secular souls
Abou el Fadl, Khaled, *Rebellion and Violence in Islamic Law* (2001) Cambridge: Cambridge University Press.
Donner, Fred M, 'Muhammad and the Caliphate: Political History of the Islamic Empire Up To the Mongol Conquest' in Esposito, John L (ed), *The Oxford History of Islam* (1999) New York: Oxford University Press, 1–61.

Lewis, Bernard, *What Went Wrong? Western Impact and Middle Eastern Response* (2003) London: Pheonix.

Kelsay, John, 'Civil Society and Government in Islam' in Hashmi, Sohail H (ed), *Islamic Political Ethics: Civil Society, Pluralism, and Conflict* (2002) Princeton: Princeton University Press, 3–37.

Chapter 5: Women as a battlefield

Abou el Fadl, Khaled, *Speaking in God's Name: Islamic Law, Authority and Women*, (2001) Oxford: Oneworld Publications.

Abou el Fadl, Khaled M, *Conference of the Books: The Search for Beauty in Islam* (2001) Lanham: University Press of America.

Abou el Fadl, Khaled, *The Great Theft: Wrestling Islam from the Extremists* (2005) New York: HarperCollins.

Ahmed, Leila, *Women and Gender in Islam: Historical Roots of a Modern Debate* (1993) New Haven: Yale University Press.

Alloula, Malek, *The Colonial Harem* (1986) Minneapolis: University of Minnesota Press.

Barlas, Asma, *'Believing Women' in Islam: Unreading Patriarchal Interpretations of the Qur'an* (2002) Austin: University of Texas Press.

Fernea, Elizabeth Warnock, *In Search of Islamic Feminism: One Woman's Global Journey* (1998) New York: Anchor Books.

Human Rights and Equal Opportunity Commission, *Ismaε – Listen: National consultations on eliminating prejudice against Arab and Muslim Australians*, available at: http://www.hreoc.gov.au/racial_discrimination/isma/report/pdf/ISMA_complete.pdf

Hussein, Shakira, 'The war on terror and the "rescue" of Muslim women' in Lahoud, Nelly and Johns, Anthony H (eds), *Islam in World Politics* (2005) New York: Routledge, 93–104.

Jameelah, Maryam, *Islam and Western Society: A Refutation of the Modern Way of Life* (1996) Delhi: Adam Publishers and Distributors.

Roald, Anne Sophie, *Women in Islam: The Western Experience* (2002) London: Routledge.

Shaikh, Sa'diyya, 'Transforming feminism: Islam, women and gender justice' in Safi, Omid (ed), *Progressive Muslims: On Justice, Gender, and Pluralism* (2003) Oxford: Oneworld Publications.

Shirazi, Faegheh, *The Veil Unveiled: The Hijab in Modern Culture* (2003) Gainesvilled: University Press of Florida.

US Department of State, 'Report on the Taliban's War Against Women' (2001) available at:
http://www.state.gov/g/drl/rls/c4804.htm

Wadud, Amina, *Inside the Gender Jihad: Women's Reform in Islam* (2006) Oxford: Oneworld Publications.

Yegenoglu, Meyda, *Colonial Fantasies: Towards a Feminist Reading of Orientalism* (1998) Cambridge: Cambridge University Press.

Chapter 6: The war on jihad

Abou el Fadl, Khaled, 'Peaceful Jihad' in Wolfe, Michael and the producers of Beliefnet (eds), *Taking Back Islam* (2002) New York: Rodale, 33–39.

Abou el Fadl, Khaled, *The Great Theft: Wrestling Islam from the Extremists* (2005) New York: HarperCollins.

Blankinship, Khalid Yahya, *The End of the Jihâd State: The Reign of Hishām Ibn 'Abd al-Malik and the Collapse of the Umayyads* (1994) Albany: State University of New York Press.

Cook, Daniel, *Understanding Jihad* (2005) Berkeley: University of California Press.

Lammers, Stephen E, 'Approaches to Limits on War in Western Just War Discourse' in Johnson, James Turner and Kelsay, John (eds), *Cross, Crescent and Sword: The Justification and Limitation of War in Western and Islamic Tradition* (1990) Westport: Greenwood Press, 51–78.

Lane, Edward William, *Arabic-English Lexicon*, (2003) New Delhi: Asian Educational Services.

Lawrence, Bruce (ed), *Messages to the World: The Statements of Osama bin Laden* (2005) London: Verso.

Lewis, Bernard, *What Went Wrong? Western Impact and Middle Eastern Response* (2003) London: Phoenix.

Sachedina, Abdulaziz A, 'The Development of *Jihad* in Islamic Revelation and History' in Johnson, James Turner and Kelsay, John (eds), *Cross, Crescent and Sword: The Justification and Limitation of War in Western and Islamic Tradition* (1990) Westport: Greenwood Press, 35–50.

Shakir, Zaid, 'Jihad is Not Perpetual Warfare', *Seasons*, Autumn–Winter 2003–4, 53–64.

Stout, Jeffrey, 'Justice and Resort to War: A Sampling of Christian Ethical Thinking' in Johnson, James Turner and Kelsay, John (eds), *Cross, Crescent and Sword: The Justification and Limitation of War in Western and Islamic Tradition* (1990) Westport: Greenwood Press, 3–34.

von Denffer, Ahmad, *'Ulūm al-Qur'ān: An Introduction to the Sciences of the Qur'ān* (1991) Kuala Lumpur: The Islamic Foundation.

Chapter 7: What is so medieval about al-Qaʻida?

Abd-Allah, Dr Umar Faruq, 'Islam and the Cultural Imperative', A Nawawi Foundation Paper (2004) available at: http://www.nawawi.org/downloads/article3.pdf

Blankinship, Khalid Yahya, *The End of the Jihâd State: The Reign of Hishām Ibn 'Abd al-Malik and the Collapse of the Umayyads* (1994) Albany: State University of New York Press.

Butterworth, Charles E, 'Al-Fârâbî's Statecraft: War and the Well-Ordered Regime' in Johnson, James Turner and Kelsay, John (eds), *Cross, Crescent and Sword: The Justification and Limitation of War in Western and Islamic Tradition* (1990) Westport: Greenwood Press, 79–100.

Campbell, Courtney S, 'Moral Responsibility and Irregular War' in Johnson, James Turner and Kelsay, John (eds), *Cross, Crescent and Sword: The Justification and Limitation of War in Western and Islamic Tradition* (1990) Westport: Greenwood Press, 103–128.

Cook, Daniel, *Understanding Jihad* (2005) Berkeley: University of California Press.

Fouda, Yosri and Fielding, Nick, *Masterminds of Terror: The Truth Behind the Most Devastating Terrorist Attack the World Has Ever Seen* (2003) Camberwell: Penguin Books.

Gray, John, *Al-Qaeda and What it Means to be Modern* (2004) Chatham: Faber and Faber.

Gray, Paul, *Nightmare of the Prophet: Why the Next Century Could be Our Most Violent Yet*, (2004) North Melbourne: Freedom Publishing Company.

Lawrence, Bruce (ed), *Messages to the World: The Statements of Osama bin Laden* (2005) London: Verso.

Lewis, Bernard, *What Went Wrong? Western Impact and Middle Eastern Response* (2003) London: Pheonix.

Masud, Muhammad Khalid, *Shāṭibī's Philosophy of Islamic Law* (2000) Kuala Lumpur: Islamic Book Trust.

Murad, Abdal Hakim, 'Bombing Without Moonlight: The Origins of Suicidal Terrorism', *Islamica Magazine*, Spring 2005, 59–76.

Qutb, Sayyid, *Milestones* (2005) New Delhi: Islamic Book Service.

Ramadan, Tariq, *To Be A European Muslim: A Study of Islamic Sources in the European Context* (1999) Leicester: The Islamic Foundation.

Roy, Olivier, *Globalized Islam: The Search for a New Ummah* (2004) New York: Columbia University Press.

Roy, Olivier, 'A Clash of Cultures or a Debate on Europe's Values?', *ISIM Review* 15, Spring 2005, 6–7.

Sonn, Tamara, 'Irreglar Warfare and Terrorism in Islam: Asking the Right Questions' in Johnson, James Turner and Kelsay, John (eds), *Cross, Crescent and Sword: The Justification and Limitation of War in Western and Islamic Tradition* (1990) Westport: Greenwood Press, 129–148.

Chapter 8: Reformists, Reformation and Renaissance

Abd-Allah, Dr Umar Faruq, 'Islam and the Cultural Imperative', A Nawawi Foundation Paper (2004) available at: http://www.nawawi.org/downloads/article3.pdf

Abou el Fadl, Khaled, *Rebellion and Violence in Islamic Law* (2001) Cambridge: Cambridge University Press.

Abou el Fadl, Khaled, *The Great Theft: Wrestling Islam from the Extremists* (2005) New York: HarperCollins.

Husain, Ed, *The Islamist: Why I Joined Radical Islam in Britain, What I Saw Inside and Why I Left* (2007) London: Penguin Books.

Kamali, Mohammad Hashim, 'Law and Society: The Interplay of Revelation and Reason in the Shariah' in Esposito, John L (ed), *The Oxford History of Islam*, 107–153.

Manji, Irshad, *The Trouble with Islam: A Muslim's Call for Reform in Her Faith* (2003) Sydney: Random House.

Masud, Muhammad Khalid, *Shāṭibī's Philosophy of Islamic Law* (2000) Kuala Lumpur: Islamic Book Trust.

Natana, J DeLong-Bass, *Wahhabi Islam: From Revival and Reform to Global Jihad*, (2004) London: I.B. Tauris.

Ramadan, Tariq, *The Messenger: The Meanings of the Life of Muhammad* (2007) London: Allen Lane.

Shakir, Zaid, 'Jihad is Not Perpetual Warfare', *Seasons*, Autumn–Winter 2003-4, 53–64.

Shakir, Zaid, 'Islam: Religion or Ideology?', *Zaytuna Institute* (2006) available at: http://www.zaytuna.org/forms/Islam%20Religion%20or%20Ideology.pdf

Qutb, Sayyid, *Milestones* (2005) New Delhi: Islamic Book Service.

Chapter 9: Searching for the human

Abdul Rauf, Imam Feisal, *What's Right with Islam is What's Right with America* (2005) New York: HarperCollins.

Cook, Daniel, *Understanding Jihad* (2005) Berkeley: University of California Press.

Jameelah, Maryam, *Islam and Western Society: A Refutation of the Modern Way of Life* (1996) Delhi: Adam Publishers and Distributors.

Maududi, Syed Abul A'la, *Al-Hijab: Purdah and the Status of Woman in Islam* (1997) Lahore: Islamic Publications.

Qutb, Sayyid, '"The America I Have Seen": In the Scale of Human Values' in Abdel-Malek, Kamal (ed), *America in an Arab Mirror: Images of America in Arabic Travel Literature: An Anthology* (2000) New York: Palgrave Macmillan, 9–28.
Qutb, Sayyid, *Milestones* (2005) New Delhi: Islamic Book Service.

Acknowledgements

One of my favourite lines in modern cinema comes from *The Incredibles*, an animated children's movie about a couple of retired superheroes who, having promised their wives they would become model family men but obviously unable to kick their superheroic habits, secretly intercept police radio signals and fight crime anonymously. Before long, they're back in costume, much to their wives' anger. When, inevitably, their renewed heroism costs family time, one is forced to plead with his wife for understanding, asking her to think of the greater good.

Her retort is swift and brilliant: 'I am your wife,' she bellows. 'I am the greatest good there is!'

I begin, then, by thanking my wife, Susan, for her patience, support and understanding; for all the times she has tolerated my writing intruding upon what little family time was left; for sharing her ideas with me, criticising and thereby elevating mine; and for exempting me temporarily from housework when deadlines approached. I wrote this book while working full time, which would have been impossible without Susan's massive sacrifices. As it happens, she never finished reading my manuscript because the extra burden gave her no time to do so (at least, that's what I prefer to believe).

This book would simply not exist without Martin Flanagan; a vessel for a golden heart, a man of humility, sincerity, honesty and integrity. It was Martin who convinced me I had something to say, and fostered in me the courage to say it – even if he didn't agree with what came out. But for his intervention, I may never have written a word.

This text bears the hallmarks of many wonderful people to whom I am profoundly indebted. Naturally, I must acknowledge the patience and skill of the team at Pan Macmillan, who cheerfully responded to my inane questions and requests, and worked tirelessly to produce the final product so rapidly. Thanks to Karen Penning for her invaluable counsel, her openness to a broad range of ideas and her suggestions on the manuscript, which always led to improvements; to Tom Gilliatt for his wide-ranging advice and for making me believe the book was worth publishing; to Annie Coulthard for managing publicity in a way that did not make me feel ridiculous; and to the numerous readers, editors and artists who worked on the project without me ever having the chance to meet them or learn their names. You know who you are, even if I don't. But your work was crucial, and I am most appreciative. I must also recognise the decisive contribution of Nikki Christer, who believed in me enough to solicit this work when a book was the last thing on my mind. I hope she feels the result has done her justice, and that this book is hers, too.

I thank Amal Awad, a wonderful emerging writer in her own right, whose editorial suggestions reflected the work of an alchemist. I have no doubt our many arguments substantially improved this text. Boundless gratitude is due to Azhar Usman, a primordial friend I only recently met, who will almost certainly not grasp the depth of the inspiration and encouragement he gave me, and will inevitably give to countless others. Azhar's legacy is already immense, and America is blessed to have him.

I am grateful to have had the opportunity to consult people

such as Dr Mohamad Abdalla, Director of the Griffith Islamic Research Unit and imam of the Kuraby mosque in Brisbane; Dr Ian Coller of the School of Historical Studies at the University of Melbourne; Reverend Jim Barr, Senior Minister at the Canberra Baptist Church; and Dr Pete Lentini of the Global Terrorism Research Centre at Monash University (and now my colleague). Each has helped me sharpen my thoughts, and inspired several revisions to the text. Of course, while each may take credit for much of this book, none bears responsibility for its weaknesses.

Penultimately, I acknowledge the array of people who selflessly reviewed and commented upon several draft chapters as though this book were their own: Sherene Hassan, Shalome Knoll, Rachel Woodlock, Mohammed El-leissy and Tasneem Chopra, all of whose feedback proved varied and crucial.

To thank my parents adequately would take a separate volume. For now, I pay tribute to my father, who taught me the value of education, and my mother, who gave me a love of grammar. I am confident there are no split infinitives in this book, and I owe that to her. God, of course, doesn't need my thanks, but I give them nonetheless.

Finally, I thank those who have disagreed with me, often aggressively so, in their public commentary, usually indirectly and without knowing it. Without intellectual tension there can be no intellectual development. Through their contributions to the public conversation, such people have taught me much and improved me considerably.